Res

a

An Introduction to Research in Counselling and Psychotherapy

John McLeod

Los Angeles | London | New Delhi
Singapore | Washington DC

SAGE

Los Angeles | London | New Delhi
Singapore | Washington DC

SAGE Publications Ltd
1 Oliver's Yard
55 City Road
London EC1Y 1SP

SAGE Publications Inc.
2455 Teller Road
Thousand Oaks, California 91320

SAGE Publications India Pvt Ltd
B 1/I 1 Mohan Cooperative Industrial Area
Mathura Road
New Delhi 110 044

SAGE Publications Asia-Pacific Pte Ltd
3 Church Street
#10-04 Samsung Hub
Singapore 049483

Editor: Susannah Trefgarne
Assistant editor: Kate Wharton
Production editor: Rachel Burrows
Marketing manager: Tamara Navaratnam
Cover design: Lisa Harper
Typeset by: C&M Digitals (P) Ltd, Chennai, India
Printed and bound by CPI Group (UK) Ltd,
Croydon, CR0 4YY

Library of Congress Control Number: 2012945340

British Library Cataloguing in Publication data

A catalogue record for this book is available from the British
Library

MIX
Paper from
responsible sources
FSC
www.fsc.org   FSC® C013604

ISBN 978-1-4462-0140-4
ISBN 978-1-4462-0141-1 (pbk)

For Julia

Contents

About the author

John McLeod is Emeritus Professor of Counselling at the University of Abertay Dundee, Scotland, and Adjunct Professor of Psychology at the University of Oslo, Norway. He is committed to promoting the relevance of research as a means of informing therapy practice and improving the quality of services that are available to clients. His enthusiastic search for finding ways to make research interesting and accessible for practitioners has resulted in a teaching award from the students at his own university and an award for exceptional contribution to research from the British Association for Counselling and Psychotherapy. His writing has influenced a generation of trainees in the field of counselling and psychotherapy, and his books are widely adopted on training programmes across the world.

Preface

We live in a society that is built on research. People in all cultures, at all times in history, have always wanted to be able to do things better. In earlier centuries, much of this effort centred on the need to survive – to develop crops that would grow, boats that would not sink. The complexity of modern industrial societies, allied to advances in science and technology, have pushed the reach of research into more and more areas of life. And unlike in the past, where new developments were largely based in specific communities and were disseminated only slowly, there now exists a massive knowledge industry, a network of universities, commercial research organisations, intellectual property lawyers, fundraisers and publishers, which ensures that information about new ideas and discoveries can spread rapidly across a global network.

Where does counselling and psychotherapy fit into all this? Unlike fields such as cancer care, consumer electronics or the defence industries, there are no multi-million-dollar research institutes devoted to the advancement of knowledge about counselling and psychotherapy. Instead, there are many pockets of relatively small-scale activity, usually groups of three or four researchers in a university department supported by the efforts of their students. The outputs of these researchers are linked together through networks of personal contact, scientific meetings and committees, and research journals. Systematic research in counselling and psychotherapy began to take shape during the 1940s. Since that time, many thousands of interesting and valuable studies have been published. Persuasive evidence has been produced for the effectiveness of psychotherapy in relation to the treatment of major psychological problems such as anxiety and depression. Counselling and psychotherapy research represents a mature field of inquiry, built around several decades of cumulative effort around the creation of appropriate research designs and techniques. Over the last 20 years, research evidence has increasingly been used by policymakers and health-service managers to inform decisions around the types of therapy, and amount of therapy, that should be provided for different groups of clients.

What does this mean for counselling and psychotherapy practitioners and trainees? Being a competent counsellor or psychotherapist requires a capacity to make use of research knowledge as a guide for practice. It is possible to identify four types of knowledge that are relevant to the conduct of therapy. *Personal* knowledge consists of an awareness and understanding, at an immediate experiential level, of basic human processes such as love, loss, fear, meaning-making and so on. *Practical* knowledge refers to 'know-how' that arises from training and supervision, working with clients, and observing other practitioners at work. *Theoretical* knowledge comprises a stock of concepts and stories that make it possible to anticipate how things may unfold, and make plausible connections between different observations. Finally, *research* knowledge comprises a communal or collective effort, on the part of the professional community as a whole, to document, sift through and evaluate the experience of therapy participants (clients, therapists, supervisors, family members, co-workers) in a wide range of settings. Each of these sources of knowledge is equally important. Personal and practical knowledge are grounded in personal experience – first-hand involvement in various forms of action. By contrast, theoretical and research knowledge are de-centred, and offer insight into perspectives and possibilities that go beyond the necessarily limited scope of what any individual person, on their own, can see, hear or feel for him- or herself.

In offering an introduction and invitation to research in counselling and psychotherapy, the present book includes updated material and themes from two earlier texts: *Doing Counselling Research* and *Practitioner Research in Counselling*. The aim is to offer a map of various fields of counselling and psychotherapy research, and to explain why they look the way they do. The present book is intended to operate as an access route into two further books, *Doing Research in Counselling and Psychotherapy* and *Using Research in Counselling and Psychotherapy*. *Doing Research* focuses on the practical issues involved in carrying out a piece of research into some aspect of therapy, and *Using Research* focuses on ways of integrating research skills and knowledge into work with clients. Taken together, these three books equip counselling and psychotherapy students and trainees to become research-informed practitioners. Key themes in these texts are explored in more depth in *Case Study Research in Counselling and Psychotherapy* (McLeod, 2010a) and *Qualitative Research in Counselling and Psychotherapy* (McLeod, 2011).

One of the strengths of training in counselling and psychotherapy is its emphasis on experiential learning. Detached, abstract knowledge is of little relevance to what happens in therapy. In the end, therapy is all about a process of contact between people, and as a result usable knowledge needs to be personally 'owned' rather than viewed as 'received wisdom' that has been handed down from authority figures. In recognition of these factors, each chapter includes personal reflection activities that provide opportunities to make links between the concepts and issues that are being discussed, and the personal meaning and practical implications of these ideas. These reflection tasks can be used as points in the text where it might be useful to pause and reflect. Alternatively, they can function as triggers for extended written reflection in a personal learning journal, or as a basis for dialogue with learning partners.

In writing this book, I have been mindful of wanting to tell the story of counselling and psychotherapy research in a way that will be accessible and interesting. I have therefore limited the number of references that are listed. In many areas of therapy research, there exist dense webs of sources and studies that lie behind almost any statement that might be made. To have tried to cite all of these sources in this book would have resulted in an end product that would be hard to follow. Instead, key sources of further reading have been identified that flag up 'where to go next' for anyone who wants to drill further down into the primary literature.

I hope that this book will convey my own enthusiasm and excitement around the value of research in counselling and psychotherapy. In the end, therapy is about helping people to get through difficult times in their lives, and therapy training is about helping students to accept and channel their own strengths and possibilities. Over and over again, across the course of a long career, I have observed many instances, in my own practice as well as in the work of colleagues, where research knowledge has contributed to more effective, responsive and caring practice. I have also observed many instances of students who have found that the discipline of research has allowed them to sharpen their understanding of complex issues, as well as providing them with opportunities to contribute to the profession as a whole.

I also hope that this book, along with its companion volumes, will be able to play some small role in refocusing the debate around research policy and practice in counselling and psychotherapy. I believe that we are at a turning point in terms of the type of research that is being done, and the ways in which research knowledge is used to inform policy and practice. The great accomplishment of the psychotherapy research community, since the middle of the 20th century, has been to demonstrate that the methods and assumptions of medical research, and experimental psychology, can be successfully applied within the field of counselling and psychotherapy, and can yield reliable and practically useful knowledge. There are signs that this image of research, and these assumptions, may have arrived at the end of their particular cycle, and are only capable of producing more of the same type of knowledge – layers of further confirmation around what is already known, rather than new insights and new responses to emerging challenges. At the same time, the economic and organisational context of research has shifted markedly in recent years. At a time of austerity, 'big ticket' research is becoming harder to justify, and what is becoming clear is that in the future, sustainable programmes of inquiry will be based in grassroots projects in which research data are generated as a by-product of routine practice rather than as a result of external funding of specialist research workers.

A brief word about the anticipated readership of this book. It seems likely that most of the people who will be interested in this book will be those who are at an early stage in training to be a counsellor, counselling psychologist, clinical psychologist, life coach or psychotherapist. The book is also relevant to students and trainees in such fields as social work, psychiatry and mental health nursing. Some users of the book may be in a position to draw on substantial prior research training, for example as part of a psychology degree. Other readers will have had little prior exposure to the forms of inquiry that have been used in therapy research. The book is mainly aimed at the latter group, and includes several sections that introduce and explain basic research concepts that may be familiar to readers who have greater experience of research.

Finally, I would like to encourage you to turn to the end of the final chapter. I mention this because I have enough experience as an author to know that few readers ever get to the end (of academic books – thrillers are different). During the period of writing this book, I was much taken with the BBC radio series *History of the World in 100 Objects*, presented by Neil MacGregor, director of the British Museum. I thought that it might be interesting to present 'the history of therapy research in 100 studies', but I feared that the publisher would balk at such an endeavour. As a compromise, right at the end I have smuggled in 'a history of therapy research in 12 studies'. Please read these items – they are wonderful pieces of work that fully deserve to be in a museum or gallery that is visited by thousands of people every day.

Acknowledgements

In writing this book I have been aware of the enormous debt I owe to the many people who have taught me about the relationship between research and therapy, particularly my students and colleagues at Keele University and the University of Abertay Dundee. For their intellectual support and challenge around research matters I would particularly like to thank Lynne Angus, Joe Armstrong, Bud Baxter, Mick Cooper, Sophia Balamoutsou, Ronen Berger, Julia Buckroyd, Edith Cormack, Robert Elliott, Kim Etherington, Dan Fishman, Soti Grafanaki, Thomas Mackrill, Denis O'Hara, David Rennie, Brian Rodgers, Rolf Sundet, Dot Weaks and Sue Wheeler. I would also like to thank Angela Couchman, Andy Hill, Nancy Rowland in the Research Department of the British Association for Counselling and Psychotherapy, and to express my appreciation for the support and encouragement offered by my long-suffering editorial team at Sage – Alice Oven, Susannah Trefgarne, Kate Wharton and Rachel Burrows. My wife, Julia, and daughters Kate, Emma and Hannah, have been a constant source of love, encouragement and reminders of the need to 'get a life' that transcends both research and practice.

Why research is important

There are many myths and fantasies about research. These often include vivid images of white coats and laboratories. People with practical skills and competencies may believe that research is something that is 'beyond' them. A very prevalent myth in the therapy world is that research is about numbers, impenetrable statistics and large samples and has no place for ordinary human feelings and experiences. Another myth is that research necessarily ignores the uniqueness of the individual. It can be hard for some therapists to identify with the role of being a researcher. The researcher is someone who is an expert, who knows. Running through these images and fantasies is a sense of research as another world, a kind of parallel universe that takes what is happening in the real world and processes it through computers.

These myths, perhaps stated here in an exaggerated form, act as a barrier that stops therapists from becoming engaged in research and making use of research-based knowledge to enrich their practice. A more constructive point of view is to start from the acknowledgement that we do 'research' all the time. Each of us has a model or map of the world, and is continually seeking new evidence with which to verify or alter that model. A therapy session with a client can be seen as a piece of research, a piecing together of information and understandings, followed by testing the validity of conclusions and actions based on that shared knowing. Over dozens of clients and hundreds of sessions, we build up our own theories of what different types of client are like and what is effective with them. These personal theories almost always have some connection to 'official' theories, but retain an idiosyncratic element originating in the unique experiences of the individual therapist.

The aim of this book is to de-mystify research, to puncture these myths, and to position research as a friend – a familiar and well-understood dimension of everyday practice. In this chapter, a pragmatic definition of research is offered, and examples are provided of some of the ways in which research knowledge and skills contribute to effective counselling and psychotherapy.

Exercise 1.1 Images of research

Take a few moments to relax and centre yourself. When you are ready, reflect on the images, metaphors and fantasies that come to mind when you think about the idea of 'research'. You might find it helpful to imagine how you might complete statements such as:

- research is …
- if a researcher was an animal, he or she might be a …
- what I like/appreciate about therapy research is …
- what I fear about therapy research is …

Take a few minutes to note down (visually and/or in words) the images and metaphors that occur to you. What do these images tell you about such issues as:

- the role of research in our culture/society;
- the reactions that clients and therapists might have if asked to take part in a research study;
- your own barriers and motivators around learning more about research.

A pragmatic definition of research

A useful working definition of research is: *a systematic process of critical inquiry leading to valid propositions and conclusions that are communicated to interested others.* Breaking this definition down into its component meanings allows some of the assumptions that lie behind it to be made explicit:

1 The concept of *critical inquiry*. Research grows out of the primary human tendency or need to learn, to know, to solve problems, to question received wisdom and taken-for-granted assumptions. These impulses are fundamentally *critical*; the need to know is the counterpoint to the sense that what is already known is not quite sufficient.

2 Research as a *process* of inquiry. Any research involves a series of steps or stages. Knowledge must be constructed, through a cyclical process of observation, reflection and acts of experimentation.

3 Research is *systematic*. There are two distinct sets of meanings associated with the notion that research should be systematic. The first is that any investigation takes place within a theoretical system of

concepts or constructs. A piece of research is embedded in a frame-work or way of seeing the world. Second, research involves the application of a method, which has been designed to achieve knowledge that is as valid and truthful as possible.

4 The products of research are *propositions* or statements. There is a distinction between research and learning. Experiential knowing, or 'knowing how', can be a valuable outcome of an inquiry process, but *research* always involves communication with others. Learning can occur at an individual, intuitive level, but research requires the symbolisation and transmission of these understandings in the public domain.

5 Research findings are judged according to criteria of *validity*, truthfulness or authenticity. To make a claim that a statement is based on research is to imply that it is in some way more valid or accurate than a statement based on personal opinion. However, every culture has its own distinctive criteria or 'logic of justification' for accepting a theory or statement as valid. For example, within mainstream psychology, truth value is equated with statements based on rational, objective experimentation. In psychoanalysis, truth value is judged on the basis of clinical experience.

6 Research is *communicated to interested others*; it takes place within a research community. No single research study has much meaning in isolation. Research studies provide the individual pieces that fit together to create the complex mosaic of the *literature* on a topic. Research can be viewed as a form of *collective knowing* that reflects the best efforts of a community to arrive at some level of agreement about how best to proceed in relation to practical concerns.

This definition of research is intended to demonstrate that there are many ways of arriving at valid propositional knowledge in the field of therapy. The definition does not imply that research must be 'scientific', nor does it make assumptions about what constitutes science. In technologically advanced modern societies, it is all too readily assumed that 'research' equals 'science' and that scientific methods represent the only acceptable means of generating useful knowledge. A great deal of research into counselling and psychotherapy has followed this route, in taking for granted the rules and canons of the scientific method and constructing therapy as a sub-branch of applied psychology or as a discipline allied to medicine. However, there are strong arguments in support of the position that therapy may be more appropriately regarded as an *interdisciplinary* activity, using concepts and methods from the arts and humanities, theology, philosophy and sociology as well as psychology and medicine. If this perspective is adopted, it is essential that research in counselling and psychotherapy is defined in such a way as to give equal weight and legitimacy to methods of inquiry drawn from *all* of these disciplines.

Another feature of the definition of research being employed here is that research is not taken to be only studies that appear in academic journals. There exists a broad continuum of research activities that lead to a diversity of research *products*. At a very local level, a therapist may critically review his or her work with a particular set of clients and report back their conclusions to a peer supervision group. Also at a local level, a counselling agency may analyse data on clients and outcomes for inclusion in its Annual Report. By contrast, international collaborative studies may involve 'cutting edge' developments in theory and practice that are written up as highly technical research reports in academic journals. It is important to be aware that, in the wider scheme of things, relatively little research ever finds its way into academic journals. The majority of studies are disseminated as limited-circulation reports and discussion papers, or are lodged in university and college libraries as student dissertations. Nevertheless, across this continuum of sophistication and ambition, all therapy researchers are faced with the same set of methodological and practical issues.

> ### Exercise 1.2 Research as conversation
>
> Adopting a pragmatic definition implies that therapy research is not a matter of arriving at an ultimate truth in relation to a question or issue, but instead operates as a vehicle for an on-going conversation or dialogue around what is involved in making effective therapy available to different types of people with different types of problem. From this perspective, research functions as an anchor-point for these conversations, which in turn lead to further research that aims to deepen or extend the conversation. In this exercise, consider the question: 'What kinds of conversations are made possible for you (or might be made possible) through your knowledge of research?' These might be actual conversations with colleagues or clients, or imaginary conversations with people you have never met, such as Carl Rogers.

Why is research important?

There are many reasons why research is important and needs to be taken seriously by anyone working as a counsellor or psychotherapist. These reasons include:

1 *Gaining a wider perspective.* Counselling and psychotherapy are largely private activities, conducted alone in conditions of confidentiality. Research studies allow therapists to learn about, and

from, the work of their colleagues, and give the profession a means of pooling knowledge and experience on an international scale.

2 *Accountability*. There is a significant level of resourcing of counselling and psychotherapy from public finances, and this financial backing brings with it a responsibility to demonstrate the efficacy of what is being offered to clients. It does not convince the public at large for counsellors to assert that, in their personal experience, most clients gain a great deal from therapy. More rigorous, objective evidence is required. If counselling/psychotherapy is to maintain its good public image, and continue to attract funding from government agencies, health providers and employers, then effective, research-based systems of accountability are essential.

3 *Developing new ideas and approaches*. Counselling and psychotherapy are new, emerging professions, and innovations in theory and technique are springing up all the time. Until the 1930s, the only form of psychotherapy that existed was psychoanalysis. There are now dozens of well-established approaches. Counselling and psychotherapy are activities where innovative interventions are continually being generated by practitioners, which subsequently need to be evaluated through research. Given that there is evidence that therapeutic interventions can do harm as well as good (Lambert, 1989), an informed awareness of the value of research in checking the value of innovations is indispensable.

4 *Offering therapy to new client groups*. Running in parallel with the development of new techniques has been the opening up of new client groups, and areas for the application of counselling and psychotherapy. The relevance and effectiveness of existing models in these new contexts is an important topic for research.

5 *Personal and professional development*. One of the chief sources of job satisfaction experienced by many counsellors and psychotherapists is a sense of continually learning about human nature in response to the lives and personal worlds that clients allow them to enter. As part of this process, practitioners may find themselves with 'burning questions' that can only be answered by carrying out research. The professional and career development path taken by experienced therapists may lead many to seek to consolidate their professional identity by making a contribution to the research literature.

6 *The external credibility and legitimacy of counselling and psychotherapy as professional activities*. Like other human service professions such as medicine, nursing, clinical psychology, teaching and social work, there is an expectation that members of the counselling/psychotherapy profession will be able to offer a rational basis for their interventions through drawing on a research-based body of knowledge. This trend is reflected in the increasing movement towards university- and college-based training for these professions,

with significant emphasis in these courses on research awareness and skills.

7 *Using research tools and instruments to collect feedback on the progress of therapy.* There has been a movement in recent years to develop ways of using brief research questionnaires to collect feedback from clients on a regular basis, as a means of generating information that can provide both client and therapist a basis for reviewing the progress of therapy. This kind of data can also give therapists a better sense of their own effectiveness with different client groups, and can feed in to supervision and training.

8 *Becoming sensitised to the experiences and needs of clients.* The professional role and status of the therapist mean that he or she has a particular perspective on the therapy process. Research studies that focus on the experience of clients can serve as useful reminders that the client may have a different perspective on what is happening. In addition, research into experiences of specific problems and conditions can help to sensitise therapists to the needs of clients from these groups.

A fundamental theme running through these reasons for undertaking research is that the knowledge base for counselling and psychotherapy practice is not fixed, dogmatic and immutable. Although therapy theories may appear solid and immovable, the history of therapy reveals that pioneers such as Freud and Rogers had to struggle to get their ideas accepted in the face of what was the accepted wisdom of their time and place. And, inevitably, even the apparent certainties of psychodynamic or person-centred theory, or CBT, will in turn be modified and overthrown at some stage.

> *Exercise 1.3 Reflecting on your own personal engagement with research*
>
> What is your own current involvement with therapy research? How many research papers do you read in a typical month? What areas of research are of particular interest to you? Do any of the list of reasons why research is important, outlined above, encourage you to extend your involvement in therapy research?

Conclusions

This chapter has introduced some of the key ideas that underpin the discussion of research that is offered in the rest of the book. The driving force of research is the area between knowing and not knowing. Something is known but it is not enough. Research that has meaning takes off from the point of a personal felt sense of a need to know. Being research-informed is an essential component of all competent counselling and psychotherapy practice, because it is not possible to be a good therapist without possessing a spirit of openness to inquiry and learning. Good research in the domain of counselling and psychotherapy always exists in a dialogue with practice. Research is a collective activity. Each study draws on what has gone before, and its inevitable imperfections and inconclusiveness will be carried forward by someone yet to come. Research encompasses different ways of collecting and analysing data. The findings of research can be disseminated through different types of research 'product'. These ideas have the effect of demystifying research. Within the educational system, and our culture as a whole, there has existed a widely held assumption that research is an elite activity that is separate from everyday life, best reserved for brainy folk. This is not a helpful assumption. It is better to think about research as similar to cooking. Yes, some people are really good at it, and are an inspiration to the rest of us. But, in the end, we can all do it, because it is something that needs to be done.

The chapters that follow attempt to build an understanding of the scope and nature of contemporary research in counselling and psychotherapy. The next chapter offers an overview of therapy research, in the form of the story of how it has evolved and changed over the past century. There then follow a series of chapters that explore the engine of therapy research: the philosophical assumptions about knowledge that have influenced researchers, the practical challenges of doing research, how knowledge is organised into a 'literature', and the nature of qualitative and quantitative modes of inquiry. The focus then turns to how these ideas and techniques have played out in relation to the two big questions that have dominated the therapy research literature: 'Does it work?' (outcome research) and '*How* does it work?' (process research). The closing chapter offers some reflections on what this all means, and where it is all going.

Suggested further reading

Cooper, M. (2008). *Essential Research Findings in Counselling and Psychotherapy: The Facts Are Friendly.* London: Sage. (This book offers a unique, accessible overview of the practical conclusions that can be drawn from research into all aspects of therapy.)

Recommended resources

Further information on any of the ideas that are introduced in the following chapters can be found in two excellent therapy research methods textbooks:

Barker, C., Pistrang, N. and Elliott, R. (2002). *Research Methods in Clinical Psychology: An Introduction for Students and Practitioners*, 2nd edn. Chichester: Wiley.

Timulak, L. (2008). *Research in Counselling and Psychotherapy*. London: Sage.

Research in counselling and psychotherapy: a historical overview

In order to understand why it is that the counselling and psychotherapy literature encompasses many hundreds of studies on certain topics, and almost no studies on other topics that may appear to be equally important, it is necessary to develop a historical perspective. The field of counselling and psychotherapy research has undergone a number of important shifts in emphasis, both in response to external social, cultural and economic pressures, and as a result of the emergence of new ideas and techniques within the academic community. An appreciation of the history of therapy research also makes it possible to gain a sense of the direction in which this field is travelling, and to take a position around the direction in which it *should* travel. The evolution of research in counselling and psychotherapy can be divided into four main stages:

- early history, using clinical cases to establish a knowledge base;
- development of systematic research based on quantitative methods;
- the therapy wars;
- back to the grassroots: the search for practice-based evidence.

The key debates and developments within each of these stages are discussed in the following sections of this chapter. It is important to keep in mind that these stages do not depict clear-cut eras of distinctive research activity, with definite start-dates and end-points. All of the ideas that characterise each of the stages are still influential. For example, the kind of clinical case studies that were used by Freud and his colleagues to establish an evidence base for psychoanalysis are still being published today. What has happened is that new ideas about what research might look like enter the field, dominate the discussion for a while, and then become part of the mix.

The account of the historical development of research offered in this chapter focuses mainly on outcome research, which has represented the arena in which key debates over the nature of therapeutic evidence has taken place. For the most part, research into the process of therapy, and into issues around training and supervision of therapists, have formed a backdrop to the struggle to determine the effectiveness of competing therapy approaches, rather than taking centre stage.

Early history: using clinical case studies to establish a knowledge base

Until around the end of the 19th century, people who were experiencing problems in living, in terms of difficult relationships with others, strong emotions of anxiety, loss or depression, or dysfunctional patterns of behaviour, would seek help from two sources: other people in their immediate family and community, or priests. As Western societies became more urbanised, industrialised and secular, various barriers began to emerge in relation to the use of these traditional sources of emotional support, and what began to emerge was a new form of help, which took the form of counselling or psychotherapy. The historical origins of counselling and psychotherapy are discussed in more detail in J. McLeod (2009). Through the first half of the 20th century, the pioneers of therapy, such as Freud or Jung, were faced with a complex set of challenges. They needed to be able to show and explain to other professionals what they could do. They also needed to reflect on what they were doing, so they could get better at doing it.

The method of inquiry that was available to the first generation of psychotherapists was the clinical case study. Throughout the 19th century, significant advances had been made within medicine through careful observation of individual patients by their doctors. This tradition provided a structure within which Freud and others were able to advance their practice through critical reflection and theory-building. Many of the case studies published by Freud and his colleagues are still influential and in print, in the Penguin Freud Library. These cases included a wealth of detailed observation, linked to theoretical analysis. They were written in a vivid and dramatic manner, in some respects more like detective novels than dry scientific reports. Although Freud recognised that, ultimately, biological and neurological evidence would need to be found to support the validity of concepts such as the unconscious and repression, he was also aware of the persuasiveness of first-hand case accounts, and the contribution that they could make to the growth of knowledge. From a contemporary perspective, it is easy to identify methodological weaknesses in the type of clinical case study that was carried out by the early psychoanalysts. The notes made by the analyst were based on memory, and selectively shaped by prior assumptions. The interpretation of the case material was made by the analyst alone, with no check on the extent to which that interpretation was in fact consistent with the evidence. However, despite these methodological flaws, it is clear that the use of evidence from clinical case studies made it possible to develop, in psychoanalysis, a theory and therapeutic approach that has remained relevant and continued to be applicable to new client groups, over a period of more than a century. The enduring influence and robustness of the psychoanalytic case study as a method of inquiry is discussed more fully by Kvale (2001).

Exercise 2.1 Revisiting the psychoanalytic case study

Select and read any one of Freud's clinical case studies (i.e. a case of an actual patient, rather than an analysis of a historical figure), such as the Wolf Man, the Rat Man or Dora. It is important to read the case report as published by Freud himself, rather than a summary or critique written by someone else. These case studies are widely available in university and public libraries, or through on-line second-hand booksellers. As you read the case, reflect on its strengths and limitations as a piece of evidence about what happens in psychotherapy. How credible was Freud's understanding and conceptualisation of the patient's life? What information might Freud have included that might have improved the validity of his conclusions? Finally, how do you evaluate the usefulness of this type of evidence as a means of informing policy and practice in counselling and psychotherapy?

During the first half of the 20th century, counselling and psychotherapy became established as professions, and became more widely accessible to potential clients and patients. The same time period saw a massive expansion in research in psychology and the social sciences, which generated a wide range of new methodologies and research technologies. The desire of the counselling and psychotherapy professions to find a respectable niche within higher education meant that it was inevitable that, sooner or later, there would be a meeting of the world of therapy practice and the world of scientific research.

The earliest attempts to go beyond clinical case study evidence, and rigorously evaluate the effectiveness of therapy over a series of cases, consisted of follow-up investigations of people who had undergone psychoanalysis. These studies, based on information collected about patients treated in a number of psychoanalytic institutes, tended to show that around one-third of patients improved a great deal, another one-third were slightly improved, while the rest had either remained the same or deteriorated (Knight, 1941). These findings were initially viewed as providing positive support for the effectiveness of psychoanalytic therapy. However, in a highly influential critique of these studies, Eysenck (1952) argued that there was plentiful evidence to suggest that neurotic people who had received no formal psychotherapeutic treatment exhibited rates of improvement over time that were similar to those found in individuals who had received psychotherapy. Eysenck drew on data gathered by Landis (1938), who had found that at that time around 70 per cent of neurotic patients were discharged from psychiatric hospitals each year in the USA categorised as recovered or improved, and by Denker (1937) who reviewed the records of 500 consecutive disability claims due to psychoneurosis from the files of the Equitable Life Assurance Company. Denker defined these cases as serious, since the claimants were required to have been away from work for at least three months to be eligible to make a claim. Of these 500 insurance company cases, 72 per cent had recovered within two years, and 90 per cent within five years.

On the basis of these findings, Eysenck (1952) asserted that many people who experience emotional crises undergo a process of 'spontaneous recovery' (sometimes described as 'spontaneous remission'), in which the life problems which were worrying them gradually fade, or they find their own ways of coping. For Eysenck and other critics of insight/relationship therapy, it was essential for any form of intervention to be able to generate improvement figures significantly higher than those attributable to spontaneous recovery (Stevenson, 1961). But, when Eysenck (1952) reviewed the recovery rates reported in the 19 therapy outcome studies available to him, he found recovery rates of 44 per cent for psychoanalysis and 64 per cent for eclectic psychotherapy, using a definition of recovery equivalent to that employed in the Denker (1937) and Landis (1938) studies.

The strong critique by Eysenck (1952, 1960, 1965, 1992) of the evidence concerning the effectiveness of psychodynamic and other insight-oriented forms of therapy had two main consequences on the field of counselling and psychotherapy research. First, it became clear that clinical case study evidence, even when aggregated over a number of cases, was not sufficient on its own to provide a secure scientific basis for therapy policy and practice. Second, Eysenck's work stimulated therapy researchers to carry out more rigorous and objective studies of the effectiveness of counselling and psychotherapy (Bergin, 1963; Rogers and Dymond, 1954), using measurement tools that were specifically designed for this purpose, and adopting the strategy of including a *control group* in their study, so that the effect of therapy could be contrasted with the naturally occurring change arising in a comparable set of people who were similar in respect of demographic profile and presenting problems but who did not receive therapy.

In evaluating the relevance and impact of early case-based research into psychotherapy, it is important to acknowledge that the limitations of this methodology, cogently made by Eysenck and others, need to be balanced against the undoubted achievements that were attained. One of the strengths of clinical case studies is that they enable the outcome of a case to be understood and explained in the context of a rich description of the therapeutic process that occurred within each case. While the shift towards controlled quantitative studies of outcome (discussed further in the following sections) made it possible to make more reliable and rigorous statements about effectiveness of different forms of therapy, this precision came at the cost of relentlessly eliminating almost all of the complexity that could be captured in a case study.

The development of programmatic therapy research based on quantitative methods

To an observer in the early 1930s, it would not have been obvious where and when the development of systematic, scientifically informed research into counselling and psychotherapy would find an intellectual and academic home. At that time in the USA, psychotherapy was a practice that was as much based in social work as it was in psychology and psychiatry. There were also strong links between the emerging domain of counselling and the academic discipline of education, for example around such areas as careers counselling and counselling in schools. As it happened, the combination of World War II, which led to massive expansion in the USA in psychological care and treatment of veterans, meant that the critical point of convergence of therapy and research took place on the territory of psychology, and the expansion of therapy research in the immediate post-war period occurred primarily within the sub-discipline of clinical psychology.

The origins of programmatic therapy research based on quantitative methods occurred in the context of the research group led by Carl Rogers at the University of Ohio in the early 1940s. As with most significant moments of cultural creativity, the achievements of this group were made possible by a combination of circumstances: increased investment by the US healthcare system in psychological treatment, a new theory (non-directive/client-centred therapy), a supportive university environment, and the drive and ambition of a charismatic leader. At Ohio, and then from 1945 to 1957 at the University of Chicago, this group were the first to make audio recordings of therapy sessions (Rogers, 1942), devise methods for measuring the occurrence of theoretically relevant processes within these records, and develop methods for systematically evaluating the effectiveness of therapy. Although Rogers was the leader of this group, it included many other highly talented individuals who went on to become key figures in the expansion of counselling and psychotherapy research and practice over the next 50 years.

It is instructive to recall some of the key themes of the work of this group. They did not seek to describe or assess clients, or organise research studies, around diagnostic/psychiatric categories. Instead, they put a great deal of effort into developing an outcome measure (the Q-sort) that attempted to evaluate the effectiveness of therapy in terms of each client's own personal definition of their problem. Although their therapy approach came to be viewed as a distinctive model in its own right (client-centred therapy), the group consistently sought to develop a trans-theoretical perspective. For example, the well-known formulation by Rogers (1957) of the 'necessary and sufficient conditions' for therapeutic change was intended to apply to all forms of therapeutic relationship, not just client-centred therapy. The underlying assumption that informed the work of this research community was that people became able to address their problems in living when they were able to take advantage of a relationship that allowed them to access their own personal resources, agency and potential for growth. At a later stage in the research programme, therapists from other approaches were invited to comment on the case material that had been collected by the group (Rogers et al., 1967). It was never the intention of Rogers, or the majority of those in the original group, to establish an independent organisational structure for client-centred therapy, in the form of a professional association or journal, and in fact no such entities were set up until the 1980s. From the start there was an effort to address the philosophical shortcomings of the experimental methods of behavioural psychology as a basis for constructing an evidence base for counselling and psychotherapy. A further distinctive feature of the programme of research into client-centred therapy was a constant attention to the interrelationships between process and outcome (Cartwright, 1957; Rogers and Dymond, 1954; Rogers and Stevens, 1968) and the experience of the client (Lipkin, 1954).

What was created within the early client-centred research community was an open, discovery-oriented position in relation to inquiry. Rogers believed that 'the facts are friendly', and was willing to follow the logic of the research process wherever it would lead him. This particular journey effectively came to an end in the period around 1965. The final collective project undertaken by this group was a study, based at the University of Wisconsin, of the process and outcome of client-centred therapy with hospitalised patients diagnosed as schizophrenic (Rogers et al., 1967; Rogers and Stevens, 1968). There was major interpersonal conflict within the team, which ended in a significant delay to the publication of the final report, owing to the appropriation of the data by one member. By this time a major international figure, Rogers decided to give up his direct involvement in research, and to move to California to be involved in other types of project. The momentum was lost.

The spirit of the client-centred research programme continued to find expression in the work of Hans Strupp and his colleagues at Vanderbilt

University. From a psychodynamic starting point, Strupp was similarly convinced that there existed cross-theoretical processes that could be identified in all forms of effective therapy. His most influential attempt to investigate this hypothesis took the form of what became known as the 'Vanderbilt I' study (Strupp and Hadley, 1979). In this project, clients (male students selected on the basis of being depressed and socially withdrawn) were randomly allocated to either psychotherapy from a highly trained clinician, or to a series of counselling sessions with a member of the university faculty chosen on the basis of their interest in student welfare, but with no counselling or psychotherapy training at all. At the end of therapy, and at follow-up, there was no difference in the overall effectiveness of the professional therapy or the lay counselling. Strupp argued that this finding demonstrated that the impact of therapy was largely due to the effect of a supportive and caring relationship, rather than the application of specialist technical interventions. An important aspect of the Vanderbilt I project was the publication of a series of in-depth case studies, which used a combination of quantitative data and analysis of therapy session transcripts to look closely at exactly what was happening on good- and poor-outcome cases (Strupp, 1980a, b, c, d). Further studies carried out within the Vanderbilt research programme explored the implications of these findings for the training of therapists.

Through the work of Rogers, Strupp and others, therapy research during the period between 1950 and 1980 was characterised by efforts to establish a rigorous methodology, which incorporated the use of outcome and process measures that were sensitive to the phenomena of counselling and psychotherapy. During this period there was an openness to identifying and evaluating therapeutic processes that occurred across different therapies, and a strong interest in exploring the processes within therapy that contributed to good or poor outcomes. This phase was also marked by a willingness to use a wide range of research strategies, such as open-ended interviews and in-depth case studies, alongside quantitative measures.

Suggested further reading

Elliott, R. and Farber, B.A. (2010). Carl Rogers: Idealist, pragmatist and psychotherapy research pioneer. In L.G. Castonguay, J.C. Muran, L. Angus, J.A. Hayes, N. Ladany and T. Anderson (eds.), *Bringing Psychotherapy Research to Life: Understanding Change Through the Work of Leading Clinical Researchers.* Washington, DC: American Psychological Association. (Carl Rogers as a researcher.)

(Continued)

(Continued)

Binder, J.L. and Henry, W.P. (2010). Developing skills in managing negative processes. In J.C. Muran and J.P. Barber (eds.), *The Therapeutic Alliance: An Evidence-Based Approach to Practice.* New York: Guilford Press. (A candid and accessible account of the evolution and achievements of the Vanderbilt research programme.)

The therapeutic alliance: an enduring topic throughout the history of therapy research

The single most important topic within the therapy-process research literature has been the nature of the client–therapist relationship. Although Rogers and Strupp were interested in outcome, what they kept coming back to, in their research and writing, was the idea that it was the quality of the client-therapy relationship, not the model of therapy being applied, that made the largest contribution to change. In the early years of therapy research, the model of 'necessary and sufficient conditions' for change (i.e. the existence of a relationship within which the clients perceived their therapist as accepting, empathic and genuine) developed by Rogers (1957) inspired a large amount of research (Watson, 1984). However, the key turning point in research on the client–therapist relationship is associated with the formulation by Bordin (1979) of the concept of the *working alliance*, followed by the development of the Working Alliance Inventory by Horvath and Greenberg (1986, 1989). The concept of the 'alliance' provided a model of the therapeutic relationship that has made sense to therapists from all theoretical schools, and has had a major influence on training and practice. Over the years, many hundreds of research studies have been carried out which have examined the influence of the alliance on client outcomes in many different therapy approaches and settings (see Muran and Barber, 2010). An appreciation of the state of research-based knowledge in counselling and psychotherapy requires an awareness that, at the same time that the 'therapy wars' were being fought (see following section), there existed a parallel, if somewhat downplayed, track of inquiry which was gradually accumulating evidence that the outcomes of therapy were highly dependent on the qualities of the therapist and the construction of a collaborative working relationship.

The therapy wars

The accomplishments of Carl Rogers and his research group in devising a repertoire of instruments for measuring the process and outcome of therapy created a situation in which it became possible for many other researchers to conduct studies of counselling and psychotherapy. However, the kind of research that was carried out soon began to move in a different direction. The willingness of researchers such as Carl Rogers and Hans Strupp to follow the research trail wherever it might lead them began to be replaced by research that was motivated to demonstrate that one approach to therapy was more effective than another. This shift was due in part to the increasingly crowded and competitive psychotherapy marketplace in the USA, particularly following the development of cognitive behavioural therapy (CBT) and other new therapy approaches in the 1970s. However, the change of emphasis and direction was also an inevitable consequence of the application of experimental methods, such as randomised clinical (or controlled) trials (RCTs). By the 1960s, RCTs were being widely used in medical research to determine the effectiveness of treatment (e.g. the efficacy of drug A vs. drug B, or the survival rates associated with surgical procedure X vs. surgical procedure Y). This kind of research design made a lot of sense to psychologists whose undergraduate education had required them to design and carry out innumerable laboratory experiments. It also made a lot of sense to mental health finding agencies who were accustomed to reviewing and supporting medical-model research proposals.

A historically significant outcome study, which was one of the first to employ a randomised control group design, was the investigation by Sloane et al. (1975) into the comparative effectiveness of time-limited (average 14 sessions over four months) behavioural vs. psychodynamic psychotherapy for neurotic clients. Closer scrutiny of this study makes it possible to identify some fundamental dilemmas associated with the application of RCT methodology in counselling and psychotherapy outcome research.

The Sloane et al. (1975) study was carried out in a university psychiatric outpatient clinic. All those seeking therapy were interviewed and assessed, with those considered too disturbed to join the waiting list, or not disturbed enough to need therapy, being excluded from the study and referred elsewhere. Three main measures of change were used: a structured interview to assess levels of social and work maladjustment, ratings by the interviewer and the therapist of the severity of the target complaints reported by the client, and an interview with a close friend or relative. At the end of therapy these measures were repeated. Follow-up interviews were held one year and two years after the initial assessment. The therapists in the study were three experienced psychoanalytically oriented therapists and three experienced behaviour therapists. Clients accepted into the study were randomly assigned to a therapist or to the waiting list, and paid for treatment on a sliding scale. The results of this study were that all three groups improved at the end of the four-month period, although the treated clients improved more than those on the waiting list. These gains were maintained at the one-year and two-year follow-up interviews.

The Sloane et al. (1975) study illuminates some of the methodological challenges associated with controlled outcome research in counselling and psychotherapy. For example, the meaning or personal significance of the experience of being allocated to a control waiting list condition was a crucial feature of this study. In order to estimate the relative effectiveness of therapy in contrast to spontaneous recovery, every third applicant for therapy was allocated to a waiting list condition. However, in acknowledgement of the ethical difficulties involved in denying help to people in need, those on the waiting list were offered plentiful reassurance that they would soon be assigned to a therapist, were given a number to call in a crisis, and were contacted several times during the four-month wait period by a research assistant who checked how they were getting on. The people on the waiting list also experienced an initial assessment interview, in which they were encouraged to talk about their problems to a skilled listener and interviewer. It can be seen, therefore, that those on the waiting list had not received *no* treatment, but had been offered at least a minimal level of support, contact and hope for the future.

It could be argued, therefore, that the level of contact and support provided for those on the waiting list meant that they had indeed received a form of therapeutic intervention. If this were true, then it would imply that the study was not really comparing therapy against a no-therapy control, or placebo, but was comparing a specific form of therapy with a brief contact 'non-specific' therapy. In these circumstances any demonstration that the former is more effective than the latter would be important, since the therapy in question would be subjected to a strong test of its effectiveness and power. However, it is equally plausible to suppose that many of the people assigned to the waiting list experienced this as rejection, and as a result felt angry or worthless. Certainly, almost one in three of the waiting list group declined the offer of therapy made by the research team at the end of the waiting time. This phenomenon could be interpreted as suggesting that the therapy has been subjected to a rather weak test, in that it has been compared to a condition that would cause a lowering of levels of adjustment and a worsening of target complaints.

Another issue arising from the design of the Sloane et al. (1975) study concerns the fact that clients were not given any choice about the kind of therapy they would receive. They were randomly allocated either to a behaviour therapist or a psychoanalytically oriented therapist. These are quite different forms of therapy, and it is reasonable to suppose that at least some clients might have definite preferences for the kind of approach they would perceive as being most relevant to them. It is possible that giving clients an informed choice about the kind of therapy they were to receive would have served to enhance their positive expectations and motivation and therefore increase the success rate.

Finally, there are questions that can be asked about the representativeness of the study. It was carried out in a high-status, well-resourced clinic, with expert, experienced therapists and carefully screened clients. These factors may not correspond to the reality experienced by most therapists and their clients in everyday practice. Moreover, only three therapists were used in each group. Were these therapists truly representative of the orientations they espoused? Closer analysis by the research team of what their therapists were actually doing revealed considerable differences in how each of them delivered their brand of therapy.

The Sloane et al. (1975) study is generally acknowledged as constituting a thorough and comprehensive piece of research that has been highly regarded and influential among other researchers in this field. The research team in this study gathered a large amount of data on each client over extended periods of time. Careful ethical and professional safeguards were observed. The resources devoted to the study were substantial. Nevertheless, despite all these ingredients, the critic or sceptic looking at it can find many reasons for questioning the validity of its findings. In response to these methodological difficulties, the counselling and psychotherapy research community inevitably began to look for ways of improving the scientific rigour of controlled studies of therapy outcomes.

The obvious way to enhance the rigour of controlled studies is to introduce more control. The technology of RCT studies gradually became more sophisticated. Rather than just deliver therapy that they considered as 'behavioural' or 'psychodynamic', therapists in controlled studies were required to undergo special training and to follow a treatment manual to improve their level of competence in the model. Adherence to the manual was evaluated through ratings of audio- or video-recordings of their interactions with clients. Gradually, waiting list or 'treatment as usual' control conditions began to be dropped from RCTs, because it was too hard to know what was happening to clients in these arms of a study. Finally, clients entering studies were more thoroughly screened, so that as far as possible they represented 'pure' diagnostic categories. The aim of these methodological advances was to produce more certainty or confidence in the findings of outcome studies, while at the same time making these studies less representative of everyday practice.

To some extent, this quest for certainty and precision was a reflection of an understandable wish on the part of scientific investigators to seek to remedy the methodological weaknesses of previous studies. But the drive for greater certainty, and an emphasis on differentiating between alternative therapies rather than building bridges between them, was also a matter of responding to the policies of major healthcare providers, first in the USA and then in most industrialised countries. As a reaction to escalating health costs in the 1970s, healthcare providers in the USA began to introduce a policy of 'managed care', in which treatment costs would only be reimbursed if a diagnosis was made and a valid treatment intervention was delivered (i.e. one that had been shown in RCTs to be more effective than rival treatments for patients with that diagnosis). The impact of this policy on counselling and psychotherapy was that, to get work, therapists needed to diagnose their clients and use a defined manualised therapy whose effectiveness had been validated in one or more randomised trials.

This set of circumstances – the combination of a capability on the part of the therapy research community to carry out good-quality RCT studies, and the policy position of managed care providers – unleashed what Wampold (2001) has described as the 'therapy wars'. Researchers had strong incentives to conduct studies that showed that their pre-ferred form of therapy was more effective than its competitors. Many hundreds of studies began to be carried out, which compared the effec-tiveness of different therapies for different client groups. On the back of these studies, methods of meta-analysis were developed that made it possible to estimate the accumulated effectiveness of different therapies over a series of studies. Within this war, there were many specific battle sites, such as the argument over which therapy was most effective for depression, for anxiety or for PTSD, and debates over whether only those training programmes should be accredited if they taught vali-dated therapies. In the UK, a major battleground in the therapy wars has been the struggle around what kind of therapy should be provided within the Improving Access to Psychological Therapies (IAPT) pro-gramme that was launched in England in 2008.

Box 2.1

National Institute of Mental Health (NIMH) Treatment of Depression Collaborative Research Program

One of the defining battles of the therapy wars was fought on the territory of the collaborative study of depression conducted by a team led by Irene Elkin under the auspices of the National Institute of Mental Health (NIMH), a government-funded research agency in the USA. This study embodied many of the lessons that had been learned from earlier attempts to conduct randomised trials of therapy. To reduce the possibility of bias, it was carried out on three sites, with leading researchers drawn from different approaches, and carefully trained thera-pists following manualised protocols. A large number of patients (250) were involved. The study aimed to resolve, once and for all, the question of the relative effectiveness of CBT, interpersonal (broadly psychodynamically oriented) therapy, antidepressant medication, and a placebo condition. Further information about the design and results of this study can be found in Elkin et al. (1985, 1989), Elkin (1994) and Shea et al. (1992). Essentially, all three of the active interventions were found to be broadly equivalent in effectiveness. Surprisingly good outcomes were also reported for the placebo condition. However, few within the research community were satisfied with the findings of this study. Over the years, multiple re-analyses of the NIMH depression data have been carried out, using alternative statistical models and examining alternative hypotheses (e.g. that differential outcomes were due to therapist effects of alliance effects).

From the 1980s until the world economic crisis of recent years, by far the largest proportion of funding for counselling and psychotherapy research has been directed towards the completion of RCTs, and carrying out meta-analyses of the increasing weight of RCT evidence in respect of the effectiveness of therapy for various disorders. Reviews of the conclusions of these studies have been published in a range of authoritative sources: the Cochrane database, the NICE guidelines, and edited volumes such as Lambert (2004) and Roth and Fonagy (2005). In turn, these reviews have had a significant impact on policy and practice.

Suggested further reading

To gain a sense of the type and volume of research that has been conducted within the era of the 'therapy wars', it may be useful to visit the depression research website that is maintained by Professor Pim Cuijpers and his colleagues at the VU University Amsterdam (www.psychotherapyrcts.org). As of the end of 2011, this site included summaries of over 280 RCT studies of psychotherapy for depression.

The era of the therapy research wars has been dominated by the contribution of the CBT research community. CBT has been a therapy approach that came into existence in the 1970s at a point where the ideas and technology needed to conduct rigorous therapy research were in place. Many of the pioneers of cognitive therapy and CBT, such as Aaron Beck and Donald Meichenbaum, have been accomplished and creative researchers who have been comfortable in making links between theory, research, practice and training. CBT has also had the advantage of drawing on intellectual roots in academic and experimental psychology, which highlighted the need for clear definition of therapeutic goals and outcomes, and the regular monitoring of patient progress. One of the important research innovations that was pioneered by CBT researchers was a variant on the clinical case study known as the 'n=1' or 'single subject' design. In this type of case study, information on the client's symptoms or problem behaviour is collected on a regular basis (possibly even hourly or daily), thus making it possible to use time-series analysis to analyse the impact of therapy, or of particular phases within therapy. This research technique has been widely used within CBT to document the effectiveness of treatment innovations. Once the potential effectiveness of a new therapy technique has been established using an n=1 case study, it is then possible to move to a full RCT in order to determine the efficacy of the intervention on a larger sample, under more controlled conditions. The CBT professional community has supported a range of research journals that have facilitated effective communication between researchers and practitioners, for example *Behaviour Therapy and Research* and *Cognitive Therapy and Research* – it is easy for CBT clinicians to know where to find the latest research findings. The existence of an extensive and thriving evidence base allows CBT practitioners to have confidence in what they do, and leads to confidence in the approach on the part of clients and policymakers. In addition, the capacity to use research as a means of evaluating the usefulness of new ideas has allowed CBT to continue to grow and develop, as illustrated in recent years by its willingness to incorporate therapeutic ideas and methods from such domains as mindfulness, forgiveness and compassion. The CBT research tradition has been open to a range of research methodologies. For example, one of the leading figures in the development of CBT for obsessive-compulsive disorder, Paul Salkovskis, has published qualitative (Bevan et al., 2010) and case study research (Challacombe and Salkovskis, 2011), as well as RCT studies (Sørensen et al., 2011).

The achievements and success of CBT, in the context of the on-going research wars, has created considerable difficulties for other approaches to therapy. Although there exist respectable amounts of research evidence to support the effectiveness of psychodynamic and person-centred/experiential therapies, the total number of studies on these approaches is much smaller than it is for CBT. This creates problems at the level of meta-analyses of effectiveness in relation to specific disorders, where large numbers of studies are needed to produce reliable conclusions. There are well-established therapies, such as transactional analysis (TA) psychotherapy, Gestalt therapy and narrative therapy, that lack an evidence base of controlled studies. While it is possible for those within the CBT camp to point out, quite rightly, that anyone can carry out and publish an RCT, the reality is more complex. As could be seen from the description earlier in this chapter of the Sloane et al. (1975) comparative study, RCTs are resource intensive, require high-level research skills, and have mainly taken place within well-established, high-status, large healthcare institutions and universities. Those who would wish to conduct RCTs on under-represented therapies tend, on the whole, to work in private practice or in underfunded community counselling agencies, neither of which are environments conducive to doing RCTs. Finally, the methodological criteria for an acceptable RCT are somewhat higher now than when many of the groundbreaking CBT-oriented RCTs were being conducted. There is a strong sense, therefore, that this is a war in which it is almost impossible for other therapies to compete at any meaningful level.

Exercise 2.2 Reflecting on the pros and cons of randomised controlled studies

What is your own position, in respect of the role that RCTs should play in the development of counselling and psychotherapy policy and practice? If you support a strong pro-RCT or anti-RCT viewpoint, what do you say to people who take an opposite position? Alternatively, if you take a balanced stance, where do you see RCTs fitting in to an overall research strategy? If you were the national commissioner for therapy research, what proportion of your funding would you allocate to RCTs, and what specific research questions would you want 'trialists' to address?

Suggested further reading

The pursuit of the therapy wars resulted in widespread disenchantment on the part of therapy practitioners around the direction that was being taken by the research community. Two influential papers that reflected these feelings are:

Morrow-Bradley, C. and Elliott, R. (1986). Utilization of psychotherapy research by practicing psychotherapists. *American Psychologist*, 41, 188–197. (A survey of therapists in the USA, which revealed considerable dissatisfaction with what was on offer from mainstream research.)

Polkinghorne, D.E. (1999). Traditional research and psychotherapy practice. *Journal of Clinical Psychology*, 55, 1429–1440. (A classic paper that offers a stimulating discussion of the relationship between research and practice, and suggests that much research does not reflect the complexities of actual work with clients.)

Back to the grassroots: the search for practice-based evidence

For reasons that are not hard to understand, there has been powerful resistance within the counselling and psychotherapy professions in recent years to many of the assumptions around which the therapy wars have been fought. There are several objections to the application of RCT methodology in counselling and psychotherapy research:

- RCTs produce biased results that support the therapy approach favoured by the director of the study.
- The process of selecting clients for inclusion in RCTs means that those who are chosen are not typical of the kind of clients seen in routine therapy practice.
- Clients are forced to express their views through fixed-choice questionnaires, and so are unable to say what they really feel about the therapy they have received.
- Therapist adherence to a treatment manual creates a situation that lacks relevance for everyday practice, because the majority of practitioners describe themselves as integrationist/eclectic in orientation.
- The most important outcomes of psychotherapy are experiences and insights that cannot be measured.
- Clients have preferences for the type of therapy that they think will help them – this factor is ignored in most RCTs.
- The evidence suggests that therapist competence and personal qualities, client motivation, and the strength of the therapist–client relationship are stronger predictors of outcome than therapy approach – RCTs are looking in the wrong place for the key to effective therapy.

Any one of these objections, if valid, would call the utility of the current therapy RCT literature seriously into question. However, adherents of RCTs are generally able to counter these objections. The supporters of RCT methodology also have a powerful weapon in their armoury, which is the argument that controlled studies may be flawed in many ways, but that efforts are continually being made to improve this methodology (which is undoubtedly true) and that there is no realistic alternative: RCTs represent the best evidence that is currently available.

Beyond critique of the inadequacies of RCT studies as a source of evidence for therapy practice, there has also been a sense that the therapy wars have not done enough to advance the quality of therapy that is offered to clients in relation to their huge cost. From the 1990s, there has therefore been a movement within the counselling and psychotherapy research community to look for alternative research approaches. For many of these researchers, this effort has been tempered by a reluctant acceptance that RCTs are here to stay, at least for the moment, because they are so solidly embedded within governmental policymaking procedures.

Rather than replace RCTs, the aim has been to supplement them with research conducted using a range of other methodologies. This position has become known as *methodological pluralism* (Howard, 1983), which can be defined as an appreciation of the role and contribution of a diversity of methodological traditions (e.g. RCTs, case studies, qualitative studies, action research, etc.).

Over the last 20 years, therefore, there has been a steady expansion in the types of counselling and psychotherapy research that have been published. Much of this work has sought to accomplish a fundamental realignment of the focus of therapy research. The scientific logic of randomised trial methodology is to create a highly controlled research space in which carefully defined and highly monitored therapy is delivered to clients who are screened on the basis of exhibiting a single disorder. The findings of RCTs therefore provide evidence of the efficacy of therapy under 'ideal' conditions. Further research then needs to be carried out on how effective this therapy is under conditions of routine practice. This research strategy attempts to mirror the approach taken by pharmaceutical companies when developing a new drug treatment: the drug is first created and tested in laboratory conditions and then tested by doctors in their everyday practice in clinics and hospitals. This set of assumptions about the relationship between research and practice can be described as an *evidence-based practice* model: practice is based on the best available research evidence. The alternative model can be characterised as a *practice-based evidence* approach: the aim is to investigate routine practice, to identify what works and what does not work, and thus make it possible to disseminate evidence of 'best practice' that can be used to improve standards.

The rationale for a practice-based evidence strategy for the development of research in counselling and psychotherapy is grounded in a set of assumptions about the nature of practical knowledge in this field:

- new ideas in therapy emerge from innovations and experiments carried out by front-line practitioners, not from university researchers or laboratory studies;
- counselling and psychotherapy are highly contextualised activities – theories and protocols need to be adapted to specific circumstances;
- good therapists are responsive and flexible in the way they work with clients, rather than strictly adhering to manuals or protocols;
- therapy is a co-constructed, collaborative activity, not a 'treatment' that is 'administered' by one person to another;
- practitioners are more likely to be influenced by stories and case reports than by statistical results;
- there can be different, yet equally valid, perspectives on what is helpful in therapy – there is no reason to expect that there is one fixed 'right answer'.

These are some of the factors that have motivated recent developments in counselling and psychotherapy research. These developments have taken a range of different methodological forms: the use of routine outcome and process measurement; the rise of qualitative research; the renewal of interest in case-based evidence; and the emergence of personal experience methodologies. Each of these research approaches is described below. The common ground, across all of them, is that they try to get close to what actually happens in therapy. They can be regarded as *grassroots* research, informed by the principle that knowledge rises from below rather than being imposed from above.

Suggested further reading

A collection of papers that provides an invaluable overview of various strands of practice-based research:

Barkham, M., Hardy, G.E. and Mellor-Clark, J. (eds.) (2010). *Developing and Delivering Practice-Based Evidence: A Guide for the Psychological Therapies*. Chichester: Wiley-Blackwell.

The use of routine outcome and process measurement

For the first 30 years of counselling and psychotherapy, research was characterised by the development of dozens of self-report rating scales and questionnaires that could be used to assess the prevalence and intensity of all imaginable aspects of therapy process and outcome. During that period, the use of these measures was largely restricted to research projects run by academic researchers in which data were collected, then analysed and written up in a research article. Most behaviour therapists and CBT practitioners collected data from their clients, but this information tended to be restricted to particular behaviour or cognitions that were the target of change for each client, and did not usually incorporate more general measures of outcome and process. Many of the measures that were available were complex to administer, and their use was restricted to those who had undergone special training in psychological assessment techniques. Many of these measures were published by commercial organisations and were expensive to purchase. From the 1990s, all this started to change. Three brief, free/low-cost outcome measures were developed for use in everyday practice: the Clinical Outcomes Routine Evaluation outcome measure (CORE), the Outcome Questionnaire (OQ) and the Outcome Rating Scale (ORS). Further information on these measures is provided in Chapter 8. These measures could be completed in a few minutes by clients at the start of every session, or regularly throughout therapy. It became possible for every practitioner, and every counselling and psychotherapy service, to evaluate the effectiveness of their work. On-line and PC-based versions of these tools were developed, which meant that data could be easily stored and analysed. Other practice-friendly scales were developed to measure aspects of the therapy process and relationships. Some practitioners and researchers began to experiment with various ways of using these measures to provide real-time immediate feedback to therapists and clients around the progress of therapy (Lambert, 2007). Databases began to be constructed, consisting of client outcome information from many clinics and agencies, thus allowing therapists and agencies to compare their success rates against sector benchmarks. The accumulation of information and the relative success rates of individual therapists opened up new possibilities for exploring the characteristics of high- and low-performing clinicians (Kraus et al., 2011). Empowered by these developments, groups of practitioners began to organise themselves into *practice research networks* that undertook collaborative research (Andrews et al., 2011; Castonguay et al., 2010b; Elliott and Zucconi, 2010; Wheeler et al., 2011). As a consequence of all this activity, training programmes for counsellors and psychotherapists were forced to devote more attention to the role of research for practice. The consequences for counselling and psychotherapy policy and practice, of the adoption of routine process and outcome measurement, are not yet entirely clear. At the present time, practitioners and agencies are still learning how to use these tools, and finding out what they can do with them. Nevertheless, this area does seem to represent a major shift in the relationship between research and practice, in that it reflects a kind of fusion of research and practice.

The shifting battleground: how valid is evidence that is derived from practice?

Box 2.2

Some of the implications of routine outcome measurement, for therapy policy-making, can be found in debate that took place around the publication of an analysis of a large database of CORE outcome scores collected from routine practice in the British National Health Service (NHS) (Stiles et al., 2006, 2007). In this study, which was published in *Psychological Medicine* (a highly influential research journal), outcome rates were assessed for counsellors in the NHS who were using either a CBT approach or were working in a person-centred, psychodynamic or integrative way with their clients. CORE outcome data were collected from over 6,000 clients in a wide range of clinical settings. Analysis of

(Continued)

(Continued)

these data showed that there were no meaningful differences in success rates across these different therapy approaches. This finding directly challenges the position of leading figures at a policymaking level in the NHS, who believed that evidence from RCTs indicated that CBT was the most effective therapy. In a critique of the CORE study, Clark et al. (2008) pointed out several ways in which there had been a lack of control around such factors as the adherence of the therapists to treatment protocols, and that these methodological weaknesses made the study worthless as evidence. A rejoinder can be found in Stiles et al. (2008). Apart from pointing up important ways in which practice-based research can be improved, this debate highlights a key issue. Who do you believe? Do you believe the results of tightly controlled studies designed and operated by academic researchers? Or do you believe in the verdict derived from evidence collected from thousands of clients and therapists?

The rise of qualitative research

In the early part of the 20th century, social science disciplines such as social anthropology, sociology, education and management studies began to develop a range of methods of qualitative research, making use of non-numerical sources of data such as interviews, informant diaries and participant observation. This narrative tradition (i.e. knowledge organised and conveyed through stories) took some time to have an impact on the field of psychology, and on research in counselling and psychotherapy. The 1990s saw special issues on qualitative research in the *Journal of Counseling Psychology* (Polkinghorne, 1994), the *British Journal of Guidance and Counselling* (McLeod, 1996), and *Psychotherapy Research* (Elliott, 1999). A further important step toward the acceptance of qualitative methods was the publication by Stiles (1993) and Elliott et al. (1999) of validity and publication guidelines for qualitative research. An overview of the scope and accomplishments of qualitative research in counselling and psychotherapy can be found in McLeod (2011). The distinctive contribution of qualitative research has been to carry out 'experience-near' studies that give voice to clients and therapists, and allow them to express in their own words the meaning of various types of therapeutic process. Qualitative researchers have also used techniques of conversation analysis, discourse analysis and narrative analysis to explore the moment-by-moment process through which clients and therapists convey and create meaning. In recent years, at least 10 per cent of published research articles on topics in counselling and psychotherapy have used qualitative or mixed method approaches, and most of these studies have explored, from various perspectives, the lived experience of routine therapy practice.

The renewal of interest in case-based evidence

Case studies have always represented a core methodology within psychology and the social sciences, because it is only within the parameters of a single case that complex processes can be examined. Case studies also make it possible to explore the relationship between a phenomenon and its context. Earlier in this chapter, the role of clinical case study evidence in the work of psychotherapy pioneers such as Freud was discussed. The methodological limitations of the clinical case study, as a means of rigorous inquiry, meant that it was largely neglected within the counselling and psychotherapy research literature for many years. However, through the mid-20th century, several groups of researchers, both within psychology as well as in other disciplines such as education and management studies, began to develop strategies for carrying out systematic case study research. Within the field of psychology, two important sources of methodological innovation were the work of Henry Murray (1938) in developing multi-method, team-based case analysis, and the use of time series analysis by researchers within the behaviour therapy and CBT community. A crucial breakthrough in the restoration of case study evidence to a lead role within counselling and psychotherapy research was the publication by Fishman (1999) of *The Case for a Pragmatic Psychology*. In this book, Dan Fishman argued that case study research was an indispensable element in any research programme that aimed to yield knowledge that would be relevant for practice. Similar arguments were being made, at that time, within other social science disciplines (Flyvbjerg, 2001). Within recent years, a growing number of therapy case studies have been published in dedicated case study journals, such as *Clinical Case Studies* and *Pragmatic Case Studies in Psychotherapy*, as well as in generic research journals. Examples of the new wave of therapy case study research can be found in McLeod (2010a) and in a special issue of *Counselling and Psychotherapy Research* (McLeod and Elliott, 2011).

Practising counsellors and psychotherapists are more likely to be influenced by case study evidence

One of the reasons that has been put forward to support the use of case study methods in research is that case studies are perceived by practitioners as being accessible and relevant. Stewart and Chambless (2010) carried out a survey of psychologists in the USA. All of these therapists had undergone training to PhD level, and were highly skilled in understanding and interpreting statistical information. Participants were sent an information package about the effectiveness

(Continued)

Box 2.3

(Continued)

of CBT for bulimia. Half of the participants received a package that included minimal case information, and mainly consisted of statistical data on treatment outcomes. The other half received a package that included some statistical information, but was mainly focused on describing a typical case of a client with bulimia who had been helped by CBT. The therapists in the second group were much more likely to be influenced by the information they had received than were those in the first group, in terms of reporting favourable attitudes toward CBT for bulimia and indicating a greater willingness to attend a training workshop on this approach.

The emergence of personal experience methodologies

A further area in which counselling and psychotherapy research has moved closer to everyday practice, in recent years, has been in the utilisation of a range of research methodologies that draw on direct recording and reflection by the researcher on his or her own personal experience. Examples of these methodologies include autoethnography (Meekums, 2008), narrative inquiry (Speedy, 2008), life history research (Etherington, 2003), heuristic research (Moustakas, 1990), relational research (Finlay and Evans, 2009), and radical practitioner inquiry (Lees and Freshwater, 2008; Macaskie and Lees, 2011). These approaches are in an early stage of development in relation to the field of therapy research, but are already making an impact in terms of highlighting the significance of researcher reflexivity as a source of knowledge (Finlay and Gough, 2003). Further information on these approaches can be found in McLeod (2011).

Box 2.4

The therapy genome project

Historically, biological science began with the classification of species of plants and animals. Later, it became clear that the observable differences between species were the result of different patterns of DNA. A crucial development in microbiology, genetics and medical science was the Human Genome Project (1990–2003), an international collaborative programme of research that sought to *identify* all the approximately 20,000–25,000 genes in human DNA, and determine how they are sequenced. The completion of these tasks then made it possible to develop new ways of intervening in diseases. A similar path has been followed within the domain of counselling and psychotherapy. Historically, the domain of therapy has been classified in terms of 'schools' or 'approaches' such as CBT, psychodynamic, person-centred and so on. More recently, several groups of researchers have been working on the identification of the underlying 'building blocks' of therapy, and how these elements are sequenced and combined (Cook et al., 2010; Jones and Pulos, 1993; McCarthy and Barber, 2009; McNeilly and Howard, 1991; Thoma and Cecero, 2009; Trijsburg et al., 2002). Just as the Human Genome Project aimed to generate a comprehensive mapping of the whole human genetic structure, the therapy genome project is aiming to move beyond studies of single therapy processes (such as empathic engagement, or challenging irrational beliefs), and develop a map of all possible therapeutic activities, techniques and interventions. Of course, the funding and person-power available to the therapy genome project is much less than the massive resources that were devoted to its biological counterpart. Nevertheless, some intriguing findings are beginning to emerge. For example, just as human beings share a high percentage of genetic material with other living creatures, most therapists tend to make use of a similar set of interventions, regardless of their espoused theoretical orientation (Thoma and Cecero, 2009).

The emergence of therapist attributes as a focus for process research

Many of the founding therapy approaches, such as psychoanalysis and client-centred therapy, placed a strong emphasis on the necessity for therapist personal development and self-awareness, for instance through participation in personal therapy. However, the research communities associated with these approaches did not follow through this issue in the form of studies that examined the identity attributes and personal qualities of more (or less) successful therapists. For example, the substantial body of research into the person-centred concept of empathy treated this factor as a general quality whose operation was observed and assessed in general terms, across a sample of therapists, rather than looking at how it played out at an individual level. The use of randomised trial research designs to compare the effectiveness of different therapy approaches led to the suppression of therapist effects, because these studies used training, manualisation and adherence procedures to ensure maximum uniformity across the therapists in a study. It was only when routine outcome measurement data began to be collected from large practice-based studies that it started to become apparent that there were important differences across therapists in the level of their effectiveness (Kraus et al., 2011; Luborsky et al., 1997; Okiishi et al., 2003; Wampold and Brown, 2005). These findings have, in turn, stimulated a great deal of interest in the contribution of therapist characteristics to the process and outcomes of therapy.

One influential line of research in this area has consisted of studies in which therapists within a given geographical area are asked to nominate the local 'master therapists' (the key question here has been:

'Who is the therapist in your community to whom you would send a member of your own family?'). Interview-based explorations of the attitudes and experience of master therapists and esteemed senior members of the profession have been conducted by Jennings and Skovholt (1999), Levitt and Williams (2010), Miller (2007) and Ronnestad and Skovholt (2001). These studies have tended to yield an account of accomplished therapists as people who are committed to lifelong learning, able to draw on their own life experience to inform their response to clients, and possessing exceptional interpersonal skills (in particular, willingness to make use of feedback from others). The limitation of this programme of research has been that the expertise or giftedness of the therapists who have been interviewed has been assessed only through reputational means, rather than on the basis of verified results with clients. It is possible that some (or all) of these 'master therapists' may be charismatic or persuasive figures whose reputations are not matched by their success in helping clients. An alternative strategy for identifying very effective therapists is to select them on the basis of percentages of clients who are clinically recovered, using standardised pre- and post-therapy measures. In a study of this type, Anderson et al. (2009) found that therapists who achieved good results with clients tended to display better interpersonal skills than their less effective colleagues, particularly in relation to responding constructively to interpersonal challenge. Kraus et al. (2011) found that therapists tended to be more effective with clients with some problems and less effective with clients who presented with other problems. In the Kraus et al. (2011) study, even the most effective therapists (who were clearly 'master therapists' by any definition) appeared to do relatively poorly with some categories of clients.

Research into therapist expertise has the potential to have a significant impact on training and practice. None of the research in this area has found that expertise is linked to age, gender, training, academic qualifications or experience. What seems to be emerging is the beginnings of an understanding of the personal attitudes, worldview and interpersonal skills of those people who possess a truly healing presence (Ronnestad and Skovholt, 2013). If these findings can be confirmed and elaborated in further research, it will begin to be possible to select candidates for counsellor and psychotherapist training with more confidence. The quality of therapy across the board can be enhanced if the mass of average-performing therapists can learn from their more gifted peers, and make even a small shift in their direction. Finally, studies of therapist expertise have found that a minority of practitioners are much less effective than their peers, and demonstrate an overall negative impact on their clients – further research should be capable of generating guidelines for identifying and supporting such individuals.

Important but neglected: research into cultural factors in therapy process and outcome

Box 2.5

The North American, European and Australasian societies within which counselling and psychotherapy have attained most prominence can all be characterised as reflecting increasing levels of cultural diversity. It would be foolish to argue that therapists and clients from different cultural, ethnic or racial backgrounds are not capable of establishing strong therapeutic relationships and working effectively together. At the same time, there exists considerable evidence that ethnic matching tends, on the whole, to exert a powerful impact on the process and outcome of therapy. Several studies have shown that therapy dyads, where therapist and client are from different cultural backgrounds, are associated with poorer outcomes (Farsimadan et al., 2007, 2011; Shin et al., 2005). In qualitative studies, clients from 'minority' groups have described their difficulties in relating to 'white' therapists (Thompson et al., 2004; Ward, 2005). A further set of studies has shown that 'culturally adapted' therapy is significantly more effective for clients from non-dominant cultures than is standard 'Western' therapy. It seems likely that these patterns also hold true in relation to social class differences (Balmforth, 2006). Although this area of research has important implications for training and practice, and the design of user-friendly counselling and psychotherapy services, it is generally disregarded by policymakers and compilers of clinical guidelines.

Exercise 2.3 Preferred directions for future research: setting the agenda

Take a few moments to reflect on what you have read in this chapter. What are the threads of research effort that seem to you to be particularly useful and relevant? What are the lines of research that you would designate as unhelpful and wasteful of resources? Imagine that you are a member of a committee that is responsible for setting the agenda for counselling and psychotherapy research for the next decade, including deciding priorities and allocating resources. What would your position be within such a collectivity? What are the areas of research, and specific research questions, that should receive urgent attention, and what are the areas that you would deem to be less important? What would be your top three priority areas/research questions?

Conclusions

A historical perspective on research in counselling and psychotherapy makes it clear that the quest to construct an evidence base for therapy has been shaped by a combination of social and economic factors, as well as by the ideas and insights of researchers. The existence of a therapy professional organised around distinct theoretical schools, alongside external pressure from healthcare systems to conform to managed care and evidence-based practice principles, and the availability of a range of sophisticated research tools and strategies, all created the conditions in the 1980s for the 'therapy wars' to break out. The fallout from these wars has taken the form of a sense that research is largely a matter of engineering victory for one's preferred therapy approach in the face of opposing forces. This attitude has had a corrosive impact on the spirit of genuine inquiry that characterised the work of pioneers of therapy research such as Carl Rogers and Hans Strupp. It has also served to concentrate a massive amount of resources and intellectual firepower on the task of measuring change through the use of questionnaire measures that, at best, capture only certain aspects of the meaning of therapy for clients. The outcome-research trench warfare that has dominated the efforts of the research community for several decades has drawn resources away from the use of potentially valuable alternative methodologies such as action research and ethnography, and from the creative development of new theories. It has also diverted attention from the exploration of critical questions around such issues as the role of psychiatric diagnosis, the importance of the person of the therapist, the limitations of culturally encapsulated models of therapy, the ways in which the meaning and use of therapy depend on stage of life course, and the impact of contextual and organisational factors on the process and outcome of therapy.

It also needs to be understood that, alongside the therapy wars, life goes on. The counselling and psychotherapy research community consists of an international network of researchers, many of whom have continued to pursue topics that have little or no relationship to the question of the differential effectiveness of therapy approaches, but that nevertheless have meaning to them and sustain a literature which is capable of inspiring and delighting readers. It is also important to acknowledge that the therapy research community encompasses several regional and national groups that have evolved distinctive traditions of inquiry. The research story told in the present chapter is largely based on the work of researchers in North America, who are responsible for the bulk of the papers that are published each year, and who have had a major influence on the direction taken by therapy research in the UK. Contrasting perspectives can be found in the work of researchers in Germany, Scandinavia, Japan and other regions.

It may be that the present moment in therapy research is one in which a shift is beginning to take place. The therapy wars require the heavy weaponry of randomised trial methodology, which is expensive. It may be that, in an economic recession and in the light of the costs of adapting to climate change and an aging population, the money to pay for that kind of research will no longer be forthcoming. What seems to be happening is that different versions of what is essentially a 'grassroots' approach to research are beginning to emerge – ways of doing research that are frugal and sustainable.

At one level, the history of research in counselling and psychotherapy reflects the interests and need to know of several generations of therapists and their academic supporters. Behind that history there is another story, which is concerned with much wider debates within Western society around the nature of knowledge, and the use of scientific methods to attain reliable knowledge. The history of therapy research can be seen as a struggle to find ways to bring order and understanding to the complexity of the process of therapy. To engage in this struggle, therapy researchers made use of the knowledge-creation strategies that were available to them in the world in which they operated. The next chapter explores the various types of knowledge-generating strategies that have been adopted by therapy researchers (and by researchers in all other disciplines). As we will see, it is by no means clear that there is one 'right' way to obtain reliable knowledge. So, finally, the lack of coherence that emerges from analysis of the history of therapy research (basically, a lot of different stuff all going on at the same time) is not a consequence of the therapy wars, but instead is a consequence of a different form of conflict: the methodology wars.

Suggested further reading

An interesting and accessible way to learn more about the development of therapy research is through the life-stories of leading researchers:

Castonguay, L.G., Muran, J.C., Angus, L., Hayes, J.A., Ladany, N. and Anderson, T. (eds.) (2010a). *Bringing Psychotherapy Research to Life: Understanding Change Through the Work of Leading Clinical Researchers.* Washington, DC: American Psychological Association.

How do we know what we know?
The philosophical context of research

'Scientists need not be objective; only science needs to be objective.' (Prochaska, 2010: 251)

'[S]cience is an evolving landscape of stories about how knowledge accumulates ... there are potentially many ways of engaging with science.' (Lane and Corrie, 2006: 7)

The statement at the head of this chapter, taken from a piece of autobiographical writing by James Prochaska, one of the most influential psychotherapy researchers of the 20th century, serves as a powerful introduction to the topic of philosophy of science. Individual scientists and researchers are typically passionate about their subject. They care, they devote their lives to a quest for knowledge, sometimes they cut corners. They are human beings. It is science as a whole, as an organised system of knowledge generation, that needs to be, in some sense, 'objective'.

It is a mistake to think about therapy research, or any type of research, as merely a straightforward matter of obeying a set of guidelines or following a recipe. There are serious splits and conflicts within the research community, associated with different conceptions or stories of what comprises valid research (Lane and Corrie, 2006), and enormously challenging moral questions around what kind of research should be carried out. As a result, in order to engage with the therapy research literature, it is important to develop some level of appreciation of underlying philosophical points of view around the nature of knowledge.

Therapy research is conducted in the context of a philosophical debate about *epistemology*, or the nature of knowledge, that has been on-going for at least 300 years. In the 17th century, the debate centred on the challenge to religious beliefs and truths that was presented by new scientific discoveries. In the 21st century, the debate still incorporates some of the same issues (now defined in terms of creationism vs. Darwin's theory of evolution), but also new issues such as the way in which scientific and technological 'progress' has resulted in the destruction of the natural world.

The fundamental questions that underlie these debates are 'How do we know what we know?' and 'How do we know that what we know is in some sense true or valid, rather than error or delusion?' In response to these questions, the field of *philosophy of science* emerged over the course of the 20th century as one of the most important branches of philosophy. Philosophers of science have attempted to analyse and understand the basic nature of scientific inquiry – how do scientists create knowledge that is so powerful that it has transformed the modern world?

The aim of this chapter is to introduce some key philosophical ideas around the nature of knowledge, and to explore their relevance for the field of counselling and psychotherapy research. The chapter offers a brief account of philosophy as a discipline, before moving on to consider a series of perspectives on philosophy of science.

Levels of philosophical analysis

Box 3.1

It is useful to be clear about some of the different logical levels at which philosophical discussion takes place. *Ontological* questions refer to debates around the ultimate nature of reality. Examples of ontological questions include: Does God exist? Can reality be divided into mind/subject and body/object? Is there a single reality, or plural realities? By contrast, *epistemological* questions refer to issues around the extent to which we can gain knowledge about the world. Examples of epistemological questions include: Are there some propositions that are self-evidently true? Is empirical observation a certain source of knowledge? To what extent is all knowledge relative to the interests and presuppositions of the knower? Can all phenomena be meaningfully subjected to mathematical analysis? Finally, there is *method*, which refers to the specific procedures (e.g. experiments, questionnaires, interviews) that are used to generate knowledge. The concept of *methodology* is used when discussing the issues that arise when various ontological, epistemological and methodical positions are combined in different ways. An example of a methodological issue associated with contemporary research in counselling and psychotherapy concerns the status of knowledge derived from qualitative methods, such as analysis of unstructured interviews. It can reasonably be argued that such knowledge is inevitably *relativist* in epistemological terms, because different interviewers will inevitably elicit somewhat different accounts of experience from

(Continued)

(Continued)

those who are being interviewed. At an ontological level, therefore, it would be logically inconsistent to claim that knowledge which is based on qualitative interviews can be interpreted as leading to a single, 'objective' conclusion. For people who believe (ontologically) that there always must be a single objectively provable answer to any question, qualitative research is therefore worthless. By contrast, for those who believe (ontologically) in a 'plural universe', the attempt to arrive at a single answer (e.g. through measurement and experimentation) around which form of therapy is most effective, is equally misguided.

The nature of philosophy

There is a growing interest among counsellors and psychotherapists in the relevance of philosophical insights and ideas for their work. As competing theories of therapy and conflicting research findings have accumulated, there has been a need to develop some kind of meta-perspective from which diverse ideas can be evaluated and sorted out. In addition, the expansion of therapy beyond its roots in European culture has meant that therapists are now working with clients who possess quite different views of the world. Even within mainstream European and North American culture, technological advances are raising questions about fundamental issues of personal identity, as exemplified by the capacity of participants in social networking sites to invent new 'selves'.

Philosophy is the oldest academic discipline, and the immense scope and range of philosophical writing can make it hard for counsellors to make meaningful use of philosophy as a resource. Professional philosophers undergo many years of scholarly training in order to achieve a mastery of their discipline, and even then will tend to specialise in a particular area. In terms of understanding what philosophy has to offer, it is important to appreciate that philosophy does not aim to generate a set of 'findings' or fixed 'truths', but instead operates as a kind of open-ended conversation about the ultimate questions of human existence. It is useful to think about the role of philosophy in terms of an active process (philosophi*sing*) that questions existing ideas and arrives at more nuanced or differentiated ways of understanding. It is possible to divide the field of philosophical analysis into three broad and overlapping domains: *ontology* (the analysis of the ultimate nature of reality), *epistemology* (the principles of arriving at valid knowledge) and *moral philosophy* (how to decide between what is right and wrong). Although debates around the basis for scientific knowledge have mainly been concerned with epistemological issues, they have also touched on ontological and moral questions at various stages.

Suggested further reading

Starting points for those who are new to philosophy:

Blackburn, S. (1999). *Think: A Compelling Introduction to Philosophy.* Oxford: Oxford University Press.

Okasha, S. (2002). *Philosophy of Science: A Very Short Introduction.* Oxford: Oxford University Press.

Making sense of science: philosophical perspectives

There have been many attempts to make sense of the process of science, and to establish an agreed framework or rules of scientific method. The following sections offer an outline of this story in terms of the historical development of some of the most influential philosophical ideas about how science operates. It is important to realise that the act of presenting these ideas in some kind of historical sequence does not mean that earlier ideas have been supplanted by later formulations. On the contrary, each of the images of science that are discussed below can still claim some support within the contemporary academic and scientific community. What has tended to happen is that challenges to older ideas have not led the adherents of these earlier ideas to abandon their positions, but instead have acted as a trigger to develop better versions of them.

The traditional view of science: bedrock empiricism

From a European perspective, the idea of systematic scientific inquiry as a means of generating new knowledge about the world probably began to take shape in the 16th century. This is without doubt a Eurocentric view of the nature of scientific development, because it does not account for the influence of earlier traditions of science that existed in Arab cultures and in China. To understand how and why scientific thinking in Europe evolved in the way that it did, it is essential to have an appreciation of the extent to which Christian religious beliefs dominated all aspects of life in the pre-scientific era. For example, the Italian scientist Galileo Galilei (1564–1642) was imprisoned in his own home for the final years of his life for daring to conduct research in physics and astronomy that challenged the teachings of the Church. In Europe at that time, it was therefore necessary for anyone who believed in rational analysis and the use of objective evidence to argue their case very carefully and cautiously in order to be able to carve out a space for scientific work to take place. The main philosophers who were in the vanguard of this movement were the British empiricists Francis Bacon (1561–1626), John Locke (1632–1704) and David Hume (1711–1776). These philosophers were not only, or even principally, concerned with the question of scientific method, but were seeking to make it possible to create a different kind of society in which people could have the freedom to think for themselves. Their ideas have been characterised as *Enlightenment* philosophy, because of their emphasis on the capacity of the individual to achieve insight and to see the world 'in a new light'.

The notion of science that these thinkers espoused was one in which the task of the job of the scientist was to collect objective facts and information, and then to arrive at general laws through a process of *induction*, or the emergence of patterns within a set of data. The major achievements of science of that time reflected this approach: the identification of chemical elements; the classification of plants and animals; the observation of disease entities. At a philosophical level, this approach to building new knowledge can be viewed as a rejection of *rationalism*. A *rationalist* perspective on knowledge assumes that we have access to undisputable truths (such as the existence of God, or the idea of causality) through rational analysis of our own thought processes. The empiricists, by contrast, were highly critical of any beliefs based on rationalist principles, and argued instead that the only reliable source of true knowledge was the evidence of our senses.

Empiricism has played a dominant role on Western culture since the 1700s, and through globalisation has come to have a powerful influence on most other cultures as well. The impact of empiricism can be seen in virtually all papers that are currently published in counselling and psychotherapy research journals. These papers are written in a manner that requires the author to show his or her empirical evidence and explain how that evidence was obtained. The basic idea that lies behind this practice is the notion that true knowledge needs to be backed up by evidence that is in principle available to anyone who wishes to observe it (e.g. by replicating the study). The high-point of empiricism arrived in the *positivist* school of thought, originating in the writings of the French philosopher and social scientist Auguste Comte (1798–1857), who argued for the unity of all knowledge and that the phenomena of the social sciences, such as sociology and psychology (and by implication psychotherapy), could ultimately be reduced to biology, genetics and the laws of physics. Comte's 'positive' science proposed that all phenomena, from physics at one extreme to human behaviour at the other, could be explained by a single set of natural laws. Von Wright (1971) has characterised the main tenets of positivism as being, first, that 'the exact natural sciences, in particular mathematical physics, set a methodological ideal or standard which measures the degree of development or perfection of all the other sciences, including the humanities' (1971: 2). Positivism also assumes a unity of scientific methods. In other words, the same methods are applicable in all fields of knowledge. Positivist thinkers are only satisfied by explanations that are framed in terms of strict 'cause-and-effect' sequences, and reject any explanatory models that employ any notion of 'purpose'. Finally, the goal of 'positive science' is to attain a capacity to predict what will happen, and exert control over future events.

Exercise 3.1 The pros and cons of positivism

What are the strengths, and also the limitations, of positivism in relation to the study of counselling and psychotherapy? What therapy topics or concepts do you consider as being amenable to positivist inquiry and measurement? Conversely, what kinds of therapy process or experience are *not* amenable to measurement?

There are few, if any, contemporary therapy researchers who are 'pure' empiricists or positivists, for reasons that are examined in later sections of this chapter. Nevertheless, a broadly empiricist approach lies at the heart of the whole enterprise of counselling and psychotherapy research. An empiricist attitude presents a challenge to therapy practice that is solely guided by theory, or by the teachings of leaders of schools of therapy. An empirical approach takes the position that 'good' therapy is not a matter of 'being person-centred' or 'working with transference', but instead is evaluated in terms of whether the client benefits from what is offered. In addition, the principles of positivism call for a willingness to define and carefully describe, and if possible measure, the phenomena of therapy. There is considerable resistance to these principles on the part of some therapy practitioners, who argue that there are important dimensions of human experience that cannot be measured, and that the aim of prediction and control leaves no possibility for choice. The empiricist response to these objections can be tracked back to the ideas that drove Locke and Hume: What kind of knowledge is it, that is not based on evidence which (at least in principle) is open to all?

A different type of empiricism: phenomenology

The underlying notion of an observation-based strategy for systematic inquiry, promoted by the empiricists, was developed in a different direction by the German philosopher Edmund Husserl (1859–1938), who introduced

(Continued)

Box 3.2

(Continued)

the notion of *phenomenology*. The key idea that informs phenomenological inquiry is that it is possible to uncover the *essence* of any experience, and build systems of reliable knowledge based on the evidence of the essential characteristics of phenomena. Husserl described a process of *bracketing-off* assumptions about a phenomenon, as a means of eventually arriving at an appreciation of what that experience really means. Phenomenological ideas have been highly influential within therapy, for example through existential therapy and the theories of Carl Rogers, and they also play a key role in qualitative research.

Beyond empiricism: the contribution of Popper and Kuhn

The image of the scientist as empiricist is deeply ingrained in the collective imagination. A scientist is someone who meticulously records observations in a big book, or enters data into a computer, and then carefully pores over this information until he or she arrives at a 'eureka' moment at which a new pattern or principle becomes apparent. Unfortunately, this idea of science is almost entirely wrong.

Exercise 3.2 Being an empiricist

In order to gain first-hand experience of the limitations of a purely empirical approach to the development of knowledge, take any aspect of the world and carry out a strictly empirical inquiry into its properties. It is sensible to try this activity in respect of a relatively narrowly defined slice of the world, such as 'The behaviour of my dog over the next 15 minutes', 'What Carl Rogers says in the Gloria tape', or 'Traffic movements in the street outside my window'. Your task, in relation to the chosen topic of inquiry, is first to *just observe* (i.e. note down everything that you see, hear, smell and so on) and then to look at your notes to identify what you have learned (or maybe what you might learn if you were to carry out this exercise for a longer period of time).

The problem with empiricism, which will probably become obvious to anyone within a few minutes of embarking on Exercise 3.2, is that it is impossible to 'just observe'. The act of observation requires a prior act of intention, which in turn is based on some kind of prior assumption about what is important or interesting. In addition, it is very hard to record observations without using categories. For instance, 'my dog moves his head in an upward direction for 3 seconds ...' is a partial and incomplete descriptive statement. What actually happened was 'my dog looked at the door'. However, 'looking' is a category that subsumes a large number of constituent observations (probably too many to record unless I have video recordings of the event from several angles). What became apparent to philosophers who analysed the process of science, therefore, was that, yes, careful observation and an empirical approach are important, but that these are always interwoven with the use of pre-existing theory or a system of concepts/categories. Although many philosophers of science have arrived at this conclusion, the most useful 'post-empiricist' analyses of how scientific knowledge is created have been contributed by Sir Karl Popper (1902–1994) and Thomas Kuhn (1922–1996).

In a series of books, Popper (1959, 1962, 1972) argued that science progresses through a process of *conjectures* and *refutations*. Popper's view was that scientists devise theories or conjectures that are then tested through experimental methods in an effort to refute them. Popper asserts that no theory can represent the complete truth, but that the best theory is the one that can stand up to the most rigorous testing. It is in this way that scientists arrive at theories that have immense power and practical value. For Popper, the role of the scientist as a well-equipped, skilful *critic* lay at the heart of the scientific enterprise. From this perspective, academic freedom is important because any restriction on the potential to criticise diminishes the possibility of advancement in knowledge. For Popper, the weakness of systems of thought such as Marxism and psychoanalysis was located in their unwillingness to open themselves to criticism. Popper saw these theories as representing *closed* systems of thought that were not open to modification on the basis of evidence, and as a result could be regarded as fundamentally totalitarian or anti-democratic. Popper can therefore be regarded as a representative of one of the major themes within Western philosophy, which has been to argue that a commitment to rationality and empirical evidence is necessary to counteract the human tendency to be seduced by illusion and dogma.

> ## Exercise 3.3 Taking the concept of critical refutation seriously
>
> There are many approaches to therapy that are currently in use: person-centred, CBT, psychodynamic, narrative and so on. Which therapy approach makes most sense to you? Can you envisage a research study that might yield results that would induce you to abandon your currently favoured approach to therapy and adopt an alternative approach? What are the points in the development of your favoured approach to therapy where the theory and practice of the approach were influenced by evidence from research?

The ideas of Popper can usefully be set alongside the work of Thomas Kuhn, who observed that, although Popper was right in identifying the crucial role of criticism and refutation in scientific progress, in practice the dominant scientific theories were very rarely ever actually refuted or overthrown. Kuhn (1962) pointed out that any powerful and influential theory usually consisted of a complex network of interlocking propositions. As a result, even if an experiment or set of observations convincingly refuted one particular part of the theory, it was usually possible to 'save' the theory by using concepts from another part of the theory to explain the contradictory results, or even to abandon one segment of the theory while retaining the theory as a whole.

Kuhn (1962) suggested that an adequate explanation of science needed to take account of how scientific knowledge and activity is socially organised. In the early years in the life of a new area of science, there would probably be many competing theories as different researchers attempted to grasp a poorly understood domain of knowledge. However, as soon as one clearly adequate theory emerged that the majority of scientists in the field could support, these researchers came together to form a scientific 'community' linked through adherence to a shared 'paradigm'. The concept of paradigm is central to the work of Kuhn, and it is a complex idea. It is possible to identify more than 20 alternative uses of the concept in *The Structure of Scientific Revolutions,* the book in which Kuhn (1962) developed the core of his model. A scientific paradigm can be seen as consisting of the whole apparatus or web of knowledge employed by the members of a scientific community: theories, concepts, methods, common educational experiences, readership of key books and journals, and participation in conferences and seminars. Kuhn suggested that, most of the time, scientists engage in what he called 'normal' science, which consists of working out a detailed analysis and application of the paradigm. Occasionally, however, it may become apparent that the theory or paradigm is not able to account for important phenomena, and the scientific community is precipitated into a crisis which is resolved through a revolution represented by the adoption of a new and more comprehensive theory. In relation to Popper's concept of science as consisting of a series of 'conjectures' and 'refutations', the key new ideas introduced by Kuhn (1962) were that, first, the process of developing scientific 'conjectures' or theories was in fact a complex undertaking that involved many people over a considerable period of time. Second, Kuhn emphasised that refutations of major ideas, in the form of 'scientific revolutions', did occur, but only rarely. Finally, Kuhn's ideas stimulated a whole new field of 'social studies of science', which has continued to examine the ways in which scientific knowledge is socially organised, rather than comprising a purely rational or logical activity.

> **Suggested further reading**
>
> Accessible accounts of the life and work of Popper, Kuhn and other leading philosophers of science:
>
> Brown, J.B. (ed.) (2012). *Philosophy of Science: The Key Thinkers.* New York: Continuum.

The ideas of Popper and Kuhn represent a compelling analysis of the nature of scientific inquiry. There are many points of contact between their concept of science and the way that therapy research is conducted. The principle of 'refutation' informs all aspects of the inquiry process. For example, research papers need to demonstrate that they have considered alternative interpretations of their findings, and are able to demonstrate that the results that have been recorded are not consistent with (i.e. refute) these other models while supporting the favoured model (i.e. the paradigm within which the study comprises an example of 'normal science'). Although it is hard to design single experiments or studies in the field of counselling and psychotherapy that might refute established theories, it is possible to identify many examples of areas in which researchers have carried out reviews of previous research, in order to determine whether the overall weight of evidence supports or refutes a theory. Areas in which this kind of endeavour has been pursued include reviews of evidence around:

- Freud's theories concerning links between childhood events and adult psychopathology;
- the theory of 'necessary and sufficient condition for change in therapy' developed by Carl Rogers;
- the proposition that CBT is the most effective form of therapy for anxiety and depression.

Each of these examples represents an area of theory and research that corresponds to the pattern of scientific progress described by Popper and Kuhn. In each area, the bold generalisations put forward by pioneering researchers were refuted, in the sense of not being strictly true. However, in each case the underlying 'paradigm' managed to survive.

Exercise 3.4 Exploring the social organisation of therapy research

Select one therapy topic that has been the subject of sustained research attention (examples might include: therapist self-disclosure, homework tasks, the therapeutic alliance, the role of metaphor in therapy, the influence of gender on therapy outcomes). Use internet search tools to collect information on who has done research on your chosen topic, where they work, where they publish, who they know, what theoretical models they refer to, and what conferences they attend. Take a large sheet of paper and create a map of the scientific community that exists around your topic. If you are a member of a learning group where other members are also undertaking this exercise, then it is of interest to compare maps – you will find that some topics are supported by coherent communities of inquiry, whereas other research topics draw on fragmented networks, or on the efforts of isolated individuals. Finally, what are the implications for you, if you are considering carrying out some research of your own on this topic? At what points might you be able to connect with, or join, the community of inquiry that supports research into your topic?

A further issue that needs to be taken into account is the extent to which the knowledge base of counselling and psychotherapy has attained the status of a 'science' in the sense intended by Kuhn. There are many competing theories of therapy: the field is far from achieving a unified paradigm. Some commentators have proposed that psychology as a whole, and therapy as a part of that whole, are at a pre-paradigmatic stage. So, although the philosophy of science developed by Kuhn, Popper and others might describe an ideal set of principles through which counselling and psychotherapy might make significant headway in creating more robust and satisfactory theories and techniques, it could be that the field is not yet sufficiently mature to enter this land of promise.

Suggested further listening

The BBC Radio 4 series *In Our Time* consists of 40-minute conversations between leading academic experts, on a wide range of topics. These conversations are chaired by Melvyn Bragg, who ensures that the discussion remains relevant and accessible to listeners who lack previous knowledge of the subject. All of these programmes are freely available on the BBC iPlayer. The programme on 'The Scientific Method' explores many of the issues examined in the present chapter. Other relevant items in the *In Our Time* archive include programmes on 'David Hume', 'Empiricism', 'Logical Positivism', 'Popper', 'Pragmatism', 'Relativism', 'Science in the 20th Century', 'Science's Revelations', 'The Enlightenment in Scotland', and 'The Scientist'.

The idea of a 'human science'

Philosophers of science such as Popper and Kuhn did not believe that there was any fundamental difference between the physical sciences, such as physics and chemistry, and the social sciences, such as sociology or economics. For them, science was science: any systematic endeavour to create reliable knowledge basically needed to follow the same set of procedures. In opposition to these views, others have argued that any attempt by the social and human sciences to mimic the methods of the physical sciences is misguided and doomed to failure. From this perspective, it makes little sense to conceptualise people and social groups as objects that can be experimentally manipulated in the same way as physical entities such as rocks or metals might be. The very aims of traditional science, centring on the prediction and control of events, could be viewed as philosophically and politically inappropriate when applied to the study of human action, which can be regarded as intentional and reflexive. The search in the natural sciences for universal 'laws of nature' are similarly regarded as mistakenly applied to elucidating culturally embedded ways of knowing in which there are many local truths but perhaps no universal truth.

Underpinning the idea that there needs to be a *human science*, which is fundamentally different from 'natural science', are a set of basic ontological questions (i.e. questions about the basic nature of reality). It makes sense to most people in Western society that an objective physical reality exists that is ultimately composed of atoms, molecules and so on. It can also be argued that alongside this physical reality, and interacting with it in all sorts of ways, is a human or social reality that is ultimately composed of human consciousness, and its expression in language and culture. The rationale for this concept of a social reality has been articulated by several philosophers who can be described as pursuing a constructivist or social constructionist perspective (Lock and Strong, 2010). The central principle that unties these thinkers is that the realm of personal and social affairs is not determined by physical forces and laws, but instead is actively co-constructed by people.

In terms of how to carry out systematic research inquiry from a constructionist perspective, the focus for much of the opposition to the dominant positivist approach to research on people has rested with the proponents of interpretive or *hermeneutic* approaches to inquiry (Taylor, 1979). The key early figure in this tradition was Wilhelm Dilthey (1833–1911), who proposed that the study of persons could only be properly carried out through a distinctive human science. The method of hermeneutic inquiry has its origins in the efforts of biblical scholars to interpret the meaning of incomplete fragments of Scripture. This approach supplies the basis for a number of research strategies that use qualitative and interpretive methods. These strategies draw in general on the kinds of research activity carried out in disciplines such as the arts, humanities and theology, in that the task of the researcher is ultimately to interpret or analyse the meanings that are conveyed or expressed in a research 'text' (e.g. a transcript of a therapy session, an interview or a client's personal diary). Unlike positivist science, the aim of this type of inquiry is not prediction and control of future events, but the construction of more powerful and illuminating ways of *understanding* lived experience. The vision of a human science has been instrumental in shaping recent developments in qualitative research, not only within the field of counselling and psychotherapy research but across all social science disciplines (Denzin and Lincoln, 2011).

The possibility of adopting a human science approach to research in counselling and psychotherapy raises a number of difficult issues. There are two main points of tension. On the one hand, by emphasising human intentionality and purpose, the role of language and history in maintaining and creating meaning, and the interconnectedness of people, qualitative research/human science and psychotherapy are talking the same language and seeing the world from a similar standpoint. On the other hand, the cost of this similarity in world-view is that it directly opens up theories of therapy, and the way that therapists think about their work, to critical reappraisal. The second point of tension relates to the social function of therapy research. Therapy is inevitably a messy business. At the best of times, there is a lot happening in a therapy session that does not readily fit into any model or protocol. A positivist-empiricist, measurement-oriented approach to research simplifies and tidies up this complexity, and presents the world with an appearance of certainty in respect to what is known. The cost of a human science approach, therefore, may be to undermine public belief in the efficacy of therapy.

There are some further factors that need to be taken into consideration. Human science inevitably leads in the direction of *reflexivity*: the researcher himself or herself can no longer be regarded as outside the game, as a detached 'objective' collector of 'data', but needs to be recognised as a person with passions and interests, who is a member of a social group that constructs the world in a particular manner. This idea leads to all kinds of trouble, for anyone committed to the notion of scientific progress.

Exercise 3.5 Reflecting on the implications of reflexivity

Identify one therapy-related research topic or question in which you have an interest. It might be valuable to use the same topic that you explored in Exercise 3.3. Take a few minutes to write down, in note form, your own personal experiences, assumptions and beliefs about this topic. If you were to conduct some research on this topic, in what ways might your own standpoint and assumptions influence the way you designed the study, the way you collected data, and the way you analysed this material? What can you do to ensure that your research on this topic comprises a meaningful process of genuine discovery, rather than merely an exercise in which you look in a mirror and 'find' what you already know?

The deconstruction of science: critical theory, social justice, feminist and postmodern perspectives

The ideas that have been introduced in the preceding sections of this chapter reflect the kind of thinking that was associated with the development of scientific methods in the 19th century, through to the high-point of scientific progress in the latter half of the 20th century. However, the closing decades of the 20th century began to see a massive cultural backlash against the view that science inevitably functioned as a positive beneficial force for progress within human affairs. The slaughter of World War I, followed by the Nazi Holocaust and the use of atomic weapons, provided vivid examples of ways in which scientific knowledge could be used for evil purposes, and might even lead to the ultimate destruction of the human race. These events have been followed by regular reminders of the negative consequences of scientific and technological 'advances': thalidomide, pesticides, Bhopal, global warming and so on. Within the philosophical and social science communities, a range of significant challenges to the hegemony of science began to emerge. These challenges centred on two main ideas. First, it was argued that scientific knowledge was intrinsically bound up with the exertion of power and control by elite groups within society. Second, it was suggested that scientific methods were intrinsically destructive of relationships between people, and between people and nature.

One of the key figures in the critical philosophy of science was Paul Feyerabend (1924–1994), who argued that 20th-century science had become part of the cultural mythology of industrial societies, and claimed to be capable of delivering a level of truth and certainty that could never be attained. In his classic text, *Against Method*, originally published in 1975, Feyerabend (2010) pointed out that all cultures possess their own systems of belief and knowledge, and that rather than regard Western science as being somehow more valid than the ideas of shamans and traditional healers, it would be more appropriate to view it merely as a belief system that happened to be consistent with the values of a particular group of people at a particular point in history. His careful analysis of the actual practices of scientists suggested to him that real-life scientists do not adhere to the rules specified by philosophers of science, but instead in reality follow an 'anarchistic' strategy in which 'anything goes' as long as others can be persuaded of its veracity.

Elsewhere, the 'Frankfurt School' of philosophical and social critique, associated with the idea of 'critical theory' and the work of writers such as Jurgen Habermas (born 1929), pointed out that the complexity and costliness of modern science meant that it was inevitably controlled by those who could pay for it, such as governments and multi-national corporations. Elsewhere, feminist researchers and philosophers argued that research knowledge predominantly emphasises the values, cognitive style and interests of men, and argued that it was necessary to develop a 'feminist standpoint' in relation to the pursuit of scientific truth (Anderson, 2011). In addition, scholars from minority and oppressed ethnic and cultural groups argued that the people whom they represented were treated as *subjects* of research, often as part of the apparatus of colonial rule, rather than as equal participants in a knowledge-producing process (Smith, 1999).

Another important source of critical philosophical analysis of science has emerged from the broad cultural movements known as *postmodernism* and *post-structuralism* (Ward, 2010). Basically, these perspectives suggest that we have entered an era of fundamental cultural change, ranging across art, literature, cinema and architecture to science and psychology. The shift that has occurred involves an unwillingness to accept the validity of the 'grand narratives' of progress and rational enlightenment that dominated the thinking of the modern world of the 20th century, and instead to embrace a stance that exhibits an eclectic choosing of possibilities that are evaluated in terms of whether they yield reliable and practical 'local knowledges'. Clearly, this position raises major questions about how to pursue scientific inquiry, and even around whether the goal of scientific knowledge is feasible or desirable. Postmodern writers such as Michel Foucault (1926–1984) have been active in *deconstructing* the assumptions on which modern systems of thought have been assembled. It is less clear, at the present time, how a postmodern perspective might be used to *reconstruct* science (or knowledge-making more widely understood) in an alternative fashion.

Finally, the social and cultural hegemony enjoyed by science has been questioned by those who argue that a scientific world-view destroys the human capacity to appreciate sacred dimensions of life, and to experience the world as enchanted. Accessible and compelling accounts of this type of stance can be found in Abram (1996) and Eisenstein (2007). These writers call for the adoption of direct forms of knowing that can be achieved through involvement in the natural world, accompanied by an appreciation of the way that conventional science leads to separation between people, and between people and nature.

Taken together, recent critiques of the role and functioning of scientific inquiry present a significant challenge to the counselling and psychotherapy research community. The mainstream sciences, such as physics and medical research, are so deeply embedded in the fabric of society, and so lavishly funded, that they can largely afford to ignore such criticisms. By contrast, counselling and psychotherapy research is less firmly established, and as a result is more open to alternative ideas. In addition, the substance of the critiques that have been outlined in the previous paragraphs makes a lot of sense for many counsellors and psychotherapists, who can see in their own therapy rooms the negative consequences of inequalities of power, gender and ethnicity, and the objectifying impact of technology. As a result, there have been several attempts within the counselling and psychotherapy research community to enlist support for radically new ways of doing research that are consistent with postmodern principles.

Critical science: the case of depression

Espousing a critical perspective on the nature of scientific research is not merely a matter of academic debate. The area of research into the effectiveness of treatment for depression provides a powerful example of the relationship between scientific knowledge and economic and political power. From the 1960s, antidepressant medication has been promoted by medical establishments around the world as an evidence-based intervention, supported by findings from hundreds of well-conducted studies. These claims have been scrutinised by the British psychiatrist David Healy (1999, 2006), who presents an alternative interpretation: major pharmaceutical companies created a market for antidepressants, overinflated the benefits of these drugs, and did not give sufficient publicity to side-effects. In the opinion of Healy (1999, 2006) and other writers such as Greenberg (2011) and Levine (2007), the profit-focused orientation of the research and development and marketing divisions of multi-national drug companies have made it almost impossible to arrive at a balanced appraisal of the usefulness of the products that they sell. This is a topic that has major implications for the health and well-being of a large proportion of people who are seen by counsellors and psychotherapists.

Box 3.3

Suggested further reading

A passionate and accessible account of the nature and development of critical perspectives on social knowledge can be found in:

Kincheloe, J.L. and McLaren, P. (2008). Rethinking critical theory and qualitative research. In N.K. Denzin and Y.S. Lincoln (eds.), *The Landscape of Qualitative Research*, 3rd edn. Thousand Oaks, CA: Sage.

Resolving the tensions arising from competing concepts of 'science': towards contextualised, pragmatic ways of knowing

In many respects, the ideas that have been introduced and discussed in this chapter reflect some of the fundamental fault-lines within modern society as a whole. The emergence of science in the 17th and 18th centuries was associated with widespread questioning of the validity of belief derived from religious faith and spiritual practice. Yet, religion and spirituality still remain hugely important aspects of the fabric of contemporary society. The growth of science has also been associated with debates around the role of measurement and mathematics in the construction of true knowledge, the possibility of everyone achieving certain knowledge, and the relative merits of theoretical reflection and analysis as against empirical observation. Again, these debates continue. Within the field of counselling and psychotherapy research, there seems to have been in recent years an increasing questioning of any attempts to claim certainty based on the application of any specific methodologies, and a general movement in the direction of a pragmatic, methodologically pluralist vision of therapy research. Influential voices within this movement have been Jerome Bruner, Dan Fishman and Bent Flyvbjerg.

Jerome Bruner has been one of the leading figures in psychology for the last 50 years. He argues that any attempt to carry out practically useful research needs to remain open to different ways of knowing:

> [T]here are two modes of cognitive functioning, two modes of thought, each providing distinctive ways of ordering experience, of constructing reality. The two (though complementary) are irreducible to one another. (1986: 11)

Bruner calls these two ways of knowing the *paradigmatic* and *narrative* modes. He characterises the paradigmatic mode as logico-scientific, which 'attempts to fulfil the ideal of a formal, mathematical system of description and explanation'. The narrative mode, by contrast, deals in 'intention and action' and works with 'good stories, gripping drama, believable (though not necessarily "true") historical accounts' (1986: 12–13). In reflecting on the role and methodologies of the human sciences, he observes that 'in contrast to our vast knowledge of how science and logical reasoning proceed, we know precious little in any formal sense about how to make good stories' (1986: 14). These ideas provide a strong rationale for the role of qualitative or human science research, which is primarily narrative in orientation, alongside more conventional quantitative (paradigmatically oriented) investigations.

Current thinking around the type of research that is most relevant within the domain of counselling and psychotherapy has also been influenced by the concept of *pragmatism*, the idea that what is important is not the creation of elegant theories, but the development of models and ways of understanding that 'work' in terms of making a difference to people's lives. Fishman (1999), an American psychologist, and Flyvbjerg (2001), a Danish social scientist, argue that knowledge that makes a difference needs to involve the analysis of individual cases, in which the operation of general processes or principles can be understood within a specific context. In response to their vision, there has been an increasing emphasis in recent years on the use of research designs that involve the *intensive* analysis of single cases, alongside designs that are based on the analysis of *extensive* samples.

Conclusions

This chapter has offered a brief introduction to some of the main strands of thought within philosophy of science. It can be seen that these ideas have some potentially major implications for the conduct of research into counselling and psychotherapy:

1 The search for reliable knowledge is no easy matter. Even after 300 years of debate, it has not been possible to arrive at an agreement around a single set of principles or procedures that will guarantee scientific progress. Although the philosophy of science has provided a valuable clarification of some knowledge-generating strategies used by some scientists in some situations, it seems clear that the advancement of knowledge and understanding depends a great deal on individual imagination and inspiration, and the willingness of researchers to devote their lives to the solution of complex problems.

2 The lessons of the history of science suggest that there is no reason to believe that any single methodology, such as randomised controlled trials or experimental studies, can prove to be the royal road to true and certain knowledge about therapy. There are well-established areas of sciences, such as the theory of evolution, or astronomy, in which experiments are not possible, or have played only a very minor role in the development of knowledge. The things that good scientists do not appear to be definable in terms of specific methodologies (such as using experiments, or using mathematical equations). Instead, productive scientific activity relies on a capacity for original critical thought and the creation of powerful and testable theory.

3 Over time, the cumulative activity of science produces complex, interlinked networks of ideas and observations. There are some ideas or concepts that sit at the centre of these networks, and are rarely altered as a result of new research. There are other ideas that exist at the periphery, and are more open to modification. Also, discrete areas of knowledge (such as physics, geology, geography, biology, sociology, psychology, etc.) connect with each other in multiple ways. It could be argued that research into counselling and psycho-therapy has, up to now, not generated the same level of complexity, coherence and interconnectedness that has been achieved in fields such as medicine or information technology.

4 Despite the undoubted importance of cognitive principles such as empiricism (look for observable evidence) and falsificationism (look for counter-examples), contemporary philosophy of science suggests that the operation of these principles always in the end comes down to a matter of agreement within groups of people. Once science emerged beyond the work of pioneers such as Newton or Faraday, it depended on the existence of international communities of scholars and researchers working together to create new knowledge. It can be argued that the field of counselling and psychotherapy research has not sufficiently embraced this notion: the therapy research literature is highly fragmented, and overdependent on the efforts of isolated individuals.

5 Almost all therapy researchers are, or have been, practitioners of therapy. Training in therapy tends to lead to strong allegiance to a particular therapy approach (e.g. psychodynamic, CBT). By con-trast, the history and philosophy of science suggests that key advances in knowledge (e.g. Darwin, Einstein) arose not through the effort to confirm what was already known, but to transcend these assumptions.

6 Increasingly, all areas of science have been required to face up to the reality that scientific research does not produce 'truths' that exist independent of social values and political choices. The social and political critique of therapy research has been muted, so far, but will inevitably occur and will lead to a reshaping of the intellectual and organisational landscape of this field of inquiry.

These are just some of the possible implications of counselling and psychotherapy research, of taking account of the contribution of studies of the history and philosophy of science. No doubt there are other lessons and implications that can be drawn. The main benefit of knowing about these matters is that it forces us to think about how we know what we know. This kind of reflection is what is required if therapy research is to be able to fulfil its role in facilitating the renewal and reconstruction of therapy theory and practice in response to on-going social and cultural change.

Questions for reflection and discussion

Box 3.4

1 In what areas of therapy research can useful knowledge be best achieved by accurate, objective measurement of variables? Are there some areas where knowledge is better achieved through attention to the complexities of everyday language?
2 Should the primary aim of research focus on the prediction of outcomes (e.g. a person with a particular diagnosis will be helped by a certain type of intervention)?
3 Which (if any) of the following constructs can be meaningfully measured: empathy, symptom reduction, irrational beliefs?
4 What is the role of theory in research? What is the relationship between theory and research?
5 To what extent should a researcher aim to be detached and objective as against being an involved participant in the lives of research participants?
6 By what criteria should the validity of research findings be judged?
7 To what extent, and in what ways, does counselling and psychotherapy research serve the interests of powerful groups in society? What might therapy research look like if it served different interests?
8 Within the field of counselling and psychotherapy research, is there a 'scientific community'? Or are there sub-communities? How might a new researcher join one of these communities?

Entering the world of therapy research: finding your way around the research literature

We live in a culture that has created, and continues to produce, an enormous amount of theoretical and research knowledge. The development of the printing press and publishing houses, the emergence of a literate citizenship, and more recently invention of the Internet have all contributed to the massive outpouring of written material. However, unlike the situation in earlier eras, for example when all the knowledge in the world could be assembled in one place in the Library of Alexandria, for contemporary readers the task of keeping in touch with ideas is much harder. It may be that some future super-internet search engine will make it possible to access all of the counselling and psychotherapy research literature in a straightforward manner. At the present time, this is not possible. The therapy research literature is complex, with pockets and strands of knowledge hidden away in all sorts of places. To engage with this literature, and to become a research-informed therapist or therapy policymaker, it is necessary to learn how to find one's way around the literature.

On the whole, research papers and books are written in a fairly dry style. They are different from newspaper or popular magazine articles, or novels, which are written in a style designed to seduce or entice the reader. By contrast, research papers are, for the most part, technical documents that have been written to provide information for people who already have an active interest in the topic that is being addressed. It is when research publications are read in order to *look for* something, when the reader is guided by a passion to expand or check out his or her own ideas, that this kind of reading material comes alive (further discussion of the functions of reading for counsellors can be found in McLeod, 1997).

The aim of this chapter is to discuss some of the ways in which counsellors and psychotherapists can gain access to, and make use of, previously published research that is relevant to their interests. The chapter explains how the research literature is organised, and how research papers are structured. There is also discussion of how to learn to appraise research reports from a position of curiosity that reflects a balance between critique and appreciation.

Exploring the literature

The literature on counselling and psychotherapy is highly fragmented and complex. There exists a very long list of academic journals that publish research into counselling and psychotherapy (see Box 4.1, which is not exhaustive). No single university library could ever carry all these journals, so in many instances access to copies of articles may require the use of inter-library loan facilities. Unlike other disciplines, as yet there is no specialised abstracting service which provides summaries of recent research in therapy. It can therefore be difficult to keep track of what has been published.

Journals that publish counselling and psychotherapy research articles

Box 4.1

American Journal of Orthopsychiatry

American Journal of Psychiatry

American Journal of Psychotherapy

American Psychologist

Annals of Behavioral Medicine

Archives of General Psychiatry

Archives of Women's Mental Health

Arts in Psychotherapy

Asia Pacific Journal of Counselling and Psychotherapy

Australia and New Zealand Journal of Family Therapy

Australian Journal of Counselling and Psychotherapy

Behavior Therapy

Behavioural and Cognitive Psychotherapy

British Journal of Clinical Psychology

British Journal of General Practice

British Journal of Guidance and Counselling

British Journal of Psychiatry

British Journal of Psychotherapy

Canadian Counsellor

Clinical Case Studies

Clinical Psychology and Psychotherapy

Clinical Psychology Review

Clinical Psychology: Science and Practice

(Continued)

(Continued)

Counselling and Psychotherapy Research

Counseling Psychologist

Counselling Psychology Quarterly

Counselling Psychology Review

Counselor Education and Supervision

Employee Assistance Quarterly

European Journal of Psychotherapy and Counselling

Family Process

Group Analysis

International Journal for the Advancement of Counseling

International Journal of Group Psychotherapy

International Journal of Transactional Analysis Research

Journal of Applied Behavioral Health

Journal of Behavior Therapy and Experimental Psychiatry

Journal of Behavioral Medicine

Journal of Brief Therapy

Journal of Clinical Psychiatry

Journal of Clinical Psychology

Journal of College Student Development

Journal of College Student Personnel

Journal of Constructivist Psychology

Journal of Consulting and Clinical Psychology

Journal of Counseling and Development

Journal of Counseling Psychology

Journal of Critical Psychology, Counselling and Psychotherapy

Journal of Humanistic Psychology

Journal of Mental Health

Journal of Mental Health Counseling

Journal of Psychotherapy Integration

Journal of Sexual and Marital Therapy

Journal for Specialists in Groupwork

Journal of Systemic Therapies

New Zealand Journal of Counselling

Nordic Psychology

Patient Education and Counseling

Person-centred and Experiential Psychotherapies

Pragmatic Case Studies in Psychotherapy

Professional Psychology: Research and Practice

Psychiatry

Psychoanalytic Psychology

Psychodynamic Practice

Psychological Medicine

Psychology and Psychotherapy

Psychotherapy

Psychotherapy and Psychosomatics

Psychotherapy Research

Qualitative Social Work

Small Group Research

Transactional Analysis Journal

Women and Therapy

Also the many other journals that specialise in specific client/diagnostic groups such as anxiety, eating disorders, depression, sexual abuse, trauma and so on.

The counselling and psychotherapy literature is organised around a number of different types of publication. Most research reports are published in the academic journals listed in Box 4.1. Typically, these journals each publish four issues per year. These issues will mainly contain a mixed collection of papers which are included in sequence of their final approval for publication. Some journals will occasionally devote a whole issue to a single-topic symposium. The *Counseling Psychologist* is typically structured around a keynote paper (usually a major study or review of the literature) followed by a series of commentaries. Alongside these academic journals are professional journals (such as *Therapy Today*) which publish some research and theory but are mainly devoted to professional issues and business. Also somewhere alongside these academic counselling and psychotherapy journals are journals from other disciplines which will nevertheless from time to time publish papers that would be of interest to psychotherapists and counsellors. Such journals would include those in adjacent fields such as nursing and social work, but also such diverse titles as *British Journal of General Practice*, *British Medical Journal*, *Social Science and Medicine* and *Sociological Review*.

It is useful to think about academic and professional journals as belonging together, because they can usually be found together in the same location in a library (the *periodicals* collection). Also, most journal articles are listed in on-line computer databases (see below) and can be searched without ever visiting a library.

Books represent a second category of published literature. It is probably sensible to think about books in terms of those that are teaching texts and those which contain new theoretical or research material. Teaching texts may be very useful in providing a 'map' or overview of an area of interest, and in supplying references. For most research purposes, however, it is necessary to use primary source material.

A third category of the literature comprises what might be called semi-published items. These are reports or monographs which are in the public domain but are difficult to get hold of because they have been published in small numbers or only distributed locally. A potentially important resource for researchers can be unpublished master's and doctoral dissertations and theses, which are normally held in the library of the university at which the person did their degree. In Britain most PhD theses can be borrowed through inter-library loans (under very strictly controlled access arrangements), and an increasing number are lodged in electronic archives that can be accessed through the relevant university website. Copies of almost all PhD theses from the USA (and some from British universities) are available through Dissertation Abstracts Online and Dissertation Abstracts International, for a price. MA or MSc dissertations can be more difficult to get hold of, because they may be stored in departmental rather than university libraries, and as a result may not be catalogued. There are many interesting and valuable research reports produced by therapy agencies and government or local authority departments. Often, these reports may be quite widely publicised at the time of publication, but thereafter can be hard to trace. Access to this kind of material is usually through writing directly to the organisation concerned. Libraries may be reluctant to stock what they regard as ephemeral material of this kind.

There exist, therefore, a number of different means of gaining access to theoretical and research papers and books. These include:

- personal 'handsearching' in a library;
- on-line databases (e.g. BIDS, PsychLit, Medline);
- reference lists of books and articles;
- consulting the index of authoritative texts such as Lambert (2013);
- asking tutors and colleagues;
- writing to authors of articles;
- website discussion pages and other internet resources.

If you find that one particular person has published useful research in your area of interest, it can be fruitful to write, asking if they could send you PDF copies of specific articles, and any additional published or unpublished papers they might have available on that topic. When a paper is published in a journal, the author receives a PDF of the article, and most researchers are quite keen to pass these on to anyone who might be studying the same area. Research can be a lonely business and it can be reinforcing to receive emails asking about one's work, so there is a good chance that a reply will be forthcoming. If you write to a fellow researcher, it is best to be clear about what you want, and not to request general advice that may demand a lengthy written response and therefore deter them from getting back to you at all.

Librarians are usually very willing to help you in developing literature-searching skills, but will not have the time to carry out an actual literature search on your behalf. It is not realistic to give a librarian a piece of paper with, say, 'the effectiveness of time-limited counselling' on it and expect them to produce a list of references for you. What is more realistic is to ask a librarian about the on-line facilities that are available. Often, libraries can offer leaflets or computer self-tutorial sessions that will teach you how to use on-line databases or the Internet. It will be helpful for a librarian if you can show them a few examples of the kind of thing you are looking for, such as specific references from journals. The librarian can then help you to find that journal, or similar journals. Remember, it is very unlikely that a librarian would be familiar with the counselling or therapy literature – they need some clues from you as to where to start. Apart from handsearching, which depends on your capacity to skim-read journal contents pages and abstracts and pick out relevant items, all the 'quick' methods such as on-line searches depend on *keywords*. To get the best yield from these searches it is important to be creative in your thinking about keywords. For example, a search for articles on 'time-limited counselling' may involve trying out a variety of alternative keywords: time-limited, time-conscious, counselling/counseling (British vs. American spelling), psychotherapy, intervention, brief, dose, treatment planning, workplace counselling, EAPs, single-session, solution-focused and so on. On-line searches *always* miss some articles, either because these articles have been published in obscure places or because they have been filed under odd keywords. An exhaustive handsearch (if you have time) will always produce some items that do not show up on computerised searches. Conversely, handsearching alone will miss a vast amount, because it is physically impossible for an individual researcher to get hold of all the journals that might potentially include relevant papers.

A note on the history of journal publishing

Historically, journals were produced as printed paper magazines, which were posted out to libraries and individual subscribers four times each year (for some journals, monthly). Although this publishing structure still exists, almost all journals are now published on-line as well as in printed format, and most readers access articles on screen. Some journals launched in recent years are published only on-line. The shift to internet-based operations has introduced important new possibilities for journals. For example, forthcoming or in-press articles are usually published on-line as soon as they have completed the review process, even if the 'official' publication in a specific issue of the journal may be several months in the future. In addition, it is now possible for journals to include lengthy appendices and supplementary material on the journal website, linked to the relevant article. On-line publication has also begun to have an impact on the economics of publishing; because it is much cheaper to produce electronic copies of articles (i.e. no printing and distribution costs), there are increasing demands for journals to follow the general ethos of the Internet and allow free access to content.

Box 4.2

It can take a substantial amount of time collecting research books and articles to arrive at the point of feeling that one has a secure overview of the work that has been done in that area. Once a useful article or two is found, the references in that paper will lead to other sources, which in turn need to be located and again may lead to yet new sources. In planning a research study it is important to allocate enough time for literature searching. Another factor which may eat up time arises from the incomplete and fragmented nature of much counselling and psychotherapy knowledge: in many areas the research just does not exist. If, for example, you are interested in carrying out research into the effectiveness of therapy for depression, or the effectiveness of counselling in primary care, your file of research articles will grow fairly rapidly. There are many papers on these topics. However, there are other topics which are very important but which have not generated a research literature. For example, it is difficult to review the *research* literature on commonplace counselling concepts such as 'respect', 'acceptance' or 'boundaries', simply because little or no research has been done. In carrying out research into these latter topics, it may be necessary to create a platform for the research by looking at studies on similar issues. For instance, an understanding of how to approach 'boundaries' from a research perspective might be pieced together by looking at work on contracts, missed appointments or therapist techniques.

When collecting research literature, it is of course essential to know when to stop. No one can know everything. To design a piece of research, or to use research to inform practice, what is important is to have a *sufficient* grasp of the literature. It is perhaps worth bearing in mind that when the NHS wishes to establish a *definitive* review of knowledge in a particular area it sets up what is known as a 'Cochrane Review', which is a team of five or six people who work for one or two years on the project.

Box 4.3

The structure of scientific reporting

The dissemination of research information handled in fields such as medicine and biotechnology is much better resourced than that in the field of counselling and psychotherapy research. In these longer-established areas, what has happened is that a wide range of different types of information outlet has been developed to ensure that scientific knowledge is effectively communicated to different audiences. For example, within most areas of science, there exist highly technical research journals whose articles may only make sense to a relatively small sub-set of researchers. There are flagship journals, which publish key findings and review articles from across the discipline. There are journals such as *New Scientist* or *Scientific American*, written for an educated lay readership. Finally, there are mass-market books, articles, TV documentaries, novels and movies that appeal to the general public. The availability of these different publication outlets means that the same information can be presented in different ways, depending on the audience. At the present time, this kind of system does not really operate within the world of therapy research. There are many valuable research findings that never reach a non-specialist audience. There are also many examples that can be found of journal articles which strive to incorporate both specific technical information and a broad readership account within the same paper – something that is very hard to accomplish in a satisfactory manner, and which authors within other disciplines would not even attempt.

What to do with research articles

Having collected some relevant research articles, it is important to work through them in a systematic manner. Many people, myself included, take the attitude that knowledge will be transferred by some kind of osmosis if articles are carried around in one's briefcase for a few days. Unfortunately this is not the case. What is crucial is to learn how to read articles *critically* and *purposefully*, so that the information and ideas contained within them can be retained for later use. Some of the key skills involved in critically reading a research paper are detailed below.

Read the abstract

First, read the abstract of the paper (a 300-word summary that appears at the beginning or end of the paper). If this seems relevant, read on. If it does not seem relevant (fairly often, the title of a paper may bear little relation to what it contains), then skim it to check whether there might be little nuggets of useful information or new references. Do not waste time reading stuff that you will not use later. If a paper subsequently turns out to be more important than it originally appeared, you can go back to it if you have kept the reference details.

Identify the plot

Any research paper is organised around a plot structure which tends to follow a pattern such as:

- This topic is important (theoretically or practically) because . . .
- Previous research has shown that . . .
- What still remains unclear, or what is wrong with this previous research, is . . .
- What we were aiming to do was . . .
- This is how we did it . . .
- This is what we found . . .
- We think these findings add to previous knowledge because . . .
- The implications of what we did for future research and practice are . . .

It is useful to think about a research paper as telling a story because this perspective opens up an awareness that there might be sub-plots ('We really did this study because we hate behaviour therapy and wanted to show that it is misguided and wrong . . .'). As in any story, there are portions of the narrative that are glossed over ('Major parts of the questionnaire didn't work out but we don't want to go into that in any detail if you don't mind . . .'). Finally, a narrative perspective gives permission to recognise that there are *other* stories that could be told about the same set of events. And this is a key point. Critical analysis of a paper means thinking about whether the results could plausibly be accounted for in other ways.

Examine the methodology

When most people begin research, and start to read research papers, they pay too much attention to the findings or results of published studies and end up assembling literature reviews that focus solely on 'facts' (e.g. 'Smith [1996] demonstrated that client-centred therapy was not effective with test-anxious college student clients' – this is a fictitious example). Treating studies as if they were little 'fact modules' leads to a rather superficial approach to the literature. It assumes that we are just piling up knowledge in an inexorable fashion. It is more useful to recognise that, although each study indeed may contribute to some great heap of knowledge, there are limitations to any study, and that debates and disagreements exist over how to interpret data. It is essential, therefore, to pay attention not only to *what* was found, but also to *how* it was found. Some of the questions that can be usefully asked about the methods used in a study are:

- Who carried out the study? What might their allegiance be? What were they trying to prove?
- What was the sample? How was it selected? Does it reflect the wider population? Might the sample have biased or skewed the results, and in what directions?
- What questions were being asked, or what hypotheses were being tested? Did the methods of data collection produce information that was relevant to the questions/hypotheses? For example, did Smith's definition of 'test anxiety' make sense in terms of anxious students I have seen in my own practice, or in terms of relevant previous theory and research?
- Was the questionnaire chosen by Smith the best technique to use? How do I know whether or not it is a good instrument?

These are the kinds of questions that allow a reader to begin to open up the methodological assumptions and choices implicit in any piece of published research. There are at least three reasons for paying close attention to methodological aspects of research papers. First, the methods used may be so flawed (in your eyes at least) that you cannot place any credence in the results of the study. Second, different findings in the literature may reflect the use of different methods. For example, the reason why an imaginary 'Brown (1997)' may be able to report positive results for client-centred counselling with test-anxious college students is that she used a different questionnaire from Smith. Third, in preparing yourself to carry out some personal research, it is necessary to decide on which methods to use. This involves considering alternative methods, and perhaps acquiring further information on them (such as writing to Smith and Brown asking for copies of their questionnaires).

Plunder the paper for useful detail

In reading a paper or chapter it may strike you that the authors have used vivid and memorable imagery or writing that would be worth quoting in your own work. There may also be some quite specific or offbeat aspects of their results that may be worth retaining for future use (perhaps Smith found that it was mainly humanities students who reported with high test anxiety).

Consider the big picture

Having read a research paper carefully, drawing on the strategies described above, it is useful to reflect on the implications of the paper, on where it fits in to the wider context. Some of the key questions here are: What does the paper add to previous knowledge on the topic? Where does the paper lead, in terms of further research? What are the implications of the paper for training, supervision or practice?

> ## Suggested further reading
>
> Greenhalgh, T. (2006). *How to Read a Paper: The Basis of Evidence-based Medicine*, 3rd edn. Oxford: Wiley-Blackwell.

Evidence-based practice: scoping reviews, practice-friendly reviews, systematic reviews and clinical guidelines

Each year, several hundred journal research articles are published on topics that are relevant to counselling and psychotherapy policy, practice and theory. It is impossible for any individual to keep in touch with all of this information, even at the level of skimming the titles of papers, or abstracts. In fact, it is hard enough to keep up to date with research that is being carried out within an area that may be of special interest. One difficult aspect of reviewing the counselling and psychotherapy research literature is that it spans several academic/professional disciplines, including psychology, psychiatry, health studies, nursing, social work and education. As a result, when conducting an on-line literature search using a psychology-focused search tool or a health-related database, retrieving a complete listing of potentially relevant studies is unlikely. It is therefore particularly important, within the field of counselling and psychotherapy, to make use of review articles and reports that are produced by people who have the time and skills to carry out the review task in a comprehensive manner. Writers of reviews play a key role within the research community, in assembling the pieces of the evidence jigsaw into a meaningful pattern. A good research review paper not only summarises the state of existing knowledge on a topic, it also provides an indication of the gaps in that knowledge and makes suggestions for further studies that might be carried out in order to fill these gaps.

As with any area of research, one of the central challenges associated with reviewing the literature is the question of bias. It is not helpful if a person assembles a research review that selectively 'cherry-picks' the studies which support his or her position and ignores the studies which contradict their views. The history of literature reviewing over the past 20 years therefore comprises a range of attempts to overcome the issue of bias. The main strategies that have been developed in order to ensure that reviewing is carried out in a balanced and valid manner include:

- providing information about the background and motivation of the reviewer;
- transparency over how articles were located and selected for inclusion on the review;
- clarity over how information in primary research papers was summarised;
- providing information on all sources of information that were used in the review so that in principle someone else could replicate its findings.

Taken together, these criteria set a high standard for published reviews. Because of the complexity of these requirements, it is probably reasonable to say that there has never been a literature review that is beyond critique, no matter how much time and effort has been devoted to it.

There are different audiences for research reviews, and different purposes that review projects may be seeking to accomplish. The main types of review that can be found within the current counselling and psychotherapy literature are:

- introductory sections of research papers;
- scoping searches;
- historical/narrative reviews;
- practice-friendly reviews;
- systematic/meta-analytic reviews;
- clinical practice guidelines.

These different types of review form a continuum. The reviews that can be found within introductory sections of research papers are usually fairly brief and focused. By contrast, the reviews that are incorporated within practice guidelines are wide-ranging and comprehensive. The following sections provide further information on the role of each of these review formats within the broader research landscape.

Exercise 4.1 Being a consumer of reviews

Identify a topic that is of particular interest to you, and carry out an on-line search to locate different types of research review that have been published on this topic. Do not be surprised if you do not find much, other than introductory sections of research papers. If you are able to come across more than one relevant review, read what you have found and reflect on the strengths and limitations of different review formats. What are each of these reviews offering you? What is it that they are not offering – are there facets of the primary knowledge base that seem to have got lost in the review process? If you have time, conduct the same exercise in relation to a frequently reviewed topic such as 'the effectiveness of psychotherapy for depression'. Finally, reflect on the contrast between the therapy research reviews you have read and product reviews that are published by organisations such as the Consumers' Association (*Which?* magazine) – which approach is more effective, and why?

Reviews within introductory sections of research papers

Authors of research papers have a dual task: reporting on the methods and findings of the specific study that they have carried out, and at the same time making appropriate connections between that study and the literature as a whole. It is usual for research papers to incorporate an introductory mini-review of the relevant literature in order to justify and set the scene for the study that is about to be described. The restricted length of this kind of mini-review (typically less than 1,500 words) means that authors need to get to the point, and offer a concise summary of the implications of previous studies. As a consequence, this form of review can often be highly useful as a means of gaining a rapid sense of what the literature has to say on a given topic. It is not hard to find research papers in which the actual findings are inconclusive, while the introductory literature review is of real value. What can also occur is that the author of a research paper may omit to mention important earlier studies; when this happens, the weakness of the argument being developed in a research project can be obvious from the first paragraph.

Scoping searches

There are some areas of inquiry in which research may have been carried out, perhaps in a fragmented and piecemeal fashion, but where the quality of knowledge that has produced has not been reviewed. In this scenario, it can be helpful to conduct a *scoping search*, which has the aim of mapping the work that has been done, and arriving at some preliminary suggestions around the possibility of conducting a more systematic review of sections of the literature, and also suggestions around future research directions. An example of a scoping review is a project that I undertook for the British Association for Counselling and Psychotherapy (BACP), to pull together the research literature around the process and outcome of workplace counselling (McLeod, 2001a, 2007, 2011). The review process was as inclusive as possible in describing and discussing every piece of research that could be located. The discussion of studies incorporated an appraisal of the methodological strengths and weaknesses of each paper. On the whole, the methodological quality of the majority of papers was not high, which is to be expected in an area of research that is at an early stage of development. This meant that very few of the papers would have been eligible for inclusion in a more systematic or meta-analytic review (see below). One of the surprises of this project was the number of studies that were found – many more than in any previous reports on workplace counselling. This surprising finding supports the value of a scoping search: in some topic areas, there may actually be more research than would be expected, but it takes a lot of effort to track down the work that has been done. It is important to acknowledge the limitations of scoping searches; the purpose of such a review is to prepare the ground for more focused reviews at a later stage.

Historical/narrative reviews

Probably the most satisfying form of literature review, from the perspective of a reader, is a historical or narrative account that tells the story of the step-by-step construction of theory and evidence in relation to particular areas of inquiry. Like any good story, a well-written narrative review communicates the passion and courage of an individual or group of people engaged in an adventure or quest. Relatively few narrative reviews have been published in recent years. As a result, the reviews literature has had a tendency to present research knowledge as a set of overlapping snapshots of 'what we know today' in a way that obscures the reality that current understandings are always built on previous ideas and always possess momentum in some direction or another. A good example of a historical review is the account by Binder and Henry (2010) of three decades of research on psychodynamic psychotherapy, carried out at Vanderbilt University in the USA under the direction of Hans Strupp.

Practice-friendly reviews

A further genre of research review is the form of review that seeks to distil, from research findings, ideas and principles that can be applied in routine practice. An important source of such writing is the series of 'practice-friendly' reviews published in the *Journal of Clinical Psychology* (Comtois and Linehan, 2006; Greenberg and Pascual-Leone, 2006; Knox and Hill, 2003; Logan and Marlatt, 2010; Lundahl and Burke, 2009; Mains and Scogin, 2003; Post and Wade, 2009; Sin and Lyubomirsky, 2009; Solomon and Johnson, 2002). The aim of the reviewer in these papers is not to arrive at an ultimate 'objective truth' in respect of the area being discussed, but instead to consider the potential practical implications of research that has been published on particular topics.

Systematic/meta-analytic reviews

The variety of literature review that has received the most attention in recent years, and has had the most impact on policy and practice, has been systematic reviews that make use of techniques of statistical meta-analysis. These reviews aim to establish the extent to which certain interventions (e.g. forms of psychotherapy) are effective with certain populations (e.g. clients with anxiety disorders). A team of reviewers adopts a rigorous approach that involves identifying poten-tial sources of research evidence (articles in peer-reviewed journals), then evaluating the methodological adequacy of each study. The findings of those studies that meet the criteria for methodological adequacy are then analysed in terms of the overall level of change (the effect size) reported for each sub-group of clients receiving the intervention (or assigned to control conditions). To conduct this kind of review at an acceptable level of competence requires time, training and considerable statistical ability. There have been hundreds of sys-tematic reviews of the effectiveness of different kinds of counselling and psychotherapy, for different conditions. These reviews have been published in a wide range of books and journals. Widely cited collec-tions of reviews can be found in Roth and Fonagy (2005) and Lambert (2004). A particularly influential source of high-quality systematic reviews is the Cochrane Library (www.thecochranelibrary.com), which comprises an on-line database of state-of-the-art reviews of the effectiveness of most medical interventions. The Cochrane Library includes a review conducted by Peter Bower and colleagues of studies into the effectiveness of counselling in primary care. This review showed that counselling is more effective than treatment as usual (i.e. speaking to a GP) in the short term, but that no long-term benefits of counselling, over usual care, could be identified. This review has had a major impact on health policy in the UK in questioning the value of counselling in primary care settings. All Cochrane Reviews are regularly updated, and are accessible on-line. One of the myths of counselling and psychotherapy research is that reviews of outcome studies only provide support for the effectiveness of CBT. While there is certainly plentiful review-based evidence of the effectiveness of CBT, there are also systematic reviews that highlight the effectiveness of person-centred and experiential therapy (Elliott, 2002b) and short-term psychodynamic psychotherapy (Lewis et al., 2008). An influential review by Cuijpers et al. (2011) found little difference between the effectiveness rates of different types of therapy for depression.

Clinical practice guidelines

If you have had the opportunity to read any of the systematic meta-analytic reviews mentioned in this paper, or other similar reports, you will understand that these are complex technical documents, which place heavy demands on readers in terms of time and technical knowledge. Busy practitioners rarely have the time or patience to work their way through such reviews. In order to bridge the gap between reviews that carefully analyse what is known about the effectiveness of an intervention and the learning needs of practitioners who implement these interventions, a range of *clinical practice guidelines* have been developed by various organisations. Typically, these guidelines are constructed by committees of experts, who look at the findings of sets of review papers (rather than sets of original research articles). A good example of a clinical guideline is the *Depression in Adults* guideline that is published by the UK-based National Institute for Health and Clinical Excellence (NICE; www.nice.org.uk). This guideline is primarily aimed at doctors, but is also relevant for any counsellors and psychotherapists who receive referrals from doctors. The guideline includes a full report, which explains how evidence was located and evaluated. There is a 'quick reference guide', which explains what depression is, and the recommended role of drug and psychological interventions for different levels of severity of depression. There is also a guide for patients. A similar guideline is produced by the medical profession in Scotland (the SIGN guidelines). These guidelines are regularly updated, and published on-line. The 2010 version of *Depression in Adults* recommends the following types of psychological intervention for patients exhibiting moderate depression: individual or group-based CBT, interpersonal psychotherapy, behavioural activation therapy, and behavioural couples therapy. Various types of antidepressants are also recommended.

Exercise 4.2 Reading clinical guidelines

Read through the summary sections (brief reference guide and patient guide) of the NICE CG90 *Depression in Adults* guideline (available at www.nice.org.uk) or the equivalent Scottish guideline (available at www.sign.ac.uk). If you have time, you might also be interested in looking at the full guideline. How useful do you think that these documents might be as resources for practitioners and service users? What did you learn that might inform your own practice? How could these guidelines be improved?

One of the issues associated with the proliferation of clinical practice guidelines in recent years has been that practitioners do not necessarily adhere to them. In research carried out in the UK by Gabbay and le May (2010), consultations between general practitioners (GPs) and patients were observed, and GPs were invited to comment on the sources of information that they had used to inform their clinical decisions with each patient. These doctors made little use of clinical practice guidelines. Instead, they drew on rich networks of contextualised information, which they obtained from a wide range of sources. They were vaguely familiar with published guidelines, but found that the realities of practice required a more personalised approach.

Conclusions

The broad acceptance of the principles of evidence-based practice, within the fields of healthcare, education and social work, means that counsellors and psychotherapists are increasingly called upon to demonstrate that what they do is evidence-based. It is not realistic for practitioners to read all of the relevant studies that are published each year. Various types of research review fulfil the function of summarising and critically analysing the results of research studies as a means of informing practice. Competence as a counsellor or psychotherapist requires familiarity with the different types of review that are available, and a willingness to make time to read reviews and reflect on their implications for practice.

Doing research: practical and ethical issues

The research literature tends to offer a neat and tidy representation of what research is like. The aim of a research article is to report, as clearly and succinctly as possible, on the results of a study that has been undertaken. As a consequence, the sometimes messy process of actually doing research is usually hidden from view. The aim of the present chapter is to open up the realities of doing research. This information is essential for anyone who is thinking about carrying out his or her own research study. It can also be viewed as potentially valuable information for anyone who is a reader or consumer of research: to develop a critical perspective on the findings of a published research study, it is important to be able to have a sense of the kinds of challenges that were faced by the researcher, and the kinds of practical compromises that he or she might have been forced to take.

The chapter begins by considering the experience of becoming a researcher, then provides an outline of the sequence or cycle of activity that is involved in conducting a research study. A discussion is offered of the ethical issues that need to be addressed by counselling and psychotherapy researchers. The chapter concludes by reflecting on the implications of these practical and ethical issues for the evidence base of counselling and psychotherapy as a whole.

Suggested further reading

Detailed guidelines for conducting different types of research study can be found in:

McLeod, J. (forthcoming). *Doing Research in Counselling and Psychotherapy*. London: Sage.

Becoming a researcher

Counselling and psychotherapy research is carried out by people who have a wide range of backgrounds and interests, who may work in very different research environments, and who may have been exposed to very different research training experiences. The standard route to becoming a therapy researcher is to take a psychology degree, then complete a Doctorate in Clinical or Counselling Psychology, or a research PhD, before being appointed to a teaching position in a university. However, it is not hard to find examples of people who have made important contributions to the field of counselling and psychotherapy research who have not followed this pathway. Les Greenberg (Greenberg et al., 1993), a leading figure in research in experiential psychotherapy, completed a degree in engineering before being trained as a psychologist. Julia Buckroyd, who has carried out significant research on therapy for eating disorders (Buckroyd and Rother, 2008), gained a PhD in history before being trained as a psychotherapist. Kim Etherington, whose work on narrative approaches to trauma (2003) has been highly influential, was an occupational therapist before being trained as a counsellor. Linda Finlay, a major leader in the field of qualitative research in psychotherapy (Finlay and Evans, 2009) was also originally an occupational therapist. Philip Cushman, author of a comprehensive historical study of the emergence of psychotherapy (Cushman, 1995) is a psychologist but has never held a full-time academic position. This diversity represents one of the strengths of the counselling and psychotherapy research community, by ensuring receptivity to new ideas. In addition to these variations in personal and professional background, almost all counselling and psychotherapy researchers also maintain some kind of therapy practice, and are therefore exposed to different kinds of client issues.

The training experiences of those who undertake research in counselling and psychotherapy can also vary a great deal. Researchers with a first degree and doctorate in psychology gained in North America, most European countries or Australia will almost certainly know a great deal about quantitative methods and statistics, but may know very little about qualitative methods or philosophy of science. Researchers with a background in social work, social anthropology, a health profession such as nursing or occupational therapy, or in the humanities may have had substantial training in qualitative methods, and be highly sensitive to the limitations of quantitative approaches. At the present time, there are relatively few researchers who are equally competent and confident in both qualitative and quantitative styles of research.

Exercise 5.1 Getting started as a researcher

The best way to learn about the research process is to get involved and actually carry out a research project. However, many novice researchers make things hard for themselves by using their first research project to try to explore burning questions that they believe have not been satisfactorily addressed within the research literature. What makes this hard is that it leads to a situation where a new researcher is seeking to: (a) define or conceptualise a topic or phenomenon; (b) devise ways of collecting data on that topic; at the same time as (c) learning how to do research. What tends to be much more satisfying, for new researchers, is to carry out a replication or partial replication of an existing study. Walking in the footsteps of those who have gone before, in the spirit of an apprenticeship, is usually the best way to learn any practical skill. From this perspective, what existing study or studies would you be most interested in replicating? In what ways could the experience of carrying out this work function as a platform for developing your own ideas?

The majority of research studies that are published in research journals are derived from the work of students who are undertaking master's or doctoral research. In some instances, these students may in effect be undertaking a research apprenticeship, in which their work is closely guided by an experienced senior researcher, or is part of a larger programme of research. However, other students may enjoy only very limited supervision, or may be pursuing a research topic that falls outside the main research interest of their supervisor. In any of these scenarios, it is important to keep in mind that these studies are being carried out by researchers with limited experience. It is often difficult for more experienced researchers, for instance those who have achieved faculty positions on completion of their doctorate, to find the time to engage in hands-on personal research. There are no research institutes in the field of counselling and psychotherapy research. Unlike the situation in many areas of pharmaceutical and medical research, nowhere in the world is there a building full of salaried career psychotherapy researchers. The nearest the counselling and psychotherapy research community come to a critical mass of researchers in one place is in some university departments of psychology in which two or three therapy researchers, along with maybe up to a dozen students, pursue a co-ordinated programme of research. However, this is an unusual arrangement – for the most part, therapy researchers work in isolation.

A further crucial aspect of the process of becoming a counselling and psychotherapy researcher concerns the extent to which the researcher has discovered his or her own niche, or voice, within the research community as a whole. In general, those individuals who have made the most significant contributions to the therapy research literature are people who have worked on topics that possess a deep level of personal or professional meaning.

When therapy researchers reflect on their careers, all of them make strong connections between the research questions they have pursued, and aspects of their personal life or professional experience (see, for example, the chapters in Castonguay et al., 2010b; Hoshmand and Martin, 1995; Soldz and McCullough, 2000). There have been many researchers, such as Carl Rogers, Aaron Beck, Les Greenberg and Steven Hayes, who have used research to elaborate and promote their vision of how therapy should be practised. Other researchers have had careers that have centred on particular topics, such as the client's experience of therapy (Rennie, 1992) or the dynamics of the therapeutic alliance (Safran, 1993). It can be hard for new researchers to maintain a balance between learning about research skills and exploring their own agenda. Often, psychology training can be quite regimented, with the result that doctoral graduates possess good research skills but are not in touch with their own passion. By contrast, those who complete counsellor or psychotherapist training before learning about research may find it difficult to subject their strong ideas about how therapy should be conducted to the discipline of systematic inquiry.

An appreciation of the process through which people become therapy researchers makes it possible to make sense of some frustrating aspects of the therapy research literature. For example, research evidence in the field of counselling and psychotherapy research is very slow to accumulate, because there are no high-level research institutes that can immediately carry out the next study that would be required to fill in a gap in the literature. Also, many research studies lack passion and come across as technical exercises that have little meaning to the researcher (never mind to his or her readers). This is because they *are* technical exercises that have been conducted for the purpose of gaining a degree. These aspects of therapy research may be seen as reflecting some of the disadvantages of the way in which therapy research training is currently organised. By contrast, one of the strengths of the present system lies in its openness to new ideas. Because therapy research is fragmented, and (at least round the edges) open to other academic disciplines, each year there are a few studies published that are surprising and delightful, even if they are only loosely connected to what has gone before.

Exercise 5.2 Your own research identity

How do you understand your own research identity, at this point in time? What are the research skills and methods with which you feel comfortable? What are the burning research questions that have particular meaning for you? What is your preferred pathway towards becoming a more effective researcher? What kind of support, or research environment, do you need in order to develop further?

Research as a cyclical process

It is useful to think about research in terms of a cycle of inquiry (see Box 5.1). Any research begins with a period of reflection, reading, discussion and general question-finding. This leads to the formulation of a research plan (what is sometimes called the *research design*), leading to data collection and analysis, and a written report which is seen by other people. The feedback of these readers, along with the researcher's own reflections on the study, then generate further ideas, which are tested and elaborated in a subsequent piece of research. This is a cycle which may be repeated several times in the lifetime of a single research project. For example, there may be a very preliminary cycle based on testing out some vague ideas against what is available in the published literature, and then writing a paper for agency or clinic management, or for a research supervisor, that floats a general proposal for research into a particular topic. There may then follow another cycle of inquiry in the form of a pilot study in which an interview schedule or questionnaire is tried out with two or three selected participants. Having reflected on the results of the pilot study, the researcher will be ready to enter into the cycle that represents the 'proper' study. But even this will almost always generate loose ends or new ideas that demand further cycles of inquiry. For instance, presenting the results of the study at a conference or professional meeting may trigger questions that call for further research. It is important to realise that the model of the research cycle presented here describes stages in the research process which may in reality overlap and run into each other. In some research, for example when carrying out qualitative interviews, some of the most useful analytic ideas may occur when actually doing the interviews (data collection). Similarly, reflecting on the meaning and implications of the research may, and should, take place at all stages.

Box 5.1

The research cycle

Stage 1 Immersion and gestation. Reflecting on personal experience on the topic. General reading. Discussion with others. Question-finding.

Stage 2 Planning. Being explicit about the research question and how it will be answered. Addressing ethical issues. Formulating a timetable and plan of action.

Stage 3 Data collection. Gathering relevant information. Storing and cataloguing data.

Stage 4 Data analysis. Making sense of the data. Drawing conclusions.

Stage 5 Writing up. Bringing the findings of the project into a written report.

Stage 6 Dissemination of results. Publicising the findings of the study through publications, conference papers and workshops.

Stage 7 Reflecting on what has been learned, and starting again.

The image of the *designer* can be both helpful and unhelpful in making sense of the research process. It is helpful because it evokes a sense of being like an architect creating a blueprint for a building which will meet the specifications of various groups of people – the property owner, the builders, the neighbourhood, the building inspectors. But once the building work actually commences, unforeseen problems may arise and the design may need to be modified. The notion of the researcher as designer captures well the need for careful planning, consideration of the interests of different groups of people, working to a budget and timescale, and anticipating problems. Where the image of the researcher as designer is less satisfactory is when some psychology or psychology-oriented research methods textbooks include chapters on research design that are highly prescriptive in specifying a limited set of designs which (in their view) meet the requirements of scientific rigour (the equivalent of the building inspectors). This approach to research design is, I would argue, derived far too much from a tradition of laboratory experimentation where the researcher can aspire to some sort of absolute control over his or her 'subjects'. In practitioner research, it is important to be creative and flexible in planning and conducting research and to recognise that conventionally defined 'rigour' is only one among several sources of value. Another important factor in practitioner research is that collecting data normally requires co-operation and approval from other people. For example, if a study is carried out in a therapy agency or clinic, then there will almost certainly need to be quite lengthy negotiations with managers, administrators and clinicians. Some of the organisational and political issues involved in setting up research are discussed by Hardy (1995) and Barker et al. (2002). Resistance to research is not uncommon in therapists and therapy organisations, on the grounds that the activity of data collection may undermine the process of therapy or lead to breaches of confidentiality.

An appreciation of the cyclical nature of knowledge-building makes it possible to develop a better understanding of the rationale and meaning of particular research studies. The significance of a specific research study, in relation to its contribution to the research literature as a whole, may arise from the role that the study has played within a much longer sequence of studies. Reading a research study in isolation can only provide a preliminary sense of the contribution of that study – it is also essential to know about what has gone before (usually indicated in the introduction to the article, but maybe not in a way that tells the whole story), and what comes after. This factor also makes it possible to understand why studies carried out by inexperienced researchers (such as students) may lack impact. Even though an inexperienced researcher may be technically competent and work hard, if he or she does not grasp the bigger picture, then their work is unlikely to resonate with readers.

Organisational ability as a key element in effective research

It is a mistake to assume that good quality research is a matter of being well-informed about research skills and methods, having an ability to develop a critical perspective on the research literature, being theoretically imaginative and being able to write. These academic competencies are certainly valuable. But what is also central to the job description of an effective researcher is a capacity to be meticulous and well-organised. Even at the level of a student research project, it is crucial to be able to keep track of information, keep channels of communication open, and engage in realistic time planning. At a more advanced level, large-scale funded research studies, such as randomised controlled trials, place an enormous demand on the organisational and managerial skills of the principal investigator. It is no surprise that people who have an existing track record around being able to handle these pressures are favoured by funding bodies when it comes to allocating resources.

Suggested further reading

Hardy, G. (1995). Organisational issues: Making research happen. In M. Aveline and D.A. Shapiro (eds.), *Research Foundations for Psychotherapy Practice.* Chichester: Wiley.

Practice research networks

In recent years, one of the most significant developments in relation to the way that counselling and psychotherapy research is organised has been the emergence of *practice research networks* (PRNs). A practice research network consists of a collaborative agreement between university-based researchers and practitioners, sometimes with the support of relevant professional associations and therapy agencies. The motivation for the establishment of practice research networks has come from a range of sources. There is a widely held view that there exists a gap between researchers and practitioners, which has resulted in accusations by the latter that much of the research that is published lacks relevance for practice (Morrow-Bradley and Elliott, 1986). Some practitioners, who have acquired a passion for research during their master's or doctoral work, are keen to find ways to remain involved in the world of research. There are societal pressures on universities to demonstrate that the research carried out by academics and students has a meaningful impact on real-world problems. Finally, the series of economic crises that hit most industrialised societies from around 2008 have meant that there is a diminishing amount of both state and charitable funding for research, which has led many researchers to look for unfunded or minimally funded strategies for collecting data.

Most practice research networks are co-ordinated by university-based researchers, so that the activities of the network can be supported by university library and other resources (Elliott and Zucconi, 2010; Parry et al., 2010). Counsellors and psychotherapist members, and organisational members, register their interest in the network, and thereafter can be involved at different levels of commitment. Some network members may merely play a supportive and advisory role, others may collect data within their own practice, and yet others may initiate and direct projects. Most networks are organised around a website and regular meetings, possibly including an annual conference. There can also be temporary research networks that are set up to support specific projects.

SuPReNet: an example of a practice research network

A good example of a practice research network is the *Supervision Practice Research Network* (SuPReNet), established in 2008 for the purpose of supporting and co-ordinating research into clinical supervision in counselling and psychotherapy. One of the early achievements of the network was to evaluate and make available a set of questionnaires that could be used by anyone engaged in research on supervision. Further information about the activities of this network can be found in Wheeler et al. (2011) and at www.bacp.co.uk/research/SuPReNet/index.php.

Box 5.3

It is likely that practice research networks will become an increasingly important feature of the counselling and psychotherapy research environment. At the present time, the potential of the practice research network concept has yet to be fully realised, because none of the networks currently in existence have been in operation for a sufficiently long period of time. In principle, research networks are able to bring research and practice much closer to each other, and should enable more high-quality research to be published. Practice research networks also largely take the major political stakeholders (government departments, health providers) out of the equation, and create a situation that can allow large-scale, policy-oriented research to be under the control of local groups. It is clear that counsellors and psychotherapists do not spend all their time seeing clients, and support their direct client work through a range of activities such as supervision, personal therapy, on-going training, continuing professional development, and reading. For many therapists, participation in a practice network is becoming a further option within this list.

> **Suggested further reading**
>
> Castonguay, L.G., Nelson, D.L., Boutselis, M.A., Chiswick, N.R., Damer, D.D., Hemmelstein, N.A., Jackson, J.S., Morford, M., Ragusea, S.A., Roper, J.G., Spayd, C., Weiszer, T. and Borkovec, T.D. (2010). Psychotherapists, researchers, or both? A qualitative analysis of psychotherapists' experiences in a practice research network. *Psychotherapy: Theory, Research, Practice, Training*, 47, 345–354. (A fascinating account of the challenges and rewards of involvement in a practice research network.)

Exercise 5.3 Being aware of your personal research values

The following section of this chapter consists of a discussion of ethical issues in counselling and psychotherapy research. Before starting to read this section, take a few minutes to reflect on your own values as a counsellor or psychotherapist, and the implications of these values for your participation in research. Some of the value positions that can be relevant to assessing the worth of a piece of research include:

- *Truth*: what is important is to proceed on the basis of certain knowledge.
- *Aesthetic quality*: a theory needs to be elegant.
- *Social justice*: knowledge is only worthwhile if it leads to greater social equality.
- *Pragmatism*: what is important is what works, or gets the job done.
- *Relational connection*: the purpose of any form of inquiry is to bring people together in collegiality and fellowship.

Which of these values has most (and least) meaning for you? In what ways might these value positions inform your ethical decision-making when designing and carrying out a research study?

Ethical issues

In a sense, all aspects of a research plan or proposal reflect ethical or moral issues. There are always specific ethical issues that relate to maintaining the well-being of participants. Beyond this, the basic coherence of a study is also a moral issue, in that a study which produces no new knowledge or understanding is basically wasting people's time. It can be argued that the moral dimension of counselling and psychotherapy research has not been sufficiently discussed within the field. There is an assumption that general codes of research ethics within psychology, social science and health adequately address the ethical dilemmas that arise in therapy research.

However, although it is certainly true that all research takes place within a general framework of shared moral understanding and ethical practice, the context of therapy can generate distinctive ethical challenges.

Exercise 5.4 Grounding research in a professional perspective

Most counselling and psychotherapy researchers are members of professional bodies such as the American Psychological Association, British Psychological Society, British Association for Counselling and Psychotherapy, or similar organisations. Students or trainees who are doing research are usually enrolled in colleges and universities that are in turn affiliated to professional organisations. Each of these bodies publishes ethical codes that are designed to guide members in relation to working with clients, and also conducting research that involves clients. Familiarise yourself with the code of research ethics produced by the professional association to which you are affiliated (you should be able to find a copy on their website). Then read the research ethics code published by at least one other similar organisation. How accessible and informative did you find these documents? As you read them, were you aware of ethically problematic situations that were not discussed in a way that was sufficiently explicit for you to be able to know how best to deal with it?

Within the general professional ethics literature, a set of core ethical principles have been identified. These are:

- *beneficence* (acting to enhance client well-being);
- *non-maleficence* (avoiding doing harm to clients);
- *autonomy* (respecting the right of the person to take responsibility for himself or herself);
- *fidelity* (treating everyone in a fair and just manner).

Taken separately, each of these moral principles can be seen to embody values with which most people would agree. However, in practice there are situations where two or more of these principles can come into conflict. There are also other situations where it is difficult to live up to these ethical ideals.

Suggested further reading

Kitchener, K.S. (1984). Intuition, critical evaluation and ethical principles: The foundation for ethical decisions in counseling psychology. *The Counseling Psychologist*, 12, 43–55. (A classic paper which set the parameters for all subsequent discussion of ethical issues in research in counselling and psychotherapy.)

Ethical good practice always involves external scrutiny

It is a mistake to assume that maintaining ethical standards depends on the personal integrity of the individual who is carrying out a study. Certainly, personal responsibility is always a factor. For example, if a researcher loses research data, then he or she is responsible for any risk that private information about research participants will be publicised. But the adoption of an ethically sensitive approach is primarily a *collective* responsibility. All research carried out by faculty members or students in a university, or staff in a therapy clinic, needs to be approved by an ethics committee (often described in North American contexts as an 'institutional review board' or IRB), which provides an independent view of the arrangements for safeguarding the interests of research participants and ensures that the study adheres to general principles of ethical soundness that are espoused by the organisation as a whole. Beyond this general level of external scrutiny, all researchers need to make use of a supervisor or consultant, with whom they discuss any ethical dilemmas that arise on a day-to-day basis. Why are these forms of external scrutiny important? The fact is that no individual researcher (or even a small research team) has the capacity to think about all the ethical angles that might be relevant to their work. This is not because they are ignorant of ethical principles, but because they are too close to the project. Although it can often seem like a time-consuming hassle to submit a research proposal to an ethics committee or IRB, these groups will almost always be able to identify some area of ethical concern that has escaped the attention of the researcher or research team, or will suggest ways in which consent and other procedures can be tightened up. The topic of research ethics serves as a reminder that the pursuit of knowledge is always a collective endeavour.

Many of the ethical questions faced by practitioner-researchers are the same as those encountered by anyone carrying out psychological or social science research. However, there are two distinctive ethical dilemmas which arise for practitioners who carry out studies of their own clients, or of clients within the agency or clinic in which they work. First, for the most part researchers have restricted their moral responsibility to that of avoiding harm, whereas counsellors and psychotherapists seek to go beyond non-maleficence in striving to enhance client well-being (beneficence). It would therefore be morally wrong for a therapist or therapy agency to compromise beneficence in the interests of research, even if the project were carefully designed in order to avoid harm.

A second distinctive ethical dilemma in therapy research is associated with the creation of *dual roles*, for instance when the person who is the counsellor or psychotherapist to a client also becomes a researcher and asks permission to use a session tape-recording for research purposes. Many people have written about the problems thrown up by dual roles in therapy (Gabriel, 2005; Lazarus and Zur, 2002; Pope, 1991). There are some dual roles (e.g. when a counsellor also provides nursing care to a person) where both roles involve the 'counsellor' acting solely in the interests of the client. The problem in these situations may be that the counselling process could become diluted and lose its focus, or that the therapeutic contract may be unclear. There are other dual relationships where one of the roles requires the client acting in the interests of the counsellor or psycho-therapist. For example, a client who is a lawyer may then give free legal advice to their therapist. The risk here is that the acceptance of personal benefits may induce the therapist to step outside their duty of care to the client. For example, the therapist may start to ask legal questions at the end of therapy sessions, thus preventing the client from engaging in the normal process of reflecting on the impact of the session. A therapist who is also researcher to his or her own cli-ents is in this kind of situation; the research data are a benefit to the therapist, not to the client. The therapist gains from getting a PhD or a publication. The client only gains from getting good therapy.

In counselling and psychotherapy research, as in other types of research on people, the main procedures that are used to ensure ethical standards are *informed consent, confidentiality* and *avoidance of harm.*

Informed consent

Informed consent arises from the principle of autonomy. The person is regarded as having the right to choose whether or not to participate in research, and therefore must be given the information necessary for this choice in a non-coercive manner. One of the key ethical issues, in relation to the application of this principle in therapy research, is that the client may be in a (temporary) state of vulnerability or dependency at the time of being asked for consent. For example, if a counsellor asks a client to participate in research, how possible is it for the client to refuse? Clients may seek to please someone who has helped them. They may be afraid of the consequences of refusing. Can the client believe the counsellor when he or she asserts that withdrawing from the research at any time is perfectly acceptable? Much of this also holds, although perhaps to a lesser extent, when the researcher is known to be a colleague of the counsellor. A further dilemma that is associated with the principle of informed consent is the extent to which it is pos-sible to provide full and detailed information about what might hap-pen in therapy, or in a research interview that asks the client to explore his or her experience in therapy.

Confidentiality

In most therapy agencies, personal information that could identify clients is very carefully controlled and restricted. Any kind of research involves information passing outside this secure loop. An independent researcher can possess client data that can be made thoroughly anonymous, by identifying cases only with code numbers and never allowing the researcher access to names. For a therapist who is researching her own clients, however, the identity of the research participant is always known. In talking about research findings to different audiences, the therapist-researcher can find herself in situations where the identity of the client may inadvertently be disclosed. Clearly, any therapist would take great pains to avoid such a disclosure. Nevertheless, he or she is in a position of knowing much more about the client when in the role of therapist than in the role of researcher. It can sometimes be quite hard to keep these 'knowledges' separate. For example, when giving a research presentation at a conference, an independent researcher would be asked questions based only on the actual data, because it would be obvious that this data comprised the only knowledge that he or she had about research participants. It is quite common for practitioner-researchers to be asked questions along the lines of 'With your counsellor hat on, . . .?' or 'From a practitioner perspective, . . .?'. In attempting to respond to such questions it is difficult to avoid drawing on personal experience rather than sticking to research data. There are some forms of therapy research, such as qualitative studies of the client's experience of therapy and intensive case studies, that rely on being able to provide the reader with insights into the client's unique story – confidentiality is much harder to guarantee in these situations compared to quantitative research studies that collect large amounts of statistical data.

Box 5.5

The ethics of case study research

Case study research plays an important role within the range of methodologies that are available to counselling and psychotherapy research, because it is particularly well suited to exploring complex processes and taking account of the context of therapy. However, case study research is also ethically sensitive, because it is hard to disguise the identity of the client or therapist when presenting information about the whole of a case. Further discussion of the ethical challenges of case study research, and how they can be resolved, can be found in Josselson (1996) and McLeod (2010).

Avoidance of harm

In most therapy research investigations, the moment of data collection is explicitly separated from the moment of therapy. For example,
at the end of a session a client may leave the therapy room and go into
another room where they complete a questionnaire for 15 minutes.
The questionnaire may be given to the client to take home. Within
this framework, what happens in the therapy room is clearly marked
off from what happens in the research study. The research does not
actively intrude into the therapy session. Even when a session is taped,
the goal is to make this as much of a 'passive intrusion' as possible.
The tape is switched on and then forgotten. If the therapist is the
researcher, then none of this is possible because he or she is aware of
the aims of the research and of how what is happening in the therapy
session is relevant to the research. If, for instance, a therapist is taping
sessions because he or she is interested in the role of metaphor and
figurative language in facilitating therapeutic change, surely they will
be super-alert for the occurrence of metaphors in their own and the
client's language. He or she may suppress his own metaphors for fear
of over-influencing the study, or exaggerate them, to produce something that can be analysed later. Can this kind of intrusion into the
therapy process be harmful for clients? As far as I know, no one has
studied this issue, but it is clearly possible that therapist involvement
in research may skew the therapeutic process in directions that may
not be helpful for clients. Again, this is a situation where the same
issues arise even when it is not the actual therapist but a colleague
who is the primary researcher. It is highly unlikely that a therapist
could be unaware of the research interests or hypotheses of one of his
or her colleagues.

   In passing, it is perhaps worth reflecting on the fact that all three of
these ethical problems are highlighted in one of the oldest and most
influential of practitioner research methods in the therapy world –
psychoanalytic case studies. Psychoanalysts do not seek informed
consent (certainly not in advance) around any research intentions
they may have in relation to client material (see McLeod, 2010). They
have no data apart from their own clinical notes and memories. They
are free to pursue their own theoretical/research interests in their
interpretations of client material. So, although psychoanalytic case
studies have been hugely successful in generating a coherent body of
knowledge (see Kvale, 2001), they carry with them some worrying
ethical issues.

   I have intentionally constructed a rather gloomy picture of the depth
of ethical dilemmas faced by counsellors and psychotherapists who

decide to research their own practice. This is because I believe that it is indeed possible to harm clients by 'using' them for research. It is bleak too because there are other, non-ethical, issues that also need to be faced here:

- How honest will a client be when interviewed by their counsellor for research purposes? To what extent can a client be critical of the counselling process?
- How valid is a counsellor's understanding of a client, or of their own work with that client? As an involved participant in a relationship with a client, it can be very difficult for a counsellor to take a detached view of what is happening, or has happened. The actual experience of being the counsellor is so powerful that it is hard to go beyond this experience and develop an understanding that actually makes use of research data.

The point at stake is that it can be very difficult to evaluate or interpret the results of practitioner research into their own clients, notwithstanding any ethical issues. The critique of the psychoanalytic case study method by Spence (1989) offers further elaboration of this question for anyone wishing to explore it in greater depth.

Returning to the ethical challenge represented by avoiding the possibility of harm to clients, in practitioner research into their own clients, there are a number of ethical strategies that can be introduced in order to safeguard the well-being of the client:

1 Seek informed consent in advance, before therapy has started, and make it absolutely explicit that receiving therapy is not contingent on participating in the research.
2 Ask for consent at various stages in therapy, and at the end, to make it possible for the client to withdraw from the study if, for instance, they feel that the material they are disclosing is too sensitive.
3 Make sure that the client has the name of an independent consultant or advocate whom they can contact if they feel under pressure to take part in the research, or are unhappy with any aspect of the arrangements.
4 Collect data that can be analysed by others (e.g. recordings rather than process notes) so that the therapist's interpretation of the material, and his or her impact on the research process, can be checked.
5 If possible, employ a collaborative or dialogical research approach which treats the client as a co-researcher.

Finally, it is important to keep in mind the idea that ethical integrity and good research go hand in hand. Research participants are more likely to open up and contribute good-quality information if they trust you and feel safe. Also, at a personal level, there is always ambivalence associated with the role of researcher. This ambivalence can be greatly heightened if, in the back of one's mind, there are worries about whether one is being exploitative or may be damaging research participants. Further discussion of these issues can be found in McLeod (2010).

Exercise 5.5 Ethical dilemmas in therapy research

Drawing on your own values, what you have read in professional codes of ethics, and your understanding of basic ethical principles of beneficence, non-maleficence, autonomy and fidelity, how would you deal with the ethical dilemmas outlined below?

The management committee of the therapy organisation where you practise has decided that the only way to gain recognition for its way of working with clients is to carry out a randomised controlled trial (RCT) in which clients are evenly allocated to either the therapy approach developed in the clinic, or CBT. Some therapists who are employed by the agency argue that this study would be unethical, because it would be good practice in any clinic where there were two alternative therapies on offer to explore fully with the client their feelings about what was available and to let the client make the choice. What can be done to address these concerns, within the procedures of the proposed RCT? Or does the RCT need to be abandoned?

You work in a counselling service that collects a lot of data from clients, for example asking them to complete an outcome measure every week as a means of monitoring their progress. For the last year, you have been recording all of your therapy sessions with clients, as part of an advanced training in which you have been participating. You realise that one of the clients with whom you worked during this time, and who has now finished therapy, would make a valuable case study because certain aspects of the process of therapy were unexpected and did not correspond to existing theoretical understanding. However, at no point during this client's involvement with the counselling service was he ever asked to give permission for information on his therapy to be used for research purposes. What are the ethical issues that need to be taken into consideration when deciding whether or not it is acceptable to invite this client to allow his story to be written up? What procedures might need to be put in place to ensure his well-being?

You have designed a study that involves carrying out follow-up interviews with clients, three months following the end of their therapy. These are not your own clients, but have been in therapy with colleagues who are known to you. During one of the interviews it becomes apparent to you that the participant is describing a series of events that constitute serious professional malpractice and incompetence on the part of her therapist. She describes herself as having been disappointed with the therapy she had received, but does not give any indication that she regards her therapist as having been culpable. What should you do?

Suggested further reading

These sources explore some of the ways in which ethical issues permeate all aspects of the research process:

Cornforth, S. (2011). Ethics for research and publication. In K. Crocket, M. Agee and S. Cornforth (eds.). *Ethics in Practice: A Guide for Counsellors.* Wellington, NZ: Dunmore.

Etherington, K. (1996). The counsellor as researcher: Boundary issues and critical dilemmas. *British Journal of Guidance and Counselling*, 24, 339–346.

Grafanaki, S. (1996). How research can change the researcher: The need for sensitivity, flexibility and ethical boundaries in conducting qualitative research in counselling/psychotherapy. *British Journal of Guidance and Counselling*, 24, 329–338.

Conclusions

This chapter has examined some of the things that happen 'behind the scenes' in counselling and psychotherapy research. The issues discussed in this chapter include: the developmental stage and needs of the researcher; the point in the research cycle at which a study is carried out; the type of organisational support that is available to those who are conducting research; and the adequacy with which ethical safeguards are implemented. These factors are rarely highlighted in published research articles, yet the way that they are handled can make an enormous difference to the quality of the research that is carried out. In order to attain a balanced and comprehensive understanding of what they read, consumers of research evidence need to be able to see beyond the logical and rational account of the research process that is conveyed in research articles, and imaginatively reconstruct the sometimes messy reality of what actually took place. At the same time, it is not helpful to retreat to a sceptical or even nihilistic position that views all research-based knowledge of therapy as irredeemably compromised by the need to simplify the enormously complex interactions that take place between researchers, research participants and representatives of the organisations within which research is conducted. As we saw in Chapter 3, all research knowledge is socially constructed in some way or another, including in the physical sciences just as much as the human sciences.

6

Understanding quantitative methods

Historically, research into counselling and psychotherapy has largely been carried out by people trained in the disciplines of psychology and psychiatry. Within these disciplines or professions, there has existed a powerful adherence to a concept of science represented by practices such as experimentation, objectivity and accurate measurement of variables. Counselling and psychotherapy, by contrast, can be viewed as multi-disciplinary activities carried out by practitioners drawn from a range of primary professions such as the arts, education, religion and social work as well as psychology and healthcare. Therapists whose original intellectual training emphasised sociological and philosophical analysis, interpretive approaches to understanding, appreciation of aesthetic quality, or action research frequently have difficulties in appreciating the contribution that quantitative methods can make to the inquiry process. At the same time, researchers socialised into the institutionally dominant quantitative and statistical model may fail to appreciate the validity of criticisms of their approach made by proponents of other methodological perspectives.

The nature of measurement in counselling and psychotherapy research can be illustrated by imagining a study in which an investigator is interested in the way that the feelings a client has during sessions might change over the course of counselling. For example, the investigator could be attempting to test the hypothesis that clients are more likely to feel anxious in early sessions because of the unfamiliarity of the situation, and will only be able to express underlying feelings such as anger or grief once the establishment of a good relationship with the counsellor has enabled these initial anxieties to fade into the background. A research study of this kind could produce results that are of relevance to counsellor training, the preparation of clients for counselling, and the construction of models of the counselling process. But how might such a study be carried out?

One possibility for the researcher would be to meet with the client after each session for a tape-recorded interview, and ask him or her to talk about what they felt during the session. This research strategy would yield a rich descriptive account or story, probably containing metaphors ('I felt as though I was going to explode') and idiosyncratic references to personal experience ('I felt just like I did when I was told I had lost my job'). This type of data is 'qualitative': experience is encoded through an infinitely flexible language system. However, although qualitative data can be evocative and meaningful, it is difficult and time-consuming to move from the richness of an individual story to a systematic comparison across stories. If the researcher intends to compare the experiences reported by this informant with those elicited from other participants in the research, or wishes to test the hypothesis that feelings change at different stages in counselling, a different approach will almost certainly be required. In such a situation, the application of quantitative methods makes it much easier to collate data across a number of people.

The aim of this chapter is to offer a balanced account of the role of quantification in counselling and psychotherapy research. Consideration is given to the advantages of quantification in relation to the pursuit of certain types of research question, and also the limitations and dilemmas arising from attempts to quantify human experience.

Exercise 6.1 Your own position on quantification

What is your own attitude towards the use of quantitative methods in the study of therapy process and outcome? Do you regard it as essential, or as misguided? Or do you adopt a more balanced viewpoint? What are the sources of these attitudes, in terms of your life experience and education? If possible, discuss this topic with colleagues whose position differs from your own. What have you learned from these exchanges?

The possibilities of quantification

Quantitative data consist of information about some aspect of human experience, or some personal attribute, that has been transformed into numbers. Always, when quantitative methods are being used, it is essential to remember that what is being measured can also be described in words. For instance, we can say that one person is 'tall' and another is 'short' and therefore that one of them is 'taller' than the other. Quantitative methods allow these kinds of statement to be made with greater precision. We can then say that the first person is 185 cm in height and the second person is 170 cm in height and that the difference between them is 15 cm. The application of quantitative methods in research has a number of advantages:

1 Statements can be made over which there is a large degree of inter-subjective agreement. We may dispute just what counts as 'tall' (does 180 cm count as 'tall'?), but we can all agree on what we mean by a foot or an inch. Quantification therefore introduces objectivity and reliability into research.

2 Quantification makes it easier to make aggregate statements that sum up the characteristics of large numbers of people. Say, for example, a researcher wished to explore the relationship between the therapeutic alliance and outcome in counselling. He or she might interview a large number of clients and collect lots of verbal descriptions of their experience of being in a relationship with their counsellor. Analysing and making sense of this would be interesting but highly time-consuming. It is much easier to administer the Working Alliance Inventory (Hatcher and Gillaspy, 2006; Horvath and Greenberg, 1986, 1989), which provides a standardised set of questions that yield an overall measure of the quality of the thera-peutic relationship.

3 Quantitative methods make it easier to carry out comparisons between different groups of people. Staying with the example of therapeutic alliance research introduced above, it might become clear that there were some clients who had benefited a great deal from counselling, and others who had not. However, it would be difficult to tease out any contrasting experiences of the therapeutic relationship between the members of these two groups using open-ended qualitative interviews. This is because the people being inter-viewed would most likely all be using the same words to describe their experience ('trust', 'liking', 'warmth', 'bond'), and so the researcher would need to be sensitive to perhaps very subtle nuances of difference in the way each of them talked. A researcher using quantitative methods, on the other hand, could use a stand-ardised outcome measure to identify those clients who were 'good outcome' and 'poor outcome' cases, and then compare the Working Alliance scores of the two groups. This method would quickly detect whether there was a reliable difference between the two groups.

4 Transforming experience into numbers opens up many ways of look-ing for patterns in that experience. For instance, it could be helpful to look at whether male or female clients had better relationships with their counsellors, or whether the strength of the relationship was associated with the total number of sessions used, or the num-ber of appointments missed. Statistical techniques make it easy to check whether such patterns exist in a quantitative data set.

5 Quantification allows researchers to estimate the confidence with which they can claim that their results are reliable or representative. A researcher using the Working Alliance Inventory, for example, can look at the 'norms' or average scores of clients in other studies, and will then be in a position to tell whether his or her particular sample is unusually high or low in terms of relationship factors. If a researcher finds that there is a difference in scores between good or poor outcome groups, there are statistical techniques that will show whether this difference is reliable (i.e. would be likely to occur again) or is due to chance.

There are therefore a number of good reasons for using quantitative methods in counselling and psychotherapy research. However, it is essential to be aware of the strengths and weaknesses of quantitative methodology. There are some things it does well and others that it does badly.

Exercise 6.2 Turning your own experience into numbers

Find a copy of any one of the widely used therapy outcome scales, which asks you to indicate the extent to which you have recently experienced various symptoms of psychological distress. Information about how to access these scales on-line can be found on pp. 138–9. Complete the questionnaire as if you were a client attending a counselling centre or psychotherapy clinic for the first time. As you answer the questions, be aware of the thoughts and feelings that are triggered for you. It may be useful to make brief notes as you proceed. On completing the questionnaire, add up your score and compare it with any published norms to which you have access. Afterward, reflect on this experience, and if possible discuss your reactions with colleagues or learning partners. To what extent did the questionnaire enable an accurate rendering of your experience? Further exploration of the psychological processes that may occur during the activity of completing this kind of scale is available in McLeod (2001b).

Applying quantitative methods in counselling and psychotherapy: key research areas

What have counselling and psychotherapy researchers done with numbers? The most basic way in which quantification is used in therapy research has been in relation to the measurement of outcome and process factors. A wide range of measurement scales have been developed to assess levels of distress or symptomatology in areas such as anxiety, depression, post-traumatic stress, occupational stress, burnout, marital satisfaction, interpersonal difficulties, well-being, self-esteem and much else. There also exists a range of scales that have been developed to assess levels of key process factors such as empathy, working alliance and emotional experiencing. Some of these scales (e.g. the Beck Depression Inventory or BDI – Beck et al., 1961, 1988) are copyrighted and must be purchased through commercial publishers. Other scales are freely available on-line (see p. 138 for details of relevant websites). Increasingly, copies of copyrighted scales can also be found on the Internet. Standardised measures such as these are often described as *psychometric* instruments, because they have been constructed in accordance with widely accepted principles of psychological measurement ('psychometrics' = 'measuring the mind'). Typically, scales are regarded as 'validated' if systematic information has been published that verifies the capacity of the scale to measure what it is supposed to measure (validity) and its robustness in terms of yielding stable scores under different assessment conditions (reliability). Further information on the procedures that are used to establish the validity and reliability of a scale can be found in McLeod (forthcoming) and Rust and Golombok (2008).

The development of psychometric scales has made available a sophisticated technology for assessing the outcomes of therapy, based on a substantial research and development effort within the professional community. For example, over the first 25 years of its use, the BDI generated over 100 studies to determine its validity and reliability with different client groups, and it has been used in more than 1,000 substantive clinical studies (Beck et al., 1988). Since that time, many further studies have been added to this list. Many other process and outcome scales can boast similar levels of scrutiny and usage. These scales are the workhorses of therapy research, and have made a massive contribution to the accumulation of an evidence base for the profession.

Operationalisation: the bridge between theory and measurement

The concept of *operationalisation* is central to the way that quantitative research on counselling and psychotherapy is carried out. At a theoretical level, it is easy to hypothesise that CBT will be more effective in alleviating anxiety than treatment as usual from a GP. However, in order to conduct a quantitative test of this hypothesis, it is necessary to find some way of measuring constructs such as 'anxiety', 'CBT' and 'treatment as usual'. The process of devising some means of quantifying a construct is known as 'operationalising': an abstract concept is transformed into an objectively observable and repeatable set of 'operations' which yield numerical data. When reading any quantitative study, it is important to pay attention to the adequacy with which constructs have been operationalised. There is a widespread complaint that research on human intelligence is lacking in credibility and relevance because 'intelligence has been defined merely as what IQ tests measure'. The same critique can be applied to much of counselling and psychotherapy research: do widely used measures of empathy, anxiety or depression *really* reflect the true meaning of these concepts?

Box 6.1

An important sub-set of psychometric measures comprises *adherence scales* (Nezu and Nezu, 2007a; von Consbruch et al., 2012), which are used in counselling and psychotherapy outcome studies to assess the extent to which the therapists in the study are actually delivering the type of therapy that is being evaluated. As well as playing a vital role in ensuring the rigour of outcome research, adherence scales also offer trainees as well as more seasoned practitioners a valuable means of learning about the key features of different kinds of intervention (Najavits et al., 2000), or checking whether their work with clients is actually consistent with the theoretical model that they espouse (Fonagy, 1999). Usually, adherence measures consist of rating scales that are used by trained judges to assess audio recordings of therapy sessions, in terms of the occurrence and quality of specified therapist activities within the session.

Another type of scaling that has been used in therapy research has involved the construction of attitude scales, to collect information around client, therapist and public beliefs, attitudes, expectations and preferences in relation to various aspects of therapy (see, for example, Anderson and Brownlie, 2011; Liddle, 1997; Swift and Callahan, 2009; West and Reynolds, 1995). Unlike psychometric measures, these scales are not standardised tools that are necessarily used unchanged in several studies. Instead, attitude scales draw on principles of attitude measurement that have been developed within sociology and social psychology, on the basis that each scale is specially designed for the specific study within which it will be used.

Further examples of quantification within counselling and psychotherapy research can be found in measures that do not involve anyone completing a questionnaire or rating scale, but which seek to assess behaviour patterns or physiological states. For example, within the area of counselling for workplace stress, there have been several studies that have examined the impact of counselling on sickness absence (see McLeod, 2010b). Other behavioural measures that have been collected by therapy researchers include counts of school attendance, weight, alcohol intake and cigarettes smoked per day. There have also been therapy studies that have collected quantitative data on biological markers of emotional distress, such as heart rate and skin conductance.

Levels of measurement

At the beginning of this chapter, the nature of measurement in therapy research was illustrated through an imagined example of a study in which an investigator was interested in the way that the feelings a client has during sessions might change over the course of counselling. It was suggested that, in a research situation of this kind, the application of quantitative methods would make it much easier to collate data across a number of people. However, it is important to recognise that different types of *levels* of measurement exist, which have implications for the type of analysis that can be carried out.

The simplest kind of measurement which could be applied in this study would be to give the client a checklist of feeling words, such as 'worried', 'sad', 'angry' and so on, and ask him or her to tick the ones that applied during the preceding session. This information is readily quantifiable, for instance by going through the list and coding 'worried' as '1', 'sad' as '2' and 'angry' as '3'. This kind of measurement is known as *nominal* or categorical, since it involves attaching numbers to named qualities or attributes. A very common kind of nominal measurement in research arises when people are asked to indicate their gender, and the researcher codes 'female' as '1' and 'male' as '2'. Nominal measurement represents the most basic variety of quantification. Here, numbers are merely used as category labels in an arbitrary way; it would make just as much sense to code 'worried' as '3' and 'angry' as '1'. There is no relationship between numerical values in nominal scaling. For example, it would not be possible to argue that a score of 3 was 'more than' a score of 2. Nominal measurement merely allows the researcher to count up the number of times a particular quality or attribute (such as 'worried' or 'male') appears in a particular sample of people, in a format that enables information to be readily entered into a spreadsheet or database.

It should be apparent that there are serious limitations to nominal scaling of information about a psychological phenomenon such as feelings. One serious drawback is that, in the study being discussed, the client might tick 'sad' and also 'worried' because he or she had felt slightly sad at one point and had been deeply worried throughout the whole session. Nominal scaling only codes whether something is there or not, and has nothing to say about the intensity or amount of the quality being measured. Another option for the researcher might therefore be to ask the research participant to rank order the list of feeling words in order of which was felt most intensely or most often during the session. The client would be instructed to give '1' to the most powerful feeling, '2' to the next most powerful, continuing through the whole list of words. This kind of measurement is known as *ordinal*, because the numbers reflect a continuum with the largest amount of the quality at one end and the least amount at the other. In ordinal scaling there exists a relationship between numbers, and so more complex operations can be carried out on them. For example, in this study the rank order of feelings reported by one client could be compared, using a *correlation* statistic, with those reported by another client, to give an indication of the level of similarity between the two.

Ordinal measurement is like asking a room full of people to line up with the tallest at one end and the shortest at the other end. A more subtle way of assessing height, however, would be to measure each individual in terms of a standard unit of measurement such as inches or centimetres. The use of standard measurement units is known as *interval* scaling, since the attribute being measured is assessed by units of measurement, each of which represents an equal interval on a continuum. Within the field of psychological measurement, interval scaling is often achieved by using a rating scale. For example, a client could be asked to rate how angry he or she feels on a 7-point scale ranging from, say, 'extremely angry' to 'not at all angry'. Alternatively, the client may be asked to indicate the extent to which he or she agrees or disagrees with a statement such as 'during the last counselling session there were times when I felt angry' using a 5-point scale of 'strongly agree' to 'strongly disagree'. There is a special case of interval scaling known as the *ratio* scale, which applies to measurement scales in which the units of measurement are anchored in an absolute zero point.

Much of the time human attributes measured on an interval scale will form a *normal distribution*. The normal distribution is the familiar bell-shaped curve, indicative of the fact that, on most human or social phenomena, most people are clustered round the middle of the range, with fewer people at the extremes.

Different levels of measurement are associated with different forms of statistical analysis. Within the realm of statistics used by behavioural researchers, an important distinction is made between *parametric* and *non-parametric* statistics. Parametric statistics are operations that can be carried out on data which have achieved interval scale measurement and which is normally distributed. Non-parametric statistics are operations that can be applied to data that reflect ordinal or nominal levels of measurement. (The concept of the normal distribution has no meaning in relation to ordinal or nominal measures.) Parametric statistics make it possible to carry out much more complex and powerful forms of quantitative analysis.

Is everything quantifiable?

It is widely assumed within disciplines such as psychology and psychiatry that all constructs or concepts that are of interest to researchers can have numbers attached to them and so can be 'measured'. However, this assumption may not be valid. The Australian psychologist Joel Michell (1999, 2000, 2013) has argued that the criterion for true quantification to take place is that units of measurement must be capable of being added. Thus, for example, it is possible to quantify the number of therapy sessions a client has attended because five sessions plus another five sessions gives ten sessions. The implication is that a client who has attended ten sessions has received twice as much therapy as a client who has only seen their therapist on five occasions. However, does a score of 20 on the BDI represent 'twice as much' depression as a score of 10? Clearly, a score of 20 indicates that a person is *more* depressed than if they recorded as a score of 10. But 'more than' is not the same as quantification. For Michell (2000), quantification (in the sense of making it possible to conduct mathematical and statistical analyses) would require each 'unit' of depression to be of equivalent value. Michell's (2000) position presents a powerful challenge to many of the basic assumptions that have informed psychological research over the last 50 years.

Analysing quantitative data: practical steps

The series of sub-tasks involved in analysing quantitative data is set out in Figure 6.1. Decisions need to be made at each of these stages. The initial data collection procedure must be designed in such a way as to produce numbers that are appropriate for the kinds of statistical analysis that are intended. For example, employing questionnaire items with simple dichotomous yes/no responses restricts the type of analysis that can be carried out. In most circumstances a 5-point or 7-point scale opens up more possibilities for subsequent analysis.

1   Collect quantitative data (e.g. scores on questionnaire scales).
2   Enter data into a spreadsheet or matrix, usually in a computer statistics package.
3   Decide on which statistical operations are appropriate in testing particular hypotheses.
4   Apply statistical tests.
5   Interpret the results of statistical tests.
6   Display and report data.

Figure 6.1   Steps in quantitative analysis of data

Once the data are collected, it is necessary to enter them into a data matrix for ease of analysis. A matrix can be created on paper or on a computer spreadsheet, and comprises rows and columns in which the variable being measured (e.g. age, gender, number of counselling sessions, anxiety score, working alliance score, etc.) are arrayed in the first row along the top and the case numbers are listed in the first column on the left. The data for each person or 'case' can therefore be read by looking along the row that begins with their case number. The range of scores for each variable can be examined by looking down the column headed with that variable name. Each cell or box in the matrix can only include one number. While you are free to write text in these cells or boxes (and most computer packages will allow this), these qualitative data clearly cannot be 'added up' or analysed numerically. If you have collected only a limited amount of data (fewer than 30 variables) on a relatively small number of people (again, fewer than 30), *and* only plan to carry out a descriptive analysis – see below – then it is easiest to create the data matrix on a large piece of paper or several sheets of paper taped together. For larger data matrices, or when inferential analysis (see below) is to be carried out, it is better to use a statistics package on a personal computer (PC). Many desktop PCs and laptops come supplied with spreadsheets that will handle simple statistical operations. Anything more ambitious will need a purpose-designed software package such as the Statistical Package for the Social Sciences (SPSS). The expense of buying a statistics package may be a factor for some practitioner-researchers. All colleges and universities make these packages available on open-access PCs and may be willing to allow community members to use them. Alternatively, most medium to large organisations will possess, somewhere, a PC or laptop loaded with such a package (and may even employ someone who knows how to use it). Increasingly, open access equivalent packages have started to become available on the internet.

Box 13

Learning SPSS

SPSS has been widely adopted with universities and colleges, and there are several excellent user-friendly books that provide step-by-step guides on how to enter and analyse data using various SPSS tools. The best way to learn SPSS is through hands-on practice, either in a stats lab class or through individual tuition. The person who teaches you SPSS will introduce you to their preferred text. If they do not, some possibilities include:

Field, A. (2009). *Discovering Statistics using SPSS*, 3rd edn. London: Sage.

Pallant, J. (2010). *SPSS Survival Manual: A Step-by-Step Guide to Data Analysis Using SPSS*, 4th edn. Maidenhead: Open University Press.

Analysing statistical data

Once the data are in a matrix, there are basically two different kinds of statistical operations that can be carried out: *descriptive* and *inferential*. Descriptive statistics aim to provide a summary of the main characteristics of the scores that have been collected. Examples of descriptive statistics are:

- *Mean*: the average score of all subjects on one variable.
- *Median*: the score which represents the mid-point of the sample, with 50 per cent scoring higher and 50 per cent lower.

- *Mode*: the value that is recorded most frequently within the data.
- *Range*: the highest and lowest scores that were recorded.
- *Standard deviation* (abbreviated as s, sd or s.d.): an indicator of variability; two-thirds of people in a sample will have scores that are one sd above or below the mean.
- *Variance*: an estimate of how spread-out the scores are; a low level of variance indicates that scores are clustered tightly around the mean, whereas high variance indicates that scores are distributed across the whole range.

Another piece of statistics terminology that is used in describing a sample is '*n*' or '*N*' – the number of people in the study.

The concept of effect size

One of the main applications of standard deviation statistics in therapy research has been through the concept of *effect size* (ES). An understanding of the concept of ES is central to an ability to interpret the findings of studies of the outcome of counselling or psychotherapy. At an individual level, ES can be defined as the level of change reported by a client, divided by the standard deviation found for that measure when it has been administered to a group of clients. In a randomised trial where two therapies are being compared, ES is usually defined as the difference between the means of experimental (treatment) and control (no treatment) groups, divided by the standard deviation of the control group (or the pooled sample of experimental and control groups taken together). An effect size of 1.00 would indicate that the therapeutic intervention being evaluated had been highly successful, because the mean (average) score of the client group had shifted by the amount of one standard deviation in the direction of 'health'. ES represents a useful 'shorthand' way of summarising the level of effectiveness of different interventions. Further reading on the concept of ES, and how it is deployed in therapy research, can be found in Trusty et al. (2004) and Ellis (2010).

Box 6.4

Inferential statistics, by contrast, are used to answer questions or to test hypotheses. For example, a research hypothesis may be that women clients report better therapeutic alliance scores than do male clients. It is fairly easy to work out the mean therapeutic alliance scores of the male and female clients respectively. What is harder is to know whether the difference between their mean scores reveals a real difference, or merely reflects random or chance differences in the particular groups of men and women that have been included in the study. After all, another sample of women clients would yield a slightly different mean score. What inferential statistics make possible, in this kind of situation, is to estimate the degree of confidence with which a result can be regarded as due to chance. All inferential statistics, one way or another, function to calculate the probability with which a particular pattern of scores might be obtained by chance. If the statistical calculation shows that it is relatively unlikely that the result would be found by chance, then we can accept that what we have found is (in some sense) a 'true' difference.

The way in which a statistical programme reports on the likelihood of a pattern of results being due to chance is through a *probability* figure. Statisticians have decided on a convention in which an absolute certainty that something will happen (e.g. the Sun rising tomorrow) is reported as a probability of 1, whereas an absolute impossibility (e.g. Elvis Presley being discovered alive) is reported as a probability of 0. An event that is very unlikely is indicated by a number close to zero and an event that is highly likely is indicated by a number close to 1. For example, when tossing a coin the chance of getting a head or a tail is even, so the probability of either is 0.5 (it will happen 5 times in 10). The chances of Scotland winning the World Cup are, alas, remote, and so this event may be said to have a probability of 0.01 (one chance in 100).

In research on counselling and psychotherapy it is generally accepted that if a pattern of results is shown to be likely to occur by chance more than 1 time in 20 (a probability of 0.05), then it cannot be taken to be a 'true' result. When reading research reports and articles, you will find that the terminology generally used is $p < .05$. This means that the probability of the result being due to chance is *less than* 1 in 20 (0.05) and that therefore on balance we can assume that the result is due to a real difference between the groups rather than attributable to chance factors. (In some studies probabilities of 0.01 – one in 100 – are used, which are more rigorous still.) The p value is known as the *significance level*, and results that meet the $p < .05$ criterion are regarded as *statistically significant*. In some research reports, the probability that a particular result has been obtained through chance is indicated through *confidence intervals*, which refer to the range of values (i.e. maximum and minimum) within which a plausible (or statistically significant) result might occur.

Statistical tests have been designed to assess the significance of differences found when data are analysed in a variety of ways. For example, it is possible to compare the mean scores of one group of people with those of another. The statistical test used here is the *t-test* or *analysis of variance* (ANOVA). This type of statistical technique indicates the degree of confidence with which differences in scores recorded by different groups can be regarded as genuine effects, or are so small that they are more likely to have been produced by random variation within each group. Sample size represents an important consideration when using this kind of technique. If there are only five clients in a sample, their average or mean score on a measure of depression is likely to be quite highly influenced by the individual characteristics of each of them. For example, if one other client were recruited to the study, and the score of this sixth person happened to be high in depression, then the mean for the group would shift to an appreciable extent. By contrast, if there are 50 clients in a sample, it is very unlikely that the score of a 51st member (no matter how high or low) will make much of a difference to the overall mean. When designing a study, it is therefore important to take account of the level of statistical *power*: is there a sufficiently large sample size to provide confidence that differences between groups will be reliably detected?

ANOVA in action: the Sheffield Psychotherapy Project

An example of the use of analysis of variance in a piece of therapy research can be seen in the work of the Sheffield Psychotherapy Project (Shapiro et al., 1990). This research team has carried out a number of studies of the process and outcomes of brief therapy, looking at the effects of both length of treatment and treatment mode on clients who were depressed white-collar workers. In the study reported in Shapiro et al. (1990), 48 clients were randomly assigned to either prescriptive (cognitive-behavioural) or exploratory (relationship-oriented) therapy, and received either eight or 16 sessions. This type of research design is called a '2 x 2' factor design, since there are four separate groups of subjects: eight sessions of prescriptive therapy (8P), eight sessions of exploratory therapy (8E), 16 sessions of prescriptive therapy (16P), and 16 sessions of exploratory therapy (16E). The change scores that were gathered for these clients on a range of standard measures revealed substantial levels of benefit for all four groups. To explore the contribution to outcome of different factors, analysis of variance (ANOVA) was used to examine the effects of treatment mode (i.e. prescriptive vs. exploratory therapy) and duration of treatment on each of these change measures. This statistical test allowed the researchers to inquire whether the overall variance in change scores, or spread of scores, recorded on the BDI (or any of the other outcome measures employed in the study) were associated with mode of treatment, length of treatment or the interaction between the two. The capacity of ANOVA techniques to deal with interaction effects is particularly relevant here. For example, it might be expected on theoretical grounds that prescriptive therapy would be more effective in the context of very focused, eight-session therapy, while exploratory therapy would be more effective in the 16-session condition. In fact, in this study only minor differences in improvement rates due to mode, duration or their interaction were found. This is an interesting result, since it suggests that clients benefit equally from contrasting types of therapy over different lengths of time.

Box 6.5

On other occasions it may be more relevant to look at whether high scores on one variable (e.g. strength of the therapy alliance) are associated with high scores on another variable (e.g. amount of change reported at the end of therapy). The test used for this purpose is the *correlation* coefficient. When reporting correlations, the convention is that a correlation of 1 indicates a perfect correspondence (high scores on the alliance are matched by higher change scores). A correlation of –1 indicates a reverse relationship (high scores on the alliance are associated with *low* higher change scores). Note that a correlation of +1 or −1 both signify a strong relationship between two variables. By contrast, a correlation coefficient of 0 signifies no consistent relationship between two variables. In reality, correlations of +1 or −1 are never found: a correlation of around plus or minus 0.7 is usually taken as indicating a meaningful association between two factors (although how this is interpreted will depend on sample size – a correlation of plus or minus 0.2 can indicate a meaningful or statistically significant relationship, if the sample size is large enough). An absolutely crucial piece of information that is essential for understanding the use of correlation coefficients is that *correlation does not imply causality*. For example, a positive correlation between therapeutic alliance and amount of change does *not* necessarily mean that a good alliance is responsible for beneficial change at the end of therapy. It is quite possible, for instance, that therapists who are good at delivering appropriate techniques are (a) rated by their clients as having a good alliance with them, *and* (b) have clients who get well. In this instance, it is not that the alliance leads to outcome, but that both alliance and outcome result from a third factor: therapist technical competence.

Another note of caution in the use of correlational analysis is that this test can only indicate the extent of a *linear* relationship between two variables. It is feasible that in some situations a strong relationship might exist between two factors but that it was curvilinear in nature. A probable example of a curvilinear relationship is the correlation between therapist self-disclosure and client outcome. On the whole, there does not appear to be any consistent association between these variables. However, it makes sense to suppose that clients find moderate levels of therapist self-disclosure to be helpful, while high levels are overwhelming and a distraction, and very low levels make the therapist appear distant and inhuman.

Correlation statistics in action

The use of correlational statistics is illustrated by a series of studies by Combs (1986) into the personal qualities of effective counsellors. In this research, Combs assessed the 'perceptual organisation' of groups of trainee counsellors. By 'perceptual organisation', he meant the degree to which these trainees perceived the world from a person-centred perspective. His technique for doing this allowed him to rank order the members of each group, for example in terms of who was most 'open to experience' to who was least. Tutors who knew these trainees well then gave independent assessments on their effectiveness as counsellors. The similarity between the two rankings of the group were then calculated using a correlation statistic. In this set of studies, consistently high correlations were found between person-centred attitudes and counselling effectiveness. This study illustrates the strengths and limitations of the use of correlational analysis. The findings of the study are easy to understand – there is an association between person-centred attitudes and counsellor effectiveness. However, the link between these factors may be due to the operation of some other variable. For instance, it is possible that students who have had more personal therapy may be more open to experience *and* more effective as therapists.

There are many statistical tests available, depending on the analysis that is required to answer the specific research question. The statistical tests that have been introduced in this section have referred to fairly straightforward situations, where a comparison is being made between patterns of score obtained for two groups (e.g. male vs. female clients). There are also more sophisticated statistical techniques that can be used to explore more complex issues. Factor analysis and multi-dimensional scaling make it possible to look at how different variables cluster together (e.g. which items in a questionnaire tend to be answered in the same way). Regression analysis makes it possible to construct models of how scores on one variable are predicted by scores on a set of other variables (e.g. relative importance of age, gender, years of experience, and length of training on the effectiveness of therapists). Any statistics textbook will provide clear guidelines on the circumstances under which particular tests can and cannot be applied. Most universities offer statistics training courses, at all levels from introductory to advanced. There are also a great deal of valuable statistics resources available on the Internet.

Box 6.7

Demystifying statistics

- Numbers and statistical tests are a really good way of summarising information that has been collected from groups of people, and looking for patterns in that information. Essentially, that is what it is all about. A typical scenario is that a sample of people complete a questionnaire. By using statistics it is possible to look at questions such as:

  o What is the average score?
  o What is the range of scores (i.e. highest to lowest)?
  o How spread out are the scores (i.e. are the scores spread out across the whole scale, or have all the participants obtained fairly similar scores)?
  o Do different groups (e.g. men vs. women; CBT clients vs. psychodynamic clients) have different scores?

- Quite often, researchers make use of advanced and sophisticated forms of statistical analysis. This is because they are working in universities and have expert statisticians to help them. It is not unusual for the researcher him/herself

(Continued)

(Continued)

to not fully understand what the stats are about. Much of the time, the majority of readers are confused too – even people who have had some statistics training.

- In any well-written paper, the author should provide a narrative summary of the findings alongside the statistical information. It should always be possible to 'skip' the numbers and pick up the thread of the study and its results by reading the non-statistical sections of the report.
- It is very unlikely, in an article published in a reputable journal, that the statistics have been calculated wrongly. This is because the figures are checked carefully before the paper is published. However, authors of papers may sometimes neglect to discuss statistical findings that do not fit their theory.
- Statistics is a language, which includes some new ideas and words. It takes a bit of time to get to grips with it. As with any other language-learning, regular practice is important, and there is always more to be learned.

Suggested further reading

Accessible, therapist-friendly introductions to statistics can be found in:

Barker, C., Pistrang, N. and Elliott, R. (2002). *Research Methods in Clinical Psychology: An Introduction for Students and Practitioners,* 2nd edn. Chichester: Wiley.

Cooper, M. (2008). *Essential Research Findings in Counselling and Psychotherapy: The Facts Are Friendly.* London: Sage.

Detailed exploration of all of the issues discussed in this chapter is available in:

Clark-Carter, D. (2009). *Quantitative Psychological Research,* 3rd edn. New York: Psychology Press.

Explanations of statistical concepts and procedures can be accessed through a wide range of statistics textbooks:

Argyrous, G. (2011). *Statistics for Research: With a Guide to SPSS,* 3rd edn. London: Sage.

Coolidge, F.L. (2012). *Statistics: A Gentle Introduction,* 3rd edn. Thousand Oaks, CA: Sage.

Salkind, N.J. (2010). *Statistics for People Who (Think They) Hate Statistics,* 4th edn. Thousand Oaks, CA: Sage.

Walker, J. and Almond, P. (2010). *Interpreting Statistical Findings: A Guide for Health Professionals and Students.* Maidenhead: Open University Press.

Exercise 6.3 Critically reading a quantitative research paper

Find a research paper on a topic that is of interest to you that makes use of quantitative methods (strategies for locating copies of research papers are introduced in Chapter 4). On your first reading of the paper, skip any sections which include statistical terminology that you do not understand. To what extent were you able to get the gist of what the study is about, and what it found? On second reading, make note of the statistical jargon and concepts that are unfamiliar to you, and follow them up using the introductory statistics texts listed above, or through internet searches. On your third reading, reflect on the strengths and advantages of using quantitative methods in the study you have selected, and also the limitations (what aspects of the topic have been downplayed or distorted through the process of quantification?).

Meta-analysis: using statistical techniques to construct rigorous literature reviews

The use of statistical techniques in counselling and psychotherapy research reaches beyond the analysis of data that are collected in the context of a specific study. *Meta-analysis* is a method for accumulating the findings of a range of studies on a particular topic, so that conclusions can be drawn from the largest possible data set, collected from as wide a range as possible of contrasting therapy settings. The first step in meta-analysis is to determine the methodological quality (and therefore credibility) of all of the studies that have been carried out around a specific question, and eliminate any studies that do not reflect a predetermined quality threshold. Then an estimate is made of the effect size (ES) reported for each intervention in each study. Finally, the overall ES, averaged across all eligible studies, is worked out. Examples of the use of meta-analysis include the work of Elliott et al. (2012) around mapping the effectiveness of person-centred and experiential therapies; Cuijpers et al. (2011) on the relative effectiveness of different therapy approaches for depression; Lewis et al. (2008) on the outcomes of short-term psychodynamic psychotherapy; and many other published meta-analytic review papers and chapters. It has been the availability of meta-analysis as a powerful tool for carrying out rigorous reviews of existing literature that has made it possible for governments and other healthcare providers to develop service delivery policies based on supporting specific therapies for specific disorders. Further information on the use of meta-analysis can be found in Borenstein et al. (2009) and Higgins and Green (2008).

Are all swans white?

In Chapter 3, a brief outline was given of the ideas of one of the leading 20th-century philosophers of science, Sir Karl Popper. One of the key contributions of Popper was to point out that the core of scientific lay in the effort to *refute* propositions or conjectures. One of the examples he used was the statement that 'all swans are white'. This proposition can be confirmed thousands of times, through observing white swans all over the world. However, these observations do not necessarily make the statement true, because all it would take is *one* observation of a black swan to refute it. The logic of refutation is relevant to the task of adopting a balanced view of the results of meta-analysis of the outcomes of psychotherapy. Meta-analyses of therapy outcome studies have shown, over and over again, that therapy is more effective than no therapy for people with anxiety, depression and other psychological problems. But some black swans have been observed. One randomised controlled trial of the effectiveness of psychotherapy found that regular organised outdoor running (Klein et al., 1985) produced as much benefit as did participation in group therapy. What are we to make of this finding? Where does it fit into the overall picture? Is it an aberrant result, or is it just that the research community has collectively chosen not to look for swans that are other than white?

Exercise 4.4 Reviewing your learning needs around quantitative methods

Having completed reading this chapter, reflect on the adequacy of your knowledge of quantitative methods in respect of your personal engagement with therapy research. Is your knowledge sufficient to allow you to read research papers that are relevant to your professional interests? Is your knowledge sufficient to allow you to carry out the kind of research that you wish to undertake? If your statistical knowledge is not adequate, then where and how can you learn more about this form of inquiry?

Conclusions

The aim of this chapter has been to introduce some of the principles involved in using quantitative methods in counselling and psychotherapy research. Some of the issues and difficulties associated with this approach have also been explored. Statistical methods represent a powerful tool in therapy research. The main advantages of quantitative methods lie in their ability to deal with large numbers of cases, examine interactions between variables, and verify the presence of cause-and-effect relationships between variables. The main limitations of quantitative research are concerned with the risk of losing sight of aspects of human experience that may not be amenable to quantification. The alternative to quantitative research, in the form of qualitative methods that focus on the analysis of patterns of language use and the meaning of the accounts that people give of their experience, is explored in the next chapter. Examples of research studies that combine both qualitative and quantitative methods in the same project occur throughout the book, for example in respect of the use of systematic case study methods. At the present time, both qualitative and quantitative methods make powerful contributions to the overall counselling and psychotherapy research literature. It is hard to gain a satisfactory appreciation of the state of research evidence in relation to any area of therapy research without being able to read and critically assess both quantitative and qualitative studies. It is therefore necessary for all research-informed therapy practitioners to possess at least a minimal level of awareness of statistical concepts and how they are used within this field.

7

Understanding qualitative methods

Qualitative methods have been increasingly used in counselling and psychotherapy research in recent years. Many therapists are excited about the potential value of qualitative methods as a means of generating new understandings of the process and outcome of therapy. At the same time, there are significant challenges associated with the task of doing qualitative research well, and in using the findings of qualitative research to inform policy decisions. The aim of the present chapter is to examine some of the assumptions that underpin qualitative research in counselling and psychotherapy. The main approaches to qualitative research are introduced, followed by a discussion of the criteria that can be applied in assessing the validity of qualitative findings. The chapter concludes by considering some critical issues associated with the application of qualitative methods in therapy research.

Defining qualitative research

Qualitative research has often been defined in terms of what it is *not*: that is, it is research that does not involve the use of measurement or statistical techniques. For example, Miles and Huberman (1994) describe qualitative data as 'words rather than numbers', while Strauss and Corbin (1998) view the qualitative approach as comprising 'any kind of research that produces findings not arrived at by means of statistical procedures or other means of quantification'. The pervasiveness of 'negative definitions' of qualitative methods reflects the fact that, historically, much qualitative research has been explicitly conducted in opposition to, or in defiance of, the dominant positivist paradigm in psychology and social science. However, to appreciate what is involved in qualitative research, it is also necessary to frame a definition that encompasses its main characteristics and goals in a more constructive manner.

Current practice in qualitative research draws upon a number of philosophical traditions, each of which has made a distinctive contribution to the development of this approach to human science: hermeneutics, phenomenology, feminism, constructivism, social constructionism, and postmodernism. As a result, the field of qualitative research is methodologically much more fragmented than is the world of quantitative methods. Positivist research, such as experimental psychology, is derived from a philosophical position that regards knowledge as unitary, and therefore attainable through a standardised set of scientific procedures. By contrast, most qualitative researchers adopt the philosophical stance that human knowledge is contextualised, and shaped by, cultural and personal factors. As a result, different qualitative researchers, influenced by different traditions, have developed a wide range of strategies for gathering and analysing data.

Suggested further reading

Extended discussion of the philosophical perspectives that underpin qualitative methods can be found in:

McLeod, J. (2011). *Qualitative Research in Counselling and Psychotherapy*, 2nd edn. London: Sage. (Chapter 2.)

Ponterotto, J.G. (2005). Qualitative research in counseling psychology: A primer on research paradigms and philosophy of science. *Journal of Counseling Psychology*, 52, 126–136.

Stiles (1993) suggests that qualitative research can most usefully be regarded as a 'natural language' label which is best defined in terms of examples or characteristic features, not all of which are applicable in every case, rather than as a phenomenon that can be strictly circumscribed. It is possible to identify a set of interlocking themes, strategies and values characteristic of most qualitative research:

- *Naturalistic inquiry*: studying real-world phenomena in as unobtrusive a manner as possible, with a sense of openness regarding whatever emerges.
- *Inductive analysis*: allowing conclusions to arise from a process of immersion in the data, rather than imposing categories or theories decided in

advance. A willingness on the part of the researcher to 'bracket-off' his or her assumptions about the phenomena being studied.

- *An image of an active human subject*: research participants are viewed as purposefully involved in co-creating their social worlds, and are similarly engaged as active co-equals in the research process.
- *Holistic perspective*: emphasis on the reciprocal inter-relationships between phenomena, rather than attempting to create explanations solely in terms of cause–effect sequences. Keeping the larger picture in mind, rather than reducing experience to discrete variables.
- *Qualitative data*: gathering mainly linguistically based data that are richly descriptive of the experience of informants. Data as a 'text' rather than an array of numbers.
- *Personal contact and insight*: the researcher is in close contact with the people being studied. The quality of the researcher–informant relationship is of critical importance. The use of the researcher's empathic understanding of informants as a source of data.
- *Process orientation*: this views the phenomenon being investigated as a dynamic system where change is constant and on-going.
- *Awareness of uniqueness*: a willingness to view each individual case as special and unique. The principle of respecting the particular configuration of individual cases even when developing general conclusions.
- *Contextual sensitivity*: findings can only be understood within a social, cultural, historical and environmental context. Part of the task of the researcher is to consider these contextual factors.
- *Design flexibility*: within a study, methods and procedures are adapted in response to new circumstances and experiences.
- *Flexible sampling*: the choice of participants in a study is determined by a range of theoretical and practical considerations, not merely by the aim of accumulating a 'representative' sub-set of the general population.
- *Reflexivity*: the idea that the researcher is his or her primary instrument, and as a result must be aware of the fantasies, expectations and needs that his or her participation introduces to the research process.
- *Empowerment as a research goal*: an awareness of the social and political implications of research, accompanied by a commitment to using the research process to benefit research participants.
- *A constructionist approach to knowledge*: taking the point of view that reality is socially constructed. The products of research are not 'facts' or 'findings' that reflect an objective reality, but are versions of an interpreted reality, or life-world, that are constructed by the researcher (or co-constructed between researcher and participants).

The field of qualitative research has evolved as a range of approaches, each of which includes in some form all of the themes and strategies listed above. The fundamental goal of qualitative investigation is to uncover and illuminate what things mean to people. A brief definition of qualitative research might be to view it as *a process of systematic inquiry into the meanings which people employ to make sense of their experience and guide their actions*. The key idea here is that of *meaning*. The qualitative researcher strives to describe understandings, and the collective processes through which people make meaning, and act with intention and purpose on what things mean to them. By contrast, the quantitative researcher attempts to measure *variables*, and to establish cause-and-effect linkages between different factors or variables as a means of building explanatory models or theories.

Suggested further reading

Denzin, N.K. and Lincoln, Y.S. (eds.) (2011). *The Sage Handbook of Qualitative Research*, 4th edn. Thousand Oaks, CA: Sage. (An authoritative source of information about the range and scope of qualitative research and current debates.)

Applying qualitative methods in counselling and psychotherapy: key research areas

Qualitative methods have been used to explore many aspects of counselling and psychotherapy. A useful means of beginning to sort out the ways in which different qualitative methodologies have been used to tackle different therapy issues is to make a distinction between three distinct research domains, defined in terms of scale: macro, mid-range and micro. Macro-level studies explore the social, cultural and historical context within which therapy takes place. Mid-range studies examine the experience of therapy for participants. Micro-level investigations consider moment-by-moment processes. Each of these units of analysis presents distinctive opportunities and challenges for qualitative therapy researchers, and is associated with the use of specific methods of gathering and analysing data. While it is certainly possible to identify studies that straddle the boundaries of these domains, for the most part it is possible to allocate the majority of qualitative therapy research to one of these categories. Some examples of qualitative therapy research that have been carried out within each of these areas are introduced below.

The context of therapy

Relatively few studies of the social and cultural context of therapy have been carried out, probably as a result of the 'individualised', psychology-oriented nature of most theory and research in counselling and psychotherapy. One of the main methodological challenges associated with this kind of study is the fact that no single informant or research participant can ever claim personal, first-hand experience of all of the aspects of the topic that is being explored. For example, when Cushman (1995) analysed the cultural and economic factors that influenced the development of psychotherapy in the USA from the early 19th century to the mid-20th century, he needed to draw on a wide range of primary documentary material, in books, pamphlets, autobiographies, magazines and newspapers, as well as on secondary sources written by historians. In his study of the ways in which CBT was delivered in the context of a prison unit for sex offenders, Waldram (2007a, 2007b, 2012) interviewed inmates, therapists and prison officers, and sat in on group therapy sessions. This study represents an ethnographic approach to combining different sources of information into a 'thick description' of a particular slice of social life. On the basis of these studies, and other research into the context of therapy, it is possible to see that the complexity of the topic being investigated means that it is not sufficient to rely solely on a single source of data, such as interviews or one type of document (e.g. newspaper articles). Instead, the researcher needs to be flexible and innovative in seeking relevant information wherever it can be located. This form of research is more like the kind of work carried out by historians, social anthropologists and political scientists than the work done by researchers in psychology.

The experience of therapy

The main area in which qualitative methods have been used in research in counselling and psychotherapy has been in relation to client and therapist experiences of the process and outcomes of therapy. What makes this kind of research so powerful, and potentially influential, is that it gives a 'voice' to the actual participants in therapy. Although quantitative research can generate valuable knowledge in many areas of therapy, the use of quantification makes it impossible to know 'what it was like' for the therapist or client. By contrast, qualitative research represents an ideal approach for gaining access to the views and experiences of participants in therapy. For the researcher, the main challenge of this kind of research involves finding ways to enable informants to provide detailed and authentic descriptions of their experience. For example, if interviews are being used to collect data, then it is unlikely that the informant will open up and talk honestly about their therapy if they do not have a good rapport with the interviewer, or if trust is absent. Even if the client is willing to open up, he or she may find it hard to recall what happened during any hour of therapy over several months. Alternatively, they may recall too much and be unable to organise their recollections in a form that answers the researcher's questions. In response to these factors, qualitative therapy researchers have tended to pay a great deal of attention to constructing interview strategies that are maximally facilitative for research participants. For example, in a follow-up study of clients who had used a women's therapy centre, Morris (2005) took great care to ensure that participants felt safe enough to talk about their experiences and understood what was being asked of them. In a study where therapy clients were being asked to compare their experiences of therapy they had received at different points in their life, McKenna and Todd (1997) used a time-line technique to enable informants to draw a visual representation of the ups and downs of their 'therapy careers'. In a study that looked at client perceptions of the therapeutic relationship, Bedi et al. (2005) were keen to go beyond generalised statements such as 'my therapist was a good listener', and made use of a *critical incident* technique – participants were asked to tell the story of specific moments in therapy when something happened that made a difference to the quality of their relationship with their therapist. Rennie (1990, 1992, 1994a, 1994b, 1994c) was interested in how clients experienced the process of therapy within a specific session. In order to help the client to talk about what had actually happened in the session (as opposed to their retrospective reconstruction of it), he made use of the *stimulated recall* technique. The therapy session was audio-recorded. During the research interview, the recording was played back to the client, who stopped it at any point where he or she remembered what they had been thinking or feeling at that moment. This strategy results in a much richer and more detailed account of the experience of therapy in comparison to accounts that are generated during standard retrospective interviews.

Qualitative research on the outcomes of therapy

Because of the dominant position of quantitative methods, it is widely assumed that research into the effectiveness and outcomes of therapy must always involve the measurement of change using some kind of scale. However, the literature contains some examples of theoretically interesting and practically significant qualitative outcome studies. Nilsson et al. (2007) used qualitative interviews to explore experiences of change in clients who had received either CBT or psychodynamic therapy. What they found was that both therapy approaches were broadly similar in effectiveness (which is also what quantitative studies have tended to report). They also found differences in the types of change reported by CBT and psychodynamic clients, and collected fascinating information on why dissatisfied clients believed that therapy had not helped them (neither of these findings had been previously reported in the quantitative literature). Further discussion of the role of qualitative research in evaluating the effectiveness of therapy can be found in McLeod (2011: Ch. 13).

Box 7.1

Micro-analysis of therapy processes

Qualitative research has proved to be an invaluable tool in relation to making sense of moment-by-moment processes that occur in therapy. On the whole, these processes are outside of the immediate awareness of the client or therapist. It is hard to collect information on micro-processes in interviews, although the kind of stimulated recall interview used by Rennie (1990, 1992) will allow access to some dimensions of micro-process. For example, clients and therapists tend to use metaphor in their communication with each other, but rarely give much conscious attention to this kind of language use, and as a result tend to forget that it happens. Angus and Rennie (1988, 1989) recorded therapy sessions, and invited clients and therapists to listen to sections in which they had used metaphoric expressions. Under these conditions, they were able to say a lot about what the metaphors had meant to them. Nevertheless, despite the undoubted value of stimulated recall techniques, what has proved to be more useful as a means of accessing information about therapy micro-processes is the analysis of therapy transcript material. In particular, two well-established qualitative methodologies have been employed for this purpose: *conversation analysis* and *discourse analysis*. A classic example of this kind of research can be found in a study by Davis (1986), which was based on an analysis of the use of language, and strategies of linguistic control, by a therapist and client in a first meeting. Davis was able to document a number of subtle ways in which the therapist redefined the client's description of her problem, so that by the end of the session it was formulated in terms of the therapist's theoretical framework. Although it is highly unlikely that either the therapist or client were consciously aware that this was happening, careful analysis of conversational patterns that could be observed in the therapy transcript enabled the unfolding of this process to be visible.

In addition to research into different levels of understanding of the practice of therapy, qualitative methods have also been used to explore a range of topics concerned with the training, supervision and development of counsellors and psychotherapists. A particularly influential area of qualitative inquiry into therapist development has focused on the characteristics of senior practitioners and 'master therapists' (Jennings and Skovholt, 1999; Miller, 2007; Skovholt and Jennings, 2004; Skovholt et al., 1997). The findings of these studies have made it possible for the profession as a whole to learn from those who are recognised as being really good at their jobs.

Qualitative research in action

The process of carrying out qualitative research can be divided into two broad types of activity: gathering data and analysing data. In practice these two activities will often be carried out as a series of cycles of inquiry, or may even appear to be happening at the same time. However, for the purpose of the present discussion, these research operations will be reviewed separately. In the space available here, it is only possible to outline qualitative research techniques in an introductory manner. The reader intending to carry out a qualitative study is recommended to consult other texts that provide more detailed accounts of qualitative research procedures, such as Silverman (2009), Smith (2007) and Willig (2008).

Gathering qualitative data

A wide range of methods have been employed in gathering data in qualitative studies. Each of these methods has its own special advantages and disadvantages, as described below.

Interviewing

The research interview is a flexible way of gathering research data that are detailed and personal. The presence of the interviewer enables on-going monitoring of the relevance of the information being collected, and enables the researcher to check out his or her understanding of what is being said. One of the principal disadvantages of interviews lies in the amount of time that can be spent in setting them up, conducting the session and then transcribing the tape recording. Some informants (and researchers) find the experience of being recorded intimidating. The quality of information obtained also depends on the level of rapport and trust between interviewer and interviewee.

Qualitative open-ended questionnaires

In some qualitative research studies, the researchers may have a list of questions to put to informants, but it may not be practicable or necessary to conduct actual face-to-face interviews. In these circumstances, the open-ended questionnaire can be a valuable research tool. A much wider coverage of informants can usually be achieved by using this technique, and short open-ended questionnaires are normally experienced by research participants as straightforward, unintrusive and unthreatening. From the point of view of the researcher, there is the big advantage that qualitative questionnaire data do not need to be transcribed.

Projective techniques

In both interviews and open-ended questionnaires, descriptive material can be supplemented and augmented through the use of projective techniques. In all projective techniques, the person is presented with an ambiguous or incomplete stimulus to which he or she can respond in any way they choose. The classic projective techniques, which have in the past been widely used in personality assessment, include the Rorschach inkblot test, where the person is asked to tell what they see in a symmetrical inkblot; the thematic apperception test (TAT), where the person tells or writes a story about a picture; and sentence completion technique, where the person writes an ending to an incomplete sentence stem. Projective techniques have a long history within psychology, and a wide range of such techniques have been invented. In therapy research, rich qualitative material can be gained from projective questions such as 'What image or metaphor would you use to characterise your sense of the process of therapy?' (Najavits, 1993).

Participant observation

A strategy for collecting qualitative material that has been employed in a wide range of studies in sociology and anthropology is participant observation. With this method, the researcher takes part in the lives of the people being studied, and gains as full as possible an appreciation of what different activities, relationships and institutions mean to them. Participant observation requires great skill, patience and persistence on the part of the researcher. Typical challenges connected with this method are those of negotiating entry to the field, maintaining relationships with informants, keeping a balance between participation ('going native') and detachment, collecting field notes, and saying goodbye to people who may have become more than mere participants in a research study. Participant observation also tends to require a great deal of time. However, it has the potential to generate detail and authentic accounts of how people conduct aspects of their lives.

Documentary research

Each of the qualitative data-gathering methods reviewed up to this point have shared the characteristic of being initiated by the researcher. These techniques can be seen as 'reactive', in that the answers given by research participants will to some extent be a reaction to the personality of the researcher, or to the way the question was asked in the questionnaire or interview. It is therefore very useful to be able to draw upon qualitative material that may have been created spontaneously by research participants completely independently of any research study. The most common data sources of this type are personal documents and official documents. Personal documents include letters, diaries, personal journals, poems and novels written by research participants. There have been a number of client case studies that have included material from the personal diaries of the client (e.g. the studies by Evans and Robinson, 1978, and Yalom and Elkin, 1974). Organisational research often makes use of memos, minutes of meetings, and organisational archives and correspondence. For example, in their study of the origins and development of the National Marriage

Guidance Council, Lewis et al. (1992) consulted a wide variety of such official documents and papers. In some therapy studies, researchers have invited clients to keep diaries (Mackrill, 2007, 2008b).

Therapy session transcripts

Audio- or video-recordings of therapy sessions, which are then transcribed, provide a powerful source of evidence for studies of the process of counselling and psychotherapy. Analysis of transcripts can focus on brief episodes within single sessions, for example the interaction between a client and therapist as they explore a particular topic. Alternatively, it is possible to identify and analyse themes that arose across the whole course of therapy. Lepper and Riding (2006) provide a valuable guide to different approaches to working with therapy transcript data.

Inquiry groups

The human inquiry group, or co-operative inquiry group, is a data collection strategy that relies strongly on productive, authentic collaboration between members of a group, who meet together to share their experience of the topic of inquiry and gradually work towards developing a shared understanding. In practice, the members of an inquiry group can employ any and all data-gathering techniques: interviewing, keeping diaries, carrying out experiments. The distinctive aspect of the approach is the way that these familiar research techniques are embedded in a collective, cyclical inquiry process. An influential example of this approach can be found in a study by Reason et al. (1992; Reason, 1988) into the development of a framework through which GPs and practitioners of complementary medicine might collaborate effectively.

Personal experience methods

In therapy, the idea that practice involves the systematic 'use of self' is widely accepted. Therapeutic concepts such as counter-transference and congruence represent the contribution that self-involvement and purposeful use of personal feelings and experiences can make to the therapeutic process. By contrast, researchers have tended to regard their own personal experience as a potential source of bias, rather than a source of insight and data. A number of approaches to qualitative research have sought to restore a place for the personal experience of the researcher. The most widely known of these approaches is the *heuristic inquiry* method developed by Moustakas (1990). This form of research requires the total personal immersion of the inquirer in the topic, to the point where a creative 'incubation' brings a new understanding of the phenomenon. The *integral inquiry* approach devised by Braud (1998) and the *intuitive inquiry* model espoused by Anderson (1998, 2004) are broadly similar to the heuristic approach, but specifically encourage a focus on transpersonal or spiritual dimensions of personal experience (Braud and Anderson, 1998). The heuristic, integral and intuitive approaches to research can be viewed as part of a broader approach to knowing which can be characterised as humanistic psychology (Schneider et al., 2001). A contrasting approach to the use of personal experience for research purposes can be found in the work of Carolyn Ellis and her colleagues (Ellis and Bochner, 2000; Ellis and Flaherty, 1992; Ellis et al., 1997). Their approach, known as *autoethnography*, is based in a sociological tradition, and combines autobiography and ethnography (participant observation) as a method for using detailed reporting of personal experience as a means of exploring broader cultural themes.

Suggested further reading

Books that capture the experience of actually carrying out qualitative research:

Fischer, C.T. (ed.) (2006). *Qualitative Research Methods for Psychologists: Introduction Through Empirical Case Studies*. San Diego, CA: Academic Press.

Kvale, S. and Brinkmann, S. (2009). *InterViews: Learning the Craft of Qualitative Research Interviewing*, 2nd edn. Thousand Oaks, CA: Sage.

Exercise 7.1 The advantages and disadvantages of different ways of collecting qualitative data

Identify a research question that interests you, which can in principle be investigated using qualitative methods (i.e. it is an open-ended and exploratory question, rather than a closed, hypothesis-testing question). Take a few minutes to consider how you might collect data that were relevant to your topic, using each of the methods described in this section (e.g. interviews, documents, therapy session transcripts). Once you have done this, reflect on the following issues:

- What are the practical implications of using each method of data collection, in terms of time and expense, willingness of people to participate, and potential ethical barriers?
- In what ways might each of these methods influence the kind of results that you will obtain? What are the aspects of your research topic that would be highlighted or hidden as a consequence of collecting different types of data?

Although it is valuable to reflect on these issues on your own, using this exercise as a basis for a group discussion is likely to lead to a wider range of perspectives and possibilities.

Analysing qualitative data

Analysis and interpretation of qualitative data present considerable challenges to researchers. Typically, the qualitative researcher will gather many thousands of words of transcripts, notes and other written material. These raw data exist in a non-standardised form. For example, a qualitative data set can consist of detailed descriptions of events from some informants, cryptic comments from others, literal accounts and metaphoric allusions, experiential 'stream of consciousness' narratives, and distanced explanatory rationalisations. It is probably fair to say that no two researchers approach the task of qualitative data analysis in quite the same way, even if they claim to be using the methods. Each of the main qualitative approaches, such as grounded theory, interpretive phenomenological analysis (IPA), consensual qualitative research (CQR) and discourse analysis, has developed its own set of procedures for analysing qualitative data; McLeod (2011) provides detailed information on the similarities and differences between these approaches. Each of these methodologies can be viewed as representing variations around a generic set of qualitative analysis strategies, outlined in Figure 7.1.

Stage 1: Immersion

The researcher intensively reads or listens to material, assimilating as much of the explicit and implicit meaning as possible.

Stage 2: Preliminary coding

Systematically working through the data, assigning coding categories or identifying meanings within the various segments/units of the 'text'.

Stage 3: Identifying general themes or categories

Questioning or interrogating the meanings or categories that have been developed. Clustering initial codes into larger groupings.

Stage 4: Triangulation

Sorting through the categories. Comparing examples to ensure that categories are being used consistently. Looking for counter-examples (information that does not fit into the emerging overall scheme). Deciding which categories are recurring and central and which are less significant. An external auditor may be consulted at this stage, to check on the credibility and thoroughness of the analysis. Alternatively, research participants themselves may be asked for feedback.

Stage 5: Interpretation

Making sense of the data from a wider perspective. Constructing a model, or exploring the relevance of the findings of the study as a means of supporting or challenging existing theoretical ideas.

Stage 6: Writing

Editing and assembling the material that has been generated, for purposes of publication and dissemination. At this stage, difficulties in writing may indicate lack of coherence in the preceding analysis of the data, and require parts of the analysis to be reviewed.

Figure 7.1   Stages in the analysis of qualitative data

The first step in any qualitative data analysis is for the researcher to become immersed in the information that he or she has gathered. The main instrument that the researcher possesses is his or her capacity to enter, in an empathic way, the lived experience of the person or group being studied. To gain a sense of the whole of that lived experience, the researcher must temporarily internalise and 'own' as much of the data as possible. Many qualitative researchers will work on coding interviews as soon as they can following an interview, so they do not lose the 'feel' of what the informant has said. Other qualitative researchers will carry around a notebook and jot down analytic themes or ideas whenever they occur to them. It is normal practice to read through field notes or interview transcripts, or listen to tapes, several times before beginning to do analytic work on them.

The process of categorising qualitative material is sometimes called 'coding' or 'classification'. Qualitative data can be viewed as essentially comprising a text or narrative. All qualitative data-collection techniques involve gathering the descriptions, accounts or stories that people create and share in relation to their experience. One of the first tasks of the qualitative researcher is to find ways of breaking down this flow of text into its component meanings. Whether the researcher segments the text into statements, thought units or larger patterns and sequences, it is necessary to assign meanings to these blocks of text in as systematic a manner as possible. The same meaning units may be assigned to as many as ten different categories, reflecting the diverse nuances and horizons of meaning associated with that piece of text. In order to achieve this awareness of alternative meanings, the researcher must develop his or her 'theoretical sensitivity'.

In order to arrive at a fresh and detailed account of an area of experience, a qualitative researcher must be willing to suspend or 'bracket-off' his or her assumptions about what is being studied. From the perspective of phenomenological philosophy, it is argued that people ordinarily 'take for granted' the experiential world within which they live; they have a 'natural attitude' which accepts that what is perceived is just 'out there'. Any qualitative researcher who is using a phenomenologically informed approach, however, is systematically trying to find new ways of seeing or understanding the object of inquiry. In practice, it is never possible to put aside all the assumptions that might be held in relation to a phenomenon. The 'essence' of the phenomenon can never be grasped. But the very process of seeking this essence yields an understanding of the various perspectives and horizons of meaning through which the experience of that phenomenon has been constructed. A technique that can be employed to assist in this process is 'imaginative variation'. Here, the researcher does everything possible to find fresh ways of looking at the phenomenon. This involves an intentional disruption of the 'natural attitude'. The outcome of an effective phenomenological exploration of a set of qualitative data is a 'thick' description (Geertz, 1973) of the life-world or experiences of the individual or group being studied. This description may be framed as a narrative or story, or it may be organised in terms of a set of categories.

Suggested further reading

The work of Linda Finlay represents an invaluable resource for any qualitative researcher who is interested in using the insights of phenomenological philosophy to enrich their sensitivity to implicit dimensions of qualitative data:

Finlay, L, (2006). The body's disclosure in phenomenological research. *Qualitative Research in Psychology*, 3, 19–30.

Finlay, L. (2008). A dance between the reduction and reflexivity: Explicating the 'phenomenological psychological attitude'. *Journal of Phenomenological Psychology*, 39, 1–32.

The concept of 'triangulation' provides a valuable way of thinking about the later stages of qualitative analysis, when themes or categories are beginning to emerge. Triangulation (sometimes also described as 'constant comparison') is the task of finding out which meanings are most valid, accurate or important. It is a process of sifting and sorting meanings. The notion of triangulation comes from map reading, where a navigator will take bearings on different known points and draw a line that intersects on his or her current location. Similarly, the qualitative researcher can look for convergence between the data produced from diverse sources, methods and investigators as a check on the validity of a statement or conclusion. For example, in a study of group therapy using diaries kept by group members, a finding that anger was not expressed in the group until the fifth session would be more credible if it was backed up by diary observations made by all or most of the people in the group, rather than just a single informant. *Method* triangulation refers to the practice of using different data-gathering techniques in the same study. For example, the experience of a client during a counselling session could be investigated using a combination of interview, open-ended questionnaire and interpersonal process recall techniques. If the conclusions generated by all three methods were in agreement, the researcher could have added confidence in what had been found. Where a research team is used, the triangulation of observations made by different members of the team can be a valuable technique for identifying recurring themes and meanings.

Some qualitative research restricts itself to the production of a *descriptive* account of what has been studied. Other researchers find it more useful or appropriate, for their purposes, to identify *patterns* within the data (e.g. categories or themes). However, there are some qualitative researchers who seek to examine the theoretical implications of their findings, or even to construct a new theoretical model. This final stage of qualitative analysis involves the use of *interpretation*.

The act of interpretation involves locating the meaning of an experience or event within the context of a larger set of meanings (Messer et al., 1988; Taylor, 1979). This larger set of meanings would normally be a formal model or theory. It is important to be aware that, as Jones (1975) has noted, all interpretation is 'aspectival': it is taken from a certain point of view. It is inevitable that there will always exist alternative interpretations, or further interpretations carried out on the initial interpretive framework offered by a researcher. The incompleteness of interpretation has been labelled the 'hermeneutic circle': every interpretation can in turn be interpreted by someone else, in a never-ending cycle or circle of meaning-making. Despite the open-textured nature of interpretive activity, it is nevertheless possible to make judgements about the adequacy of any interpretation. Does it accommodate all factual information? Does it ignore important parts of the text or is it comprehensive? Has the writer argued logically from the data to the interpretation? The final criterion for the value of an interpretation is through its use value:

> [T]heoretical ideas are not created anew in each study ... they are adapted from other, related studies, and refined in the process, applied to new interpretive problems. If they cease being useful with respect to such problems, they tend to stop being used and are more or less abandoned. If they continue being used, throwing up new understandings, they are further elaborated and go on being used. (Geertz, 1973: 27)

The evaluation of interpretations involves a process of appraisal that is both rational (Is it supported by the evidence?) and intuitive (Does it trigger a feeling of clarity and movement?).

The final stage in analysis of qualitative data consists of *writing*, or other forms of dissemination such as presenting a talk or staging a performance. It is only at the writing stage that the coherence and plausibility of the analysis can really be evaluated: Does the research report make sense to an audience or to readers? Does the researcher find himself or herself becoming blocked during the process of writing, because the analysis lacks a logical structure and as a result does not 'flow'? Can the original research participants or informants recognise themselves in what has been written about them? Unlike quantitative research reports, which generally follow a fixed format and are relatively easy to write, the writing of qualitative research can be a daunting task. It is one thing to fill notebooks with definitions of analytic categories and ideas about interpretive themes. It can be quite another matter to pull all that together into a succinct and impactful report.

These stages of qualitative data analysis – immersion, coding, identifying general themes or categories, triangulation, interpretation, and writing – can in practice be operationalised in many different ways, depending on the particular requirements of the research project and the personal ingenuity and methodological affiliations of the researcher. It is also important to note that, throughout this analytic work, the researcher needs to keep in mind the 'quality control' criteria that are discussed below.

Qualitative research as a means of hearing the voice of the client

Box 7.2

One of the distinctive strengths of qualitative research is that it can be used as a means of documenting and disseminating the experiences of clients. This kind of research can be a valuable reminder to practitioners, who have been socialised into a particular professional world-view, of the different meanings that therapy has for those who are seeking help. It can also be useful for clients to read about the experiences of other people who have sought help, as a way of placing their own struggles in context. At some level, all qualitative research has (or should have) the function of allowing the voice of the client to be heard. However, some qualitative researchers have made a special effort to function as a channel of communication between the world of the client and the world of their professional colleagues. Notable examples of this stance can be found in Levitt et al. (2006), Manthei (2006) and Perren et al. (2009).

Criteria for evaluating the validity of qualitative research

Clearly, the concepts of validity and reliability that have been developed for use in quantitative research (see Chapter 6) cannot be applied in the same way in qualitative studies. Lincoln and Guba (1989) have argued that qualitative studies should be judged on the basis of their trustworthiness. They further suggest that trustworthiness consists of four components: credibility, transferability, dependability and confirmability. These criteria correspond to the quantitative/positivist concepts of internal and external validity, reliability and objectivity. Other writers in this field have suggested that the distinctive character of qualitative research should be reflected in criteria that do more than merely mirror the positivist tradition. A classic paper by Stiles (1993) has been highly influential in the counselling and psychotherapy research community in providing a framework for thinking about how to evaluate the quality of qualitative research:

1   *Clarity and comprehensiveness of the description of research procedures employed.* In any qualitative study, it is essential to provide detailed information on how the participants were selected, what happened to them, and how data were analysed. If this kind of procedural detail is missing, it may be difficult or impossible for the reader to determine the plausibility of the findings of the study. For example, it would be hard to have much faith in a qualitative study in which each interview lasted only 15 minutes, or in which the basis for selection of informants was not explained.

2   *Sufficient contextualisation of the study.* Qualitative research is less interested in defining general scientific laws of universal applicability, and more concerned with developing knowledge that is relevant and useful at particular times and places. It is therefore essential for the qualitative researcher to contextualise the study in its historical, social and cultural location.

3   *Adequacy of conceptualisation of data.* The reader should be able to follow the line of argument and evidence that leads from data to theory. For example, has there been sufficient triangulation to allow the demonstration of links between categories and primary data? A key criterion of research quality is the extent to which a theory sup-plies a complete and coherent account of the data. Yet there are some situations in which the experiential reality that is being researched is so dense and complex that any attempt to create a comprehensive and coherent model would lead to superficiality and falseness. In these instances, it may be necessary to acknowledge the provisional and open-ended nature of the analysis, and to identify any unresolved contradictions and theoretical issues.

4   *Systematic consideration of competing explanations/interpretations of the data.* Qualitative research is frequently criticised on the grounds that researchers using these methods merely find what they knew already. For a reader of a research paper, any sense that the investigator has done little more than gather information to support his or her pre-existing biases and prejudices will lead to irritation, rejection of the study and a tendency to discount its findings. There are two main ways that qualita-tive researchers can demonstrate that they have systematically weighed up alternative explanations/interpretations of the data. The first approach is to make explicit mention of alternative interpretations within the body of any report arising from a study, and provide reasoned arguments for supporting the preferred interpretation over the others. The second strategy is to incorporate some form of external scrutiny into the analytic process, for instance by using a team of researchers to carry out analysis, and/or involving an expert auditor and adjudicator.

5 *Credibility of the researcher (reflexivity).* The main investigative tool in qualitative research is the person of the researcher, and his or her ability to form relationships with informants that encourage the disclosure and expression of relevant data. However, while in quantitative research the credibility or reliability of a test or observation scheme can be calculated using statistical techniques, it is much harder to evaluate the credibility of a qualitative researcher. An approach that is often employed to enable the consumers of research to assess the role that the researcher has played in a study is for the latter to write a reflexive account that describes the 'internal processes' (Stiles, 1993) or 'progressive subjectivity' (Lincoln and Guba, 1989) associated with conducting the research. The involvement of a research team or group of co-researchers can be helpful in this regard, by providing a context within which the biases, prejudices and unexamined assumptions of each member can be constructively challenged by colleagues. It is also useful for those undertaking qualitative studies to monitor their own personal reactions and experiences through keeping a personal journal, and making use of supervision.

6 *Experiential authenticity of the material.* In all qualitative research, a key aim is to achieve a rich, holistic description of the topic being studied. In phenomenological research, the investigator would view such a descriptive account as an end in itself, whereas in hermeneutic or grounded theory studies the description would serve as a basis for interpretation and analysis. The extent to which the descriptive account feels real and authentic is therefore an important criterion in all qualitative research. The classic studies of R.D. Laing into the experiences of people labelled as schizophrenic (Laing, 1960, 1961; Laing and Esterson, 1964), or of Erving Goffman (1968a, 1968b) into the life-world of the psychiatric patient, have retained their places in the literature for over a quarter of a century because people who read them get a strong sense that what they are writing about accurately reflects 'the way it is'. An essential test of experiential authenticity is the degree to which the research report is received as an accurate description by the actual informants, the people who were (or are) there.

7 *Use of triangulation (including negotiation with informants/testimonial validity).* The facticity of the research data can only be established by checking it against other sources of information. The procedure of triangulation is the most widely used check of factual accuracy, and one of the most important criteria that can be applied in qualitative research is the extent and convincingness of the triangulation that has been conducted. Another method for checking both factual precision and interpretive sensitivity is to take drafts or parts of the research report back to informants and ask them to comment on it. This kind of 'negotiation with informants' or 'testimonial validity' can be used to back up the legitimacy of findings. However,

in practice it is often a difficult and time-consuming process. Relatively few research informants have the interest or motivation to read through lengthy research reports. In any case, once a report is written down it may take on an 'official' status, and deter disagreement. Sometimes, research participants can become distressed at seeing things written about them that are dissonant with their conception of self. It is worth viewing the task of negotiating with informants as similar to giving feedback to counselling clients, and to follow the same principles of careful timing, tentativeness and creating conditions of trust and safety.

8 *Catalytic validity.* As Kvale and Brinkmann (2009) have suggested, a well-conducted qualitative interview can be a positive, enriching experience for research informants. Stiles identifies 'catalytic validity' as a criterion for judging qualitative research, and defines it as 'the degree to which the research process reorients, focuses and energises participants' (1993: 611). Implicit in this criterion is the idea that research should empower all those who take part in it. The implication here is that, ideally, any negotiation with informants should include not only their views on the accuracy of the research report but also their account of how taking part in the study has affected their lives. Additionally, keeping some kind of on-going contact with informants can make it possible to discover whether there are any delayed effects of the research, for example through media publicity once the report or book of the study has been published.

9 *Replicability.* The final basis for assessing the value of a piece of qualitative research relates to the extent to which it has been, or could be, replicated. A great deal of qualitative research inevitably depends on the intensive study of single cases, or small numbers of subjects, since it is not possible to do qualitative research well with large samples of people. Nevertheless, it is important for researchers to be able to show that what they have found is not an idiosyncratic result arising from one unique case, but has relevance and applicability to other cases.

Practical guidelines on how these principles can be realised within qualitative research practice can be found in Elliott et al. (1999), Morrow (2005), Williams and Hill (2012) and Williams and Morrow (2009). An appreciation of these principles (and how difficult they are to honour in practice) is essential for readers who wish to arrive at a balanced view of the value of any qualitative studies that they come across.

Conclusions: issues in qualitative research in counselling and psychotherapy

The use of qualitative methods in counselling and psychotherapy research is increasing, with around 10 per cent of recently published research articles based in this approach (McLeod, 2011). For many therapists, this is a welcome development, because it offers the promise of an evidence base that is close to the experience and practice of therapy, and as a result is able directly to inform the activities of clients and therapists. At the same time, the growth in interest in qualitative methods has begun to highlight a number of critical issues around the challenges involved in conducting and disseminating qualitative work.

The best format for the reporting of qualitative findings

Qualitative research comes into its own when it allows the reader to empathically connect with the experience of research participants. There are, therefore, important emotional, aesthetic and illuminative dimensions of good qualitative research reports (Ponterotto and Grieger, 2007). It may be that the standard journal article is not the most effective medium for conveying this type of knowledge. However, while there are other promising formats that can be used, such as monograph-length written reports, on-line materials and performance media, at the present time it is not yet clear how these other formats can be best employed.

Building cumulative knowledge through research reviews

No single piece of research is likely to be able to claim much of an impact on policy and practice. As in any area of science or human inquiry, acceptance of new information is enhanced when a research finding is replicated by different investigators in different places. In the early years of qualitative therapy research, when few studies were being published, the issue of how to build cumulative knowledge through a systematic review procedure was not a major concern. By contrast, in recent years, the increasing volume of qualitative therapy research has focused attention on how to integrate or synthesise the findings of multiple qualitative studies on a particular topic. While there have been some attempts to conduct qualitative meta-analysis or meta-synthesis of qualitative studies of therapy (Hill et al., 2012; Timulak, 2007, 2009), this endeavour is still at an early stage. It has proved to be hard to find adequate ways to arrive at summaries of qualitative findings that are succinct and at the same time retain the meaning of the original report. In addition, because good qualitative research is sensitive to the context within which participants live, a great deal is lost if the review process seeks to strip away this nuanced, contextual detail and deal only in generalised statements.

Mixed methods: combining qualitative and quantitative strategies in a single study

There exists a growing set of examples of how qualitative and quantitative methods can be combined in therapy research. At the present time, it is possible to identify three distinct templates for mixed-methods research in counselling and psychotherapy. First, researchers carrying out systematic, research-based case studies have found it useful to use qualitative methods to provide a fine-grained account of the process of therapy, along with data from quantitative measures that allow comparison with general norms (e.g. how depressed the client is, or whether he or she has 'recovered'). Examples of this approach include Elliott et al. (2009) and Råbu et al. (2011). A second mixed-methods strategy involves building an understanding of a phenomenon through qualitative inquiry, then using quantitative methods to determine the prevalence of that phenomenon, using a questionnaire measure built around themes or categories uncovered in qualitative interviews. An example of this approach is the programme of research on therapist presence pursued by Geller and Greenberg (2002) and Geller et al. (2010). A third way of usefully combining the strengths of qualitative and quantitative methods within a research programme is to take the results of quantitative research as a starting point, and then conduct qualitative studies to resolve ambiguities or fill in gaps that have been identified in the quantitative analysis. An example of this kind of research is the Allen et al. (2009) study of client experiences of mindfulness-based cognitive therapy, which was embedded within a wider randomised trial of that form of therapy (Kuyken et al., 2008). However, although these studies provide convincing evidence of the value of combining qualitative and quantitative methods, there is still a tendency on the part of therapy researchers to remain within one methodological camp or the other, with the consequence that the therapy research literature as a whole remains fragmented, and important opportunities for developing more comprehensive insights are being lost.

Providing adequate training and development opportunities for qualitative researchers

At the present time, almost all of the published qualitative research on topics in counselling and psychotherapy consists of work that has been done at master's or doctoral level by novice researchers. Qualitative research is time-consuming, and it is difficult for experienced qualitative researchers who may hold university teaching appointments to find time to be directly involved in collecting and analysing qualitative data. This situation has almost certainly had an effect on the overall quality and impact of qualitative counselling and psychotherapy research. The process of becoming a competent qualitative researcher is complex and time-consuming because it encompasses the acquisition of philosophical understanding, interpersonal skills, technical knowledge, self-awareness and literary skills (Hansen and Rapley, 2008; Josselson et al., 2003). There are few training programmes that provide an adequate grounding in all of these domains.

Taking account of researcher reflexivity

A further critical issue that underpins qualitative research concerns the depth of personal exploration and reflexivity that is undertaken by the researcher, and how this information is included in research reports. Currently, the field of qualitative research is far from reaching a consensus on this matter. The question of the function of reflexivity, and what constitutes a useful or critical reflexivity, is explored further in Finlay and Gough (2003) and McLeod (2011).

Using qualitative research findings to influence policy decisions

There is a widely held view within the counselling and psychotherapy research community that the only way to influence politicians and policymakers is to present them with statistical data from randomised trials. Certainly, there is little evidence that qualitative therapy research has had much of an impact on policy decisions or clinical guidelines. However, the lack of political impact of qualitative therapy research may be due to the fact that qualitative researchers, at least up to now, have tended not to do research that is oriented towards policy issues. In addition, much qualitative research is written in a manner that precludes clear statements around implications for policy and practice. By contrast, in fields such as education and organisation/management studies, qualitative research has proved to be capable of making a significant contribution to evidence-based decision-making. It seems fairly obvious that stories and testimonies, and descriptions of how things happen in real-life situations, have the potential to be persuasive. Within the field of psychiatry and mental health, qualitative research that draws on service user perspectives has been highly influential in recent years. It seems probable, therefore, that the counselling and psychotherapy research community will find ways to give more prominence to qualitative evidence in relation to the formulation of policy and practice guidelines.

In conclusion, it seems clear that from the point of view of counselling and psychotherapy practitioners and students, the appeal of qualitative research is that it provides the kind of detail and depth of analysis that makes its findings relevant to practice. For many therapy practitioners and researchers, there is an 'irreversible momentum' associated with the increasing acceptance and utilisation of qualitative methodologies in counselling and psychotherapy research (Ponterotto, 2002). At the same time, there is also a sense that the full potential of qualitative methodologies has yet to be fully realised, and that the counselling and psychotherapy research community is only beginning to forge a relationship with the traditions of qualitative research.

Exercise 7.2 Your own appraisal of qualitative research

What does qualitative research offer you, as a counselling or psychotherapy practitioner? Which qualitative studies have had an impact on your practice and your way of thinking about therapy? What have you learned from the present chapter that will allow you to possess a more informed, critical appreciation of the qualitative studies that you read about? What new areas of qualitative research have been suggested that would be worth following up?

Suggested further reading

Frommer, J. and Rennie, D.L. (eds.) (2000). *Qualitative Psychotherapy Research: Methods and Methodology.* Lengerich, Germany: Pabst.

Hill, C.E. (ed.) (2012). *Consensual Qualitative Research: A Practical Resource for Investigating Social Science Phenomena.* Washington, DC: American Psychological Association.

McLeod, J. (2011). *Qualitative Research in Counselling and Psychotherapy*, 2nd edn. London: Sage.

Special issues on qualitative research in the *Journal of Counseling Psychology* (Volume 52, Issue 2, 2005) and *Psychotherapy Research* (Volume 9, Issue 3, 1999).

Evaluating the outcomes of counselling and psychotherapy

One of the core questions that has motivated many hundreds of counselling and psychotherapy researchers over several decades has been the issue of 'Does it work?'. The topic of *outcome* has been a major theme in the counselling and psychotherapy research literature, and has played a major role in the history of therapy research (see Chapter 2). Some outcome studies have looked at the relative effectiveness of different types of therapy. For example, there have been many studies comparing the outcomes of psychodynamic and cognitive-behavioural approaches, or comparing each of them with almost any therapy that has ever been devised. Other outcome studies have been driven by external pressures around accountability. Increasingly, institutional purchasers of therapy services need to be convinced that what they are paying for is effective and good value for money. Yet other outcome studies have been inspired by a wish to improve services, for example by identifying those groups of clients who may or may not benefit from a particular approach, or by looking at the effects of different forms of service provision (e.g. time-limited vs. open-ended therapy). The aim of this chapter is to provide an overview of counselling and psychotherapy outcome research. The moral rationale for investigating therapy outcomes is explored, as a precursor to examining a wide range of strategies which have been used by researchers seeking to understand and define the effectiveness of different types of therapy. The chapter concludes with an exploration of the underlying methodological challenges and dilemmas associated with therapy outcome research, and a summary of the state of the art in counselling and psychotherapy outcome research at this point in time: Where have we got to, and where do we need to go next?

> Exercise 8.1 The effectiveness of therapy - your own
> personal experience
>
> Take a few minutes to reflect on your own personal experience as a consumer/
> client of counselling and psychotherapy, your experience as a counsellor/
> psychotherapist, and what you have heard from friends, family members and
> colleagues about their own direct involvement in therapy. Summing up the
> information that you possess from these sources, how would you characterise
> the effectiveness of therapy? Is it meaningful for you to arrive at an estimate
> of the percentage of good outcomes, or does it make more sense for you to
> describe outcome in other terms?

The moral rationale for counselling and psychotherapy outcome research

One of my supervisees described the experience of a young woman with whom she had worked for some time. Janice had survived a childhood that had been emotionally, physically and sexually abusive, at the cost of becoming highly mistrustful of people and unable to form close relationships. She had never told anyone about what had happened to her in her life, for fear of the consequences. Eventually, a GP with whom she was in contact guessed what had happened and managed to persuade her to see a counsellor. The first (and only) meeting with the counsellor began with a long period of silence, during which Janice felt more and more terrified at being in the presence of someone whom she regarded as being in authority and who was so lacking in warmth. At the first opportunity that presented itself, she stood up and ran from the room. It was ten years before she was able to seek help again.

The experience of Janice can be viewed as an example of a major error in therapeutic technique. There was no evidence that the counsellor was a bad person, or was acting unethically. Indeed, it is easy to imagine situations in counselling where it might be enormously facilitative to allow the client to remain silent and to begin talking only when she was ready. But this was not one of these situations. For Janice, the silent figure sitting opposite her in a small room represented a return to what had been for her an often-repeated abusive scenario. It seems fair to conclude that Janice was harmed by her first exposure to counselling – it slowed down her emotional learning and development for several years.

The counselling service that Janice visited did not employ a routine outcome evaluation system. There was no means for the counsellor or the service to learn from what happened and do better next time. There was no opportunity for Janice to have at least the minimal remedy of expressing her feelings about her treatment, by completing a questionnaire. Yes, she had the option of writing a letter to the manager of the service, or complaining to her GP, but people who lack confidence in their own right to speak do not do things like that.

There are many counselling and psychotherapy patients or clients who have negative experiences. From the very gentle, non-directive process of early client-centred therapy (Lipkin, 1954), through to more recent outcome studies of more actively interventionist therapies (Callahan and Hynan, 2005; Lambert and Ogles, 2004), there is plentiful evidence that around 30–40 per cent of the time therapy does not work, and that 5–10 per cent of clients get worse. There is also convincing evidence that therapists are not very good at knowing when things are not going well with a client. Hannan et al. (2005) carried out a study where both experienced therapists and trainees were asked to predict the progress of current clients in their caseloads. Of the 550 clients who were followed over the course of their therapy, the therapists in the study predicted that only three were deteriorating. The actual number of clients who got worse was 40. None of the experienced therapists in this study predicted that any of their clients had deteriorated over the course of therapy. Similar findings have been reported by Hatfield et al. (2010). Within the literature, the tendency for therapists to be unaware of poor outcomes has been referred to as the 'Lake Wobegon effect', after Garrison Keillor's fictitious town of Lake Wobegon, where 'all the children are above average'. There are complex reasons why counsellors and psychotherapists (and parents and educators in Lake Wobegon) might wish to talk up the progress of those in their care. There is certainly a positive aspect to this type of bias – it conveys hope and optimism about the capacity of the client to benefit from therapy, and avoids the risk of labelling the client as a failure. However, it is a source of bias that has had the result of closing off the profession to open scrutiny of its effectiveness. The studies by Hannan et al. (2005) and Hatfield et al. (2010) only considered cases in which the client engaged with therapy to a sufficient extent that they actually completed a questionnaire at the end. In addition to these cases, there are inevitably around 25 per cent of clients who stop attending therapy and who do not provide any feedback at all. Although some of these 'do not attend' cases may have felt that they got what they needed from a brief contact with a therapist, many of them would undoubtedly be less satisfied with their treatment and may have feared that continued therapy might have had a negative effect.

The moral rationale for research into the outcomes of counselling and psychotherapy is that it keeps the profession honest, in terms of acknowledging the limitations of therapy and the existence of forms of intervention that may be harmful. Even the briefest examination of the general counselling and psychotherapy literature reveals very strong claims for the power of therapy as a means of resolving life's difficulties. However, the picture that emerges from the outcome research literature is quite different. Although outcome studies have tended to show that the majority of people find therapy to be helpful, most of those who have benefited still report some problems at the end of therapy. And some people are not helped at all. This is the territory within which outcome research is necessary. It is only by evaluating the effectiveness of approaches to therapy, or specific techniques, that it becomes possible to learn how to do better therapy.

Exercise 8.2 Mapping the outcomes of therapy

Take a few minutes to create a list of all the potential outcomes (negative as well as positive) that you can imagine resulting from counselling or psycho-therapy. If possible, share these ideas with a group of colleagues or learning partners to generate as broad an understanding of potential outcomes as you can. Cluster or categorise the ideas into groupings of outcomes. As you read the present chapter, or sources of further reading that are highlighted within it, be mindful of the extent to which the outcomes that you have iden-tified have been addressed within the research literature, or have been disregarded. What are the implications, for our understanding of the effec-tiveness of therapy, of the absence of some outcome categories (or the over-representation of others)?

Strategies for evaluating the outcomes of counselling and psychotherapy

Since the 1940s, when the first follow-up studies of counselling and psychotherapy clients and patients began to be published, several thousand therapy outcome studies have been carried out. Despite this impressive level of productivity, it is essential to recognise that the investigation of therapy outcome continues to represent a challenging and problematic enterprise (McLeod, 2001b; Meier, 2008). Some of the main methodological difficulties that are associated with this area of research include:

- how to identify the specific areas of change that are significant for each particular client. For example, an instrument such as the Beck Depression Inventory (BDI) (Beck et al., 1961) may function well as a general screening tool for large samples of patients, but may not be sensitive enough to detect the idiosyncratic difficulties experi-enced by some individuals;

- how to collect outcome information on clients who drop out of therapy;
- the influence on the client's responses of being asked to complete a questionnaire (or be interviewed by a researcher) on different occasions;
- the extent to which a client is an accurate and unbiased observer or reporter of his or her own experience;
- deciding who is correct when information that is collected from the client, therapist and a third party (e.g. family member) provide differing estimates of outcome;
- the challenge of following up clients for periods of longer than a few months;
- the difficulty of knowing whether change is attributable to therapy, or to other factors. This issue gains in significance when it is realised that many people who experience emotional problems may draw on multiple sources of concurrent help (e.g. complementary therapies, advice from friends, change of diet and lifestyle, spiritual practice);
- the difficulty of knowing whether the client's difficulties are cyclical – might he or she have got better anyway?
- the question of whether clients (and therapists) who take part in outcome studies are representative of routine practice;
- realising that people who seek therapy are emotionally vulnerable, and the process of therapy requires the establishment of a trusting relationship – collecting information from the client, particularly at the start of therapy, may threaten the quality and integrity of the treatment.

Within the literature as a whole, there are at least partial solutions to all of these issues. However, there is probably no single study in which all of the solutions have been applied at the same time. As a consequence, it is important to interpret the findings of therapy outcome research with caution. The following paragraphs offer an introduction to the main methodological strategies that have been adopted in counselling and psychotherapy research.

Client satisfaction studies

A client satisfaction study is research that evaluates the benefits of counselling or psychotherapy by asking clients to complete a short, simple questionnaire once they have finished seeing their therapist. Satisfaction questionnaires may include items that invite clients to rate their overall satisfaction with therapy, their perception of their counsellor and the agency setting, the extent to which their problem had been resolved, their views on practical matters such as number of sessions or ease of making an appointment, and their readiness to recommend the service to a colleague or friend who had a similar problem. No matter which questions are included, there is a tendency for clients to respond mainly in terms of their overall or global satisfaction with their therapy experience as a whole. So, while the researcher may be interested in different elements of the therapy such as the client's relationship with the counsellor, his perceptions of the environment and administration of the counselling agency, and the extent to which his problems have been ameliorated or got worse, in reality the answers clients give are heavily influenced by a general satisfaction factor. Moreover, clients usually give very positive ratings. This may be because they have genuinely been helped, but alternatively these ratings may result from gratitude at having someone listen to them and take them seriously for several hours (perhaps a rare experience in our society), or because less-satisfied clients are less likely to complete questionnaires. For whatever reason, client satisfaction data tend to be skewed to the positive end of the scale, which can make it difficult to discriminate between sub-groups of more- or less-satisfied clients, or tease out those factors that contribute to good outcomes. Various efforts have been made by researchers to encourage clients to make more balanced responses, or to be more open about their criticisms of the therapy they have received (see McLennan, 1990). Despite these methodological problems, there are some very positive features of satisfaction studies. They are inexpensive and unobtrusive, and give all clients a chance to have their say. All therapists and therapy agencies should be collecting satisfaction data, as a basic form of accountability, no matter what other types of research they are carrying out. Useful examples of what can be achieved in a client satisfaction study can be found in Gallagher et al. (2005), Seligman (1995) and Sloboda et al. (1993). There are no standard satisfaction scales that are particularly widely used at the present time. Most therapy agencies adapt existing scales to fit their own local requirements. Examples of well-designed satisfaction scales can be found in Attkisson and Greenfield (1994), Dersch et al. (2002; see also Shumway et al., 2004) and Oei and Shuttlewood (1999).

Practice-based outcome research

Practice-based or *naturalistic* outcome studies involve collecting data on every client who is seen in a psychotherapy clinic or counselling agency. Typically, before-and-after measures of change are taken, rather than relying on a one-shot satisfaction questionnaire completed only at the end of therapy. This type of outcome research is firmly grounded in practice, and is built around routine administration of questionnaires or other data collection methods by the administrative staff or therapists working in an agency. While client satisfaction questionnaires can be completely anonymous (the client fills it in and either posts it back or places it in a box in the reception area), in an outcome study where repeated measures are employed it is necessary to use some kind of code number so that client questionnaires from different occasions can be matched up. It is also useful to keep a record within the agency of other data (e.g. client age, gender, occupation, area of residence, and perhaps also counsellor-supplied data on outcome, presenting problem, and number of sessions) against which the client questionnaires can be compared. This is important because in a typical practice-based out-come study it is not unusual for as few as 50–60 per cent of clients to return questionnaires, so it is useful to be able to estimate whether those who do complete questionnaires are representative of the group of clients as a whole.

The concept of practice-based outcome research has been highly influential in recent years (see Chapter 2). It represents a way of col-lecting outcome data that is more rigorous than a client satisfaction survey, and much more practically feasible than a randomised con-trolled trial (see below). The possibilities for practice-based research have also been enhanced by the development of measurement instru-ments that are accessible to practitioners, acceptable to clients, and easy to administer and score. There are basically two types of instru-ment that have been proved to be straightforward to integrate into routine therapy practice. First, and most widely adopted, are brief generic symptom/well-being scales that record either general levels of distress or focus on more specific problem areas that are found in the majority of clients, such as anxiety or depression. Second, some practice-based outcome evaluation studies have made use of scales that ask the client to describe their problem (or goals for therapy) in their own words, and rate the severity of the problem (e.g. how much it has bothered them in the last week). The advantage of this kind of individualised measure is that it is highly sensitive to change, because it is concerned solely with the specific area around which the client is hoping to change. By contrast, generic questionnaires may include items that describe problem areas in which the client is not seeking change, or may not incorporate questions that are attuned to the par-ticular difficulties being experienced by the client. However, using a generic scale of symptoms of depression and anxiety makes it easier to compare outcomes across groups of clients, or to make use of norms. Further information on widely used symptom scales and individual-ised measures are provided in Tables 8.1 and 8.2. Several of these instruments are available free-to-use through internet sites.

Table 8.1   Symptom and well-being measures used in practice-based outcome studies

Instrument	Factors assessed	Internet source	References
CORE (Clinical Outcome Routine Evaluation; 5, 10 or 34 items)	Overall level of psychological difficulties – sub-scales for well-being, symptoms, functioning and risk	www.coreims.co.uk/index.php	Barkham, Mellor-Clark, Connell and Cahill (2006); Barkham and Mellor-Clark (2006)
Outcome Questionnaire (OQ; 30 or 45 items)	Symptom distress (depression and anxiety), interpersonal functioning, social role functioning and risk	www.oqmeasures.com	Lambert and Finch (1999); Lambert et al. (1996)
Outcome Rating Scale (ORS; 4 items)	Global psychological difficulties	www.talkingcure.com	Miller, Duncan and Hubble (2005)
PHQ-9 (9 items)	Depression	www.patient.co.uk/showdoc/40025272/	Kroenke, Spitzer and Williams (2001)
GAD 7 (7 items)	Generalised Anxiety Disorder	www.patient.co.uk/showdoc/40026141/	Spitzer, Kroenke, Williams et al. (2006)
Hospital Anxiety and Depression Scale (HADS; 14 items)	Overall difficulties – anxiety and depression sub-scales	www.depression-primarycare.co.uk/images/HADS%20Scoring%20Sheet.pdf	Zigmund and Snaith (1983); Bjelland et al. (2002)
SCORE (15, 29 or 40 items)	Measures three dimensions of family functioning: strengths and adaptability; overwhelmed by difficulties; disrupted communication	www.psychotherapy.org.uk/score.html	Stratton et al. (2010)
Perceived Stress Scale (10 items)	Life stress	www.mindgarden.com/docs/PerceivedStressScale.pdf	Cohen, Kamarck and Mermelstein (1983)

Practice-based or naturalistic, routine outcome data collection can form the basis for monitoring and audit activities demanded by external funding bodies or for inclusion in annual reports to trustees and so on. If an agency or clinic routinely gathers outcome data, then over a period of time a number of practice-relevant questions or opinions can be addressed:

- Trends in the data can be analysed (Has the new training course had an effect? Did the introduction of a pre-counselling leaflet have an impact on the rate of no-shows?).

- Comparisons can be made between different sub-groups of clients (e.g. men vs. women, different presenting problems, postcodes, age bands) to examine whether there are types of client who may need a new approach or who might be better referred to another agency.
- Successful and non-successful cases can be selected and subjected to a more detailed case analysis.

Table 8.2   Individualised measures used in practice-based outcome studies

Instrument	Internet source	References
CORE Goal Attainment Form	www.coreims.co.uk/index.php	See website
Simplified Personal Questionnaire (PQ)	www.experiential-researchers.org/instruments.html	Elliott, Shapiro and Mack (1999); Wagner and Elliott (2001)
Target Complaint Rating Scale	Details available in journal article	Deane, Spicer and Todd (1997)
PSYCHLOPS (Psychological Outcome Profile)	www.psychlops.org.uk	Ashworth et al. (2007, 2008)
MYMOP (Measure Yourself Medical Outcome Profile)	http://sites.pcmd.ac.uk/mymop	Paterson (1996); Paterson and Britten (2000)

The answers to these can be fed back into supervision, training and policymaking, and eventually contribute to the improvement of practice. In addition, the collection of routine outcome data can make it possible to build on more focused research studies to look more closely at particular issues of interest. For example, if the outcome data indicate that, say, men appear to benefit less from counselling than women, then some male former clients can be contacted and interviewed about their experience of the help they received and what might be done to make it more useful for them.

One of the main challenges in naturalistic outcome research is to assemble a package of data collection methods that give sufficient coverage to the factors that are of interest to therapists, agency administrators and representatives of external funding bodies, but are not so lengthy, intimidating and unwieldy as to deter clients from responding or to make unreasonable demands on agency staff. Over the years, there has been much debate about the desirability of identifying a standard, all-purpose battery of questionnaires that can be used in counselling and psychotherapy settings. The existence of agreed standardised procedures for evaluating counselling and psychotherapy has the advantage of making it much easier to compare the outcomes achieved by different agencies; sector-wide 'benchmarking' becomes possible. A sensible outcome-monitoring package might include the following elements:

- *Questions on the demographic characteristics (age, gender, occupation, martial status, faith, etc.) of the client.* This kind of information is relevant in most analyses or reports that would be compiled, but also makes it possible to assess the representativeness of the sample of people who participate in the evaluation by comparing them to the total population of clients who use the agency.
- *A questionnaire which assesses the general level of 'symptoms' or 'dysfunction' in the person's life.* There are several questionnaires which do this kind of thing, for example the CORE, OQ and other scales listed in Table 8.1.
- *Client rating of the severity of their actual problem.* This enables the measurement of the specific issue around which the client has sought help. As a measure of change, this technique can be highly sensitive, and can pick up evidence of change that may be missed by other techniques. In a few cases the client may redefine the problem after a few sessions of counselling, with the result that their initial problem rating becomes irrelevant. In practice, however, this does not occur often enough to invalidate the problem-rating method. Examples of individualised measures can be found in Table 8.2.
- *Brief satisfaction scales.* In the demographics form completed at the start of therapy, clients can be asked how easy it was to contact the service, their views on the waiting time and so on. At the end of therapy, clients can be asked about their assessment of the therapy as a whole, the relationship with the therapist, their satisfaction with the number of sessions and so forth. These satisfaction questions can be drawn from the satisfaction scales described earlier in this chapter. It is helpful to include a few open-ended questions so that clients can report on aspects of their therapy that are important to them but are not covered in the quantitative ratings sections of the satisfaction scale.
- *Information collected by the therapist.* For example, the category of problem reported by the client, length of time client has had the problem, involvement of other services, previous therapy episodes, use of supervision, and therapist's rating of outcome. A good example of a therapist form can be found on the CORE website (www.coreims.co.uk).

This combination of symptom change, problem change, satisfaction, and an invitation to add anything else that they feel is relevant is viewed by most clients as a reasonable and credible way of gathering their opinions on the counselling/psychotherapy they have received. It represents a manageable package for agency staff to deal with and an invaluable resource for practitioner-researchers.

An important issue in relation to the use of routine outcome moni-toring concerns the frequency with which the client completes the symptom and individualised scales that yield the change scores that are fundamental to the operation of the system. If a client is only asked to complete these scales at initial assessment, and then at their final meeting with their therapist, then it is inevitable that end-of-therapy information will only be available for around 60 per cent of clients, because of the high frequency of unplanned endings that occur in therapy. Even the most heroic efforts of therapists and receptionists to persuade clients to complete end-of-therapy scales will only increase this proportion to 75 per cent. This level of attrition presents a major difficulty in interpreting the meaning of the change statistics that are produced. Does an unplanned ending mean that the client had got what he or she needed, and was too busy to come back for a final ses-sion? Or might it mean that he or she was dissatisfied with the progress of therapy, and stayed away rather than saying anything to their thera-pist? It is only when data completion at the end of therapy is obtained from 90 per cent or more of clients that it is possible to claim with confidence that the findings are representative of the experience of the client group as a whole. The best way to ensure this degree of data cap-ture is by asking clients to complete questionnaires each time they attend (or, in long-term therapy, at least once per month). If the client then drops out of therapy, information is available from his or her final session, so it is possible to make an estimate of the change that has occurred for that person over the course of however many sessions they have attended. Weekly or frequent completion of an outcome scale also opens up possibilities of using this information for real-time tracking of client progress and as a source of feedback for the client and therapist (see section below on client-focused outcome research).

It is always interesting, but practically difficult, to collect follow-up data from clients (e.g. 6 or 12 months after the end of therapy). This can involve mailing questionnaires to the client, completion of question-naires during a phone call, or scheduling a follow-up meeting with the therapist. It is hard to get clients to agree to any of these procedures. Some clients may have emotionally moved on and not want to revisit the scene of their therapy or the issues they explored in therapy. Ethically, it is essential to inform clients right at the start of therapy (and then remind them at the end), and secure appropriate permissions, in respect of any follow-up contact. A follow-up strategy that may be relevant in some situations is to focus effort on securing further information from a sub-sample of clients. These could be randomly selected, or comprise a group of clients who are of particular interest. Usually, follow-up data collection is scheduled for either three or six months following comple-tion of therapy. These timescales are long enough to allow the initial supportive glow of weekly meetings with a therapist to wear off, but are short enough for the client to retain some connection with the therapy service that they attended. Information from follow-up periods of one year or longer is of substantial theoretical and practical significance, but is hard to obtain.

In practice-based outcome research, there are no control groups: all the information that is collected refers to clients and patients who are receiving therapy in everyday, routine circumstances. A potential limitation of practice-based or naturalistic research, therefore, is that it is possible that changes which are observed in clients may be attributable to factors other than therapy. For example, many clients may have got well anyway even if they had not entered therapy. An important strategy for addressing this methodological issue is through the use of *benchmarking* comparisons. Benchmarking involves systematically comparing practice-based outcome data against other relevant sources of information. There are two ways in which benchmarking can be carried out. It is possible to compare practice-based evidence against the findings of highly controlled randomised clinical trials (see following section) and studies that have tracked the progress of people who are anxious or depressed and have received no treatment (Minami et al., 2007; Weersing and Weisz, 2002; Weersing, 2005). An alternative approach is to compare results against the outcome statistics reported by other organisations and groups of therapists that have published similar monitoring data (Cahill et al., 2010; Mellor-Clark et al., 2006). A study by Armstrong (2010) provides an example of practice-based outcome research in which findings from questionnaires completed by clients in a voluntary counselling agency were contrasted against published results from other sources. The Armstrong study illustrates the advantages and also the limitations of outcome benchmarking. The use of benchmarking enabled the results obtained in one practice setting to be contextualised, and therefore to make a more substantial contribution to the evidence base as a whole. On the other hand, there were aspects of the Armstrong sample (specifically, a high proportion of unemployed clients) which could not be precisely matched against any comparator studies. As a consequence, in this instance a benchmarking strategy was not able to address a crucial question: To what extent were the outcomes reported by Armstrong (2010) attributable to the counselling that was delivered, or to the effect of employment status of clients?

The widespread adoption and implementation by counselling and psychotherapy agencies over the past decade of systems for collecting routine outcome data has meant that an ever-increasing number of publications are being generated that report on the findings of such projects. Particularly influential have been practice-based studies of the effectiveness of counselling in primary care by Stiles et al. (2006, 2008) and Gibbard and Hanley (2008), and a study of long-term psychoanalytic psychotherapy by Lindgren et al. (2010). These studies have been based on large samples, and are carefully written in a way that acknowledges and addresses the limitations of this kind of research (e.g. clients not completing questionnaires at the end of therapy).

It is important to note that the administration of outcome scales to clients on a routine basis is not the only means of conducting practice-based outcome research. It is possible to collect valuable evidence about outcomes in everyday practice by carrying out systematic case studies (see below). Another approach, used by Morrison et al. (2003), is to conduct a survey of practitioners. Morrison et al. sent a questionnaire to all members of a professional network for therapists in private practice, inviting them to complete a questionnaire in which they provided information on their most recent successful case of a client with depression and a client who had an anxiety disorder.

As with any form of research methodology, practice-based outcome research is characterised by strengths and also limitations. The distinctive strengths of practice-based outcome research are that it:

- collects evidence of actual change (rather than client satisfaction);
- reflects what is happening in everyday practice in respect of factors such as variable length of treatment, therapist flexibility in response to client needs, and clients with multiple diagnoses/problems;
- comprises an affordable and cost-effective means of generating outcome data, with the implication that more research can be carried out on a wider range of therapies.

The primary limitation of practice-based outcome research lies in the fact that the researcher has very little control over what is happening in terms of ensuring that clients and therapists complete questionnaires, or in terms of being able to specify or define the actual interventions that are being used by therapists. A further limitation is that it is impossible, in this kind of research, to know with any confidence what might have happened to clients if they had not received therapy at all, or had received a different type of therapy. A succinct account of the limitations of practice-based outcome research and the implications of these factors for the credibility of practice-based evidence can be found in Clark et al. (2008). As with any area of research methodology, a cycle of methodological innovation is taking place within the domain of practice-based research. For example, many current studies have adopted a strategy of data collection at every session to address the issue of client attrition. It seems likely that future years will see further examples of methodological developments that are aimed at enhancing the rigour of practice-based outcome studies.

Suggested further reading

Barkham, M., Hardy, G.E. and Mellor-Clark, J. (eds.) (2010). *Developing and Delivering Practice-Based Evidence: A Guide for the Psychological Therapies.* Chichester: Wiley-Blackwell. (An authoritative source of information around methods of routine outcome monitoring, and also other possibilities for research that is based in everyday practice settings.)

Box 8.1

Effect size, clinically significant change and reliable change: key concepts in contemporary outcome research

Practice-based outcome studies and randomised clinical trials (RCTs) both involve the administration of a standardised scale for measuring some aspect of functioning before therapy, at the end of therapy and, if possible, at follow-up. Historically, analysis of change has relied on the use of a test of statistical significance to determine whether the change that has been observed is so small as to have been due to chance factors, or is in fact statistically meaningful (i.e. the differences found would be very unlikely to be the result of chance variations). However, if the sample of cases is large enough, a statistically significant result can be produced even when the actual amount of change in each case is slight. Statistically significant change is therefore not a particularly informative method for reporting change, because statistically significant change does not necessarily translate into meaningful clinical change. In order to provide a way of indicating the degree of change that has been produced by an intervention, an effect size (ES) calculation can be made. ES is a technique for conveying magnitude of change across a group of subjects or research participants, as a standardised metric measure (e.g. *small*, *medium* or *large* effects), and is widely employed in counselling and psychotherapy research (Fidler et al., 2005; Trusty et al., 2004). All outcome studies that use standardised scales to evaluate change in psychological functioning should be able to report their findings in terms of ES. Following Cohen (1988), an ES of 0.2 or less is considered small, an ES of 0.3 to 0.7 is considered medium, and an ES of greater than 0.8 is considered large. A further approach to reporting on the effectiveness of a counselling or psychotherapeutic intervention is to estimate the proportion of individual cases that have improved or recovered (Jacobson et al., 1984; Jacobson and Revenstorf, 1988). The concept of *clinical significance*, in relation to change resulting from therapy, was introduced by Jacobson et al. in the following terms: 'A change in therapy is clinically significant when the client moves from the dysfunctional to the functional range during the course of therapy' (1984: 340). To decide whether the changes recorded by clients are meaningful in practical terms (i.e. clinically significant), two criteria need to be met. First, the client needs to have shifted by a certain number of points on the measurement scale (*reliable change* has occurred). Second, the client needs to have moved out of the problem or 'caseness' range of scores and into the 'normal' or 'non-clinical' range (*clinical change* has occurred). The cut-off points for 'clinical' and 'non-clinical' scores can be established by administering a scale, in its development phase, to groups of people known to represent clinical and non-clinical populations. The advantage of analysing effectiveness research data in terms of clinically significant change is that it yields information on the proportions of clients who have achieved practice-relevant outcomes: *recovered* (reliable and clinical change recorded for that client), *improved* (reliable change, but not sufficient to move the client into the 'normal' range), *unchanged* and *deteriorated* (reliable level of increase in symptoms). The principles for defining clinically significant change, first stated by Jacobson in the 1980s, have been widely accepted within the counselling and psychotherapy research field, with authors being encouraged to use clinical change indicators in their reports wherever possible (Fidler et al., 2005). However, there remains some debate within the research community concerning the most appropriate techniques for determining cut-off points and estimating reliable and clinical change levels (see Atkins et al., 2005; Wise, 2004).

The concept of 'recovery'

In the contemporary counselling and psychotherapy outcome research literature, the concept of 'recovery' refers to the attainment by the client, at the end of therapy, of a level of improvement that is defined in terms of the norms of the particular measure (e.g. CORE, OQ) that has been used. Within the broader field of mental health policy and practice, the concept of recovery has a different meaning. Over the past 20 years, what is known as the 'recovery movement' has evolved as a means of promoting the potential of people with long-term mental health problems to establish meaning and purpose in their lives (Davidson et al., 2005, 2006). This alternative concept of recovery generally refers to a process through which a person actively engages with a range of other people and groups, around a multiplicity of identity issues (Brown and Kandirikirira, 2007). The meaning of 'recovery' within the recovery movement is therefore much broader that the meaning that is attributed to this term within the psychotherapy research literature. This contrast serves as a reminder of significant dimensions of change that are not currently addressed within counselling and psychotherapy outcome research.

Box 8.2

Randomised controlled trials

Practice-based research, discussed in the previous section, represents a particular way of thinking about the relationship between research and practice. Supporters of practice-based research believe that the most useful way of generating knowledge that can be used to improve the quality of practice is to collect and analyse information about what happens in routine practice, and use that information to identify principles of best practice. An alternative strategy is to adopt the procedures that are followed by pharmaceutical companies and in other life sciences. New discoveries (e.g. a new drug) are made in the laboratory, and then tried out 'in the field' through carefully controlled 'trials' on groups of patients. The underlying logic of this strategy is that it is necessary to begin by establishing the essential efficacy of a treatment in controlled or ideal conditions before assessing how well that treatment functions when confronted by the complexity and messiness of actual front-line practice. In the field of counselling and psychotherapy, the implementation of this second approach has taken the form of the use of *randomised controlled/clinical trials* (RCTs) of therapy.

A randomised trial of therapy involves first of all finding a pool of people who are all seeking help and who have a similar problem (e.g. as diagnosed through a psychiatric interview or scores on a questionnaire). These clients are then randomly assigned to different 'treatment conditions'. These conditions may comprise two or more different kinds of therapy, or a therapy compared with a control condition (e.g. remaining on a waiting list for six months), or a comparison with a placebo condition (e.g. being given regular meetings with a helper who does not use actual therapeutic skills or interventions). The client's level of anxiety, depression, phobia or other problems are assessed before therapy, at the end of therapy, and then again at a follow-up period. Any difference between groups that is found at the end of therapy can be attributed to the effect of treatment, because the process of randomisation has taken account of all other causal factors. For example, it is not possible to argue that the clients in the more effective treatment condition were more highly motivated, had less severe symptoms, or possessed any other attributes that may have made them more likely to gain from therapy. If true randomisation has occurred, clients in each of the treatment groups will display similar levels of these factors. It is this capacity to support strong causal statements that gives RCTs an advantage compared to practice-based or naturalistic studies in which change scores are collected for clients in routine therapy. Both RCTs and practice-based outcome studies can demonstrate that change has occurred, but it is only an RCT that can provide evidence that the change which has been observed is attributable to therapy rather than to something else. An example of a classic RCT, conducted by Sloane et al. (1975), is described in Chapter 2.

In principle, therefore, RCTs represent a powerful methodology for determining the efficacy of different types of therapeutic intervention. In practice, however, a high level of control over the therapeutic process is required in order to conduct a rigorous randomised trial. It can be argued that this degree of control has led to a situation in which some (or all) randomised trials of counselling and psychotherapy have become elegant and self-contained experiments with high internal validity, but which lack relevance to real-world practice (low external validity). Researcher control over the process of therapy in an RCT principally occurs in two areas: selection of clients and manualisation of therapy. An RCT that was based on all clients who applied for therapy in a particular clinic would end up with a heterogeneous mix of people who were depressed, anxious, borderline personality disorder, alcohol dependent and so on, or who possessed any combination of these characteristics. It would then be very likely that randomisation would produce unequal groups, because there would be no way of ensuring that hard-to-treat borderline personality disorder clients and easy-to-treat anxiety clients were equally distributed across the treatment conditions. As a consequence, RCTs usually aim to recruit clients who are narrowly defined, for example people with moderate levels of depression who do not have any other main diagnoses. It has been argued by Westen et al. (2004) and others that the design requirements of randomised trials of therapy inevitably create serious disjunctions between the world of research and the world of ordinary practice: the clients included in RCTs are different, in important ways, from those seen by the majority of practitioners. For example, most depressed clients also manifest other types of problem at the same time. An evidence-base that is grounded in studies of therapy with 'pure' depressed clients may not be relevant to work with clients who report depression *plus* other issues. Further discussion of methodological issues associated with RCTs can be found in Chapter 2.

A further critical feature of the design of RCTs arises in relation to the degree of precision with which the therapeutic intervention needs to be specified. In the earliest randomised trials, therapy was delivered by practitioners who had been trained in specific approaches (CBT, psychodynamic, client-centred, etc.) and who described themselves as adherents of these models. However, it soon became apparent that therapists who believed that they were practising a particular approach may in fact have been working in quite different ways. This is an important issue in any RCT. Its is essential to know that, in an RCT which compares psychodynamic therapy with CBT, it is actually these therapies that are being provided and not idiosyncratic versions of them or a generic/non-specific therapy which reflects the tendency of experienced practitioners to assimilate many different ideas and techniques over the course of their career. The solution to the issue of 'treatment fidelity' has been to create therapy manuals, which define the treatment to be provided. The therapists in an RCT are then trained to deliver the approach specified in the manuals, and their level of adherence to the protocol is assessed through supervisor ratings or analysis of therapy session recordings. Another important respect in which the design requirements of RCTs shape the kind of therapy being studied arises in respect of the length of therapy. It is hard to run an RCT if clients can have as many sessions as they wish. It is also expensive and difficult in practice to run an RCT of long-term therapy. As a consequence of these considerations, most RCTs limit the number of sessions that clients can receive. The use of treatment manuals and restriction on length of therapy can be viewed as important ways in which the kind of therapy that is studied in an RCT is different from therapy in everyday practice. It can be argued that an important characteristic of expert therapists is that they are flexibly responsive to the needs of different clients in relation to the techniques and strategies that are used and the duration of treatment (Stiles, 2009). The conditions that are created within an RCT significantly restrict the extent of therapist responsiveness and therefore the generalisability of the evidence that is derived from such studies.

Suggested further reading

Nezu, A.M. and Nezu, C.M. (eds.) (2007). *Evidence-based Outcome Research: A Practical Guide to Conducting Randomized Controlled Trials for Psychosocial Interventions*. Cary, NC: Oxford University Press. (A well-informed and accessible source of detailed information around the technical challenges involved in carrying out randomised trials of counselling and psychotherapy.)

It is important to contextualise the methodological issues associated with randomised trials of counselling and psychotherapy. RCTs are widely used in medicine, for example in trials of the effectiveness of new drug treatments. In drugs research (but not in counselling and psychotherapy research) it is possible to conduct 'double-blind' studies, in which neither doctor nor patient knows whether the drug being administered is active or is an inert placebo. It is also possible to dismantle medical interventions into readily researchable component elements in a way that is not possible in most psychological therapies. In medicine, the randomised controlled trial is regarded as the 'gold standard' in terms of credible research evidence. However, even within medicine there are vigorous debates around the role of RCT evidence (see, for example, Slade and Priebe, 2001). There is also an on-going process of refinement of RCT methodology, reflected in the Consolidated Standards of Reporting Trials (CONSORT) guidelines (www.consort-statement.org) (Trudeau et al., 2007). The existence of such debates within the medical research community makes it possible to see that dilemmas around the use of RCTs are not unique to the field of counselling and psychotherapy research and practice.

In the world of counselling and psychotherapy, many hundreds of RCTs have been carried out over the years. Reviews of the findings of therapy RCTs can be found in Lambert (2013) and many other sources. Evidence from RCTs has played a central role in informing the construction of clinical practice policies and guidelines by the National Institute for Health and Clinical Excellence (NICE) in England and similar governmental bodies elsewhere. It is clear that randomised trial methodology represents a key strategy for exploring the effectiveness of therapy. Wessely (2006) makes a passionate case that many more therapy RCTs should be carried out, on the basis that it is morally and ethically unacceptable to use therapy approaches that have not been exposed to this most stringent form of evaluation. Other leading figures within the counselling and psychotherapy research community argue with equal passion that therapy RCTs have yielded evidence that lacks practical relevance (Persons, 1998; Westen et al., 2004). A further consideration arises from the complexity and expense of the RCT method, which means that it is only possible to implement this kind of study in a well-financed elite establishment. Almost all RCTs have been carried out within university medical schools or clinical psychology departments. There are great tranches of everyday counselling and psychotherapy practice that have not and will not ever be included in an RCT, short of massive (and highly unlikely) governmental investment in therapy outcome research.

Are therapy RCTs asking the wrong questions?

Most randomised controlled trials in the field of counselling and psychotherapy have involved comparisons between different therapy approaches. This kind of comparison is technically very difficult to carry out because each approach encompasses a multitude of behaviour sequences, some of which overlap (e.g. respectful and empathic listening is a potentially powerful intervention that occurs in all therapies). It may be that one of the reasons why many people in the therapy world are sceptical about the value of RCTs is that this methodology has been used to address research questions which are too broad. There are some therapy RCTs that have sought to address narrower questions. For example, Lambert (2007) has used a randomised trial design to evaluate the effectiveness of providing therapists with feedback about client progress (this topic is discussed in more detail below), and Fluckiger and Holtforth (2008) similarly evaluated the impact of a technique intended to enhance therapist sensitivity to client strengths. In these RCTs, a single, narrowly defined intervention was added to treatment as usual in routine practice settings. As a consequence, these studies are not vulnerable to critique on the basis of artificiality or lack of external validity. Another, more radical, challenge to the

Box 8.3

(Continued)

(Continued)

RCT tradition of comparing therapies has been made by Wampold (2001) and others, who have argued that the most theoretically interesting and practically significant source of variance in therapy outcome is not due to the effect of therapies, but instead arises from differences between the effectiveness of the therapists who provide these therapies. Several studies have found variations in effectiveness between individual therapists (Kraus et al., 2011; Wampold, 2001) that are larger than differences which are reported between therapy approaches. These findings have two main implications. First, by seeking to limit and control differences between therapists, by requiring adherence to treatment manuals, designers of RCTs have systematically diverted attention from a crucially important aspect of therapy. Second, it is possible that evidence-based clinical guidelines that are informed by comparative studies of therapy approaches are not in fact offering the public the best advice in relation to where to find the best treatment for their problems. Rather than 'choose the best therapy', it may be that the advice should be 'choose the best therapist'.

Exercise 8.3 Reflecting on your own position in relation to randomised trials

What is your own personal position in relation to the use of randomised trials in counselling and psychotherapy outcome research? How convinced are you by the findings of such studies? If an RCT found that the form of therapy you practice was less effective than another approach, how likely is it that you would change your way of working with clients? Conversely, if an RCT found that your method was *more* effective than an alternative approach, how likely is it that you might draw upon this evidence to support your own model (e.g. in a debate with colleagues)? If you take the view that RCT evidence is wholly worthless, then what other types of evidence of effectiveness are more credible to you (and why)? If you take the view that RCT evidence represents a 'gold standard' of scientific quality, then what role (if any) do you attribute to other forms of outcome research?

Cost–benefit studies

There has been increasing use of *economic* measures in studies of the outcome of counselling and psychotherapy. Healthcare providers, insurance companies and other agencies who pay for therapy are concerned whether treatment produces equivalent benefit for each pound or dollar spent, compared to other interventions such as medication. This is the issue of *cost-effectiveness*. Service providers and policymakers are also interested in the *cost–benefit* analysis of counselling, where the economic savings that result from therapy are calculated. For example, employing a counsellor for car factory workers may reduce the number of days off sick of shift workers, which will save the company money. The economic analysis of therapy is a relatively recent development, and methods are still being devised to capture the complex and often subtle economic factors associated with this area. Any kind of credible economic research into the outcome of therapy relies on the participation of health economists. Further information about the strategies and techniques that are used in analysis of the economic costs and benefits of counselling and psychotherapy can be found in Miller and Magruder (1999) and Tolley and Rowland (1995).

An example of a psychotherapy outcome study that included economic analysis is an investigation by Guthrie et al. (1999), which compared the costs of treatment as usual with the costs of delivering brief psychodynamic-interpersonal therapy for psychiatric out-patients with severe and long-term difficulties. Economic data were collected for these patients for the three months prior to entering therapy, the period of therapy, and then the six months following completion of therapy, based on analysis of consultations and prescriptions recorded in their case files. Costs were calculated for each recorded consultation, contact and episode of care, including inpatient and day patient stays, outpatient visits, accident and emergency attendances, GP and domiciliary care services, day centre use, alternative therapy, and medication. Information was also gathered around non-treatment costs, such as travel, time off work to attend appointments, and loss of earnings. The costs of psychotherapy (eight weekly sessions) were calculated on the basis of 45 minutes per session, plus 30 minutes per session for note recording, plus supervision and related overhead costs. The findings of the Guthrie et al. (1999) study present a powerful illustration of the value of economic analysis of therapy outcome. In this study, the clients who received therapy reported a statistically significant reduction of symptoms compared to those in the treatment-as-usual condition. However, this shift was minimal in clinical terms, with all of the therapy cases continuing to report levels of symptoms at the end of therapy that remained in the 'clinical' range. However, the economic analysis revealed a much more positive picture of the benefits of therapy. In the three months prior to therapy, the health costs associated with each treatment group were similar. Costs were similar through the period of therapy (even though some of them were receiving specialist therapy services). During the six-month follow-up period, the psychotherapy clients, in comparison with controls, showed a significant reduction in inpatient days, GP consultations, practice nurse contacts, number of medications, and informal care required from relatives. For the six-month follow-up period, costs were significantly lower for the psychotherapy group than for the controls. What this study seems to show is that, for people with complex problems, a limited amount of therapy can produce changes in help-seeking behaviour that convert into meaningful cost savings for the healthcare system, even if these clients have not received enough therapy to fully 'recover'. This kind of evidence can be used to make a strong case for the provision of services to this client group.

Other studies of the cost-effectiveness of counselling within the NHS include research by Fletcher et al. (1995) and Sibbald et al. (1996), which investigated whether on-site general practice counsellors have an impact on psychotropic drug prescribing rates and costs. These particular studies did not find that the presence of counsellors reduced drug bills. However, the design of these studies did not make it possible to determine whether an actual causal link existed between counselling and drug costs, or whether both factors may have been the result of some other causal source. As a result, these findings could be interpreted as demonstrating that GPs who are more attuned to mental health problems may end up prescribing more anti-depressants *and* referring more patients for counselling. There have also been several studies that offer cost–benefit analyses of the provision of workplace counselling services (see McLeod, 2007). It is important to note that both health service and workplace research into the cost-effectiveness of counselling and psychotherapy has been able to make use of organisational records that record all or most of the information that is necessary to carry out a comprehensive audit of the costs associated with therapy. It would clearly be much harder to carry out this sort of record in relation to other counselling and psychotherapy settings.

Case study approaches to investigating the outcomes of therapy

The systematic analysis of single cases has made a valuable contribution to research into the outcomes of counselling and psychotherapy. Some researchers dismiss case study methods on the grounds that 'it is not possible to generalise from a single case'. For these critics, knowledge that therapy X has been successful in a single case has no implications for whether therapy X is generally effective – there is no way of telling whether the single case that has been reported is unique (i.e. the only time that therapy X has ever worked) or typical (i.e. representative of all or most cases in which therapy X has been applied). Moreover, critics of case study methodology point out that advocates of particular approaches to therapy are likely to be highly motivated to publish case examples of successful outcomes, but hold back on publication of cases in which the client did not benefit. In response to these critical perspectives, advocates of single case methodology have in recent years developed a range of techniques for enhancing the rigour and relevance of therapy case

studies. Further information about the philosophical and methodological basis of contemporary counselling and psychotherapy case study
research can be found in Fishman (1999) and McLeod (2010a). In respect
of outcome research, the essential rationale for using case studies is that
a single case can provide evidence of the potential or 'in principle' effectiveness of a new intervention. In a situation in which a new therapy
technique has been developed, or an existing approach is offered to a
new client group, it is costly and time-consuming, and ethically problematic, to carry out a large-scale study in which the effectiveness of the
new therapy is evaluated across many clients. In this context, a detailed
case study can provide sufficient evidence to justify further research
using a larger sample. At the same time, a case report includes a richly
described documentation of how the therapy works in practice which
enables practitioners to decide on whether the new therapy approach
might be relevant to their own clients.

At the present time, there exist two main approaches to conducting
outcome-oriented case study research: '*n*=1' studies and *hermeneutic single
case efficacy design* (HSCED) studies. There are a number of similarities
between these methods. For example, they both involve collection of
information from clients on a weekly basis, the use of time-series analysis in which connections across time are made between interventions
(and other events experienced by the client), and shifts in symptoms or
other outcome indicators. However, these approaches have emerged
from different research traditions and adopt quite different strategies of
data analysis.

N=1 outcome research

Single case or *n*=1 outcome studies represent a key element of the
research base for behavioural and cognitive-behavioural approaches to
counselling and psychotherapy, and other areas of behavioural intervention, for example in education and healthcare (Barlow and Hersen,
1986; Morgan and Morgan, 2009). Behavioural interventions form part
of a long tradition of behavioural and experimental psychology that
places emphasis on accurate measurement and observation in controlled experimental situations. *N*=1 studies form part of this tradition:
'*n*' refers to the number of 'subjects' in an investigation. In an *n*=1 study
of therapy, information on the client's symptoms or problems are collected at each session, or even every day or several times each day. At
the heart of the *n*=1 study is a graph which charts the change in key
problem variables over at least three phases of the therapy: a baseline
period before therapy has commenced, the period when therapy is
being received, and the period following the end of therapy. The analysis of these data does not usually involve statistics, but relies on visual
inspection of the graph. The classic *n*=1-case graph will show a high

level of problems at baseline, followed by a rapid reduction once treatment has started, remaining at or around the same low level over follow-up. In writing up a single case outcome study, the graph is used as a device to demonstrate to readers that change has occurred, with an accompanying narrative based on case notes or counsellor observations used to explain what happened during the case. Further information on this method can be found in McLeod (2010a), Morgan and Morgan (2009) and Morley (2007). A great strength of this method lies in its unique capacity to generate systematic research evidence on new or unusual forms of counselling. For example, a counsellor using time-limited counselling in a primary care setting may believe that guided imagery exercises may be helpful for some clients who are depressed. It would be unethical to begin to use imagery with all depressed clients until the process was understood better. There may not even be enough depressed clients in this counsellor's caseload to make the collection of data over several cases a feasible proposition. The $n=1$ method allows data to be collected on perhaps two or three cases where the use of imagery seemed appropriate to the counsellor and her supervisor, and the client was keen on this approach. Using the $n=1$ format, the success of imagery would be revealed by clients' depression ratings being stable (and high) in the sessions before imagery, and falling in the weeks following the imagery intervention. By applying a single case method, the counsellor is able to explore in some detail what has happened in these cases, and is able to communicate her findings in a way that is more convincing than a simple descriptive case study that relies on the counsellor's case notes. Examples of $n=1$ studies that demonstrate how this approach is used in practice include Addy (2007), Christodoulides et al. (2008) and Egan and Hine (2008). In principle, the $n=1$ approach is very practitioner-friendly, and indeed was first developed in the USA in the 1950s as a means of enabling practitioners to carry out research as part of their everyday work. However, the idea of collecting regular information on such things as ratings of target problems may not sit easily with some counsellors and psychotherapists. A behaviourally oriented therapist can perhaps see many advantages in a socially anxious client keeping a diary of how often they spoke to people each day. Yet a therapist aiming to work with this client around the unconscious meaning of his relationships might well regard such a diary as counter-productive. However, it can be argued that, even when using a relationship-oriented or insight-oriented approach, the success of therapy depends on finding a *focus* for the work. In the end, the $n=1$ method only requires that this focus be scaled in some manner that is meaningful for the client. Viewed in this light, $n=1$ research methods have a lot to offer therapy practitioners interested in documenting and evaluating innovatory or 'newsworthy' practice. Although it is a method that originated in behavioural psychology, it is flexible enough to be applied in many other counselling and psychotherapy settings.

Box 8.4

Finding case studies

Systematic, research-based case studies are published in many leading therapy research journals, including *Counselling and Psychotherapy Research*, *Psychology and Psychotherapy* and *Psychotherapy Research*. In addition, two journals have been established for the purpose of building an archive of case material: *Clinical Case Studies* and *Pragmatic Case Studies in Psychotherapy*. The latter title is an on-line open access journal.

Hermeneutic single case efficacy design (HSCED) outcome research

A recently developed approach to rigorous case study research into therapy outcome that builds on the $n=1$ tradition is a method known as the hermeneutic single case efficacy design (HSCED). This methodology was devised by two leading figures in humanistic/experiential therapy, Art Bohart and Robert Elliott, and makes use of a radical new way of thinking about how to arrive at justifiable or 'warranted' conclusions about single cases or events. Essentially, HSCED is based on a quasi-judicial perspective on the construction of valid knowledge that follows principles of legal argument. In an HSCED study, a rich case record is compiled, which consists of detailed qualitative and quantitative information about a case. A typical rich case record might include data from outcome and process questionnaires that the client completed each week, therapist notes, and a lengthy follow-up interview with the client carried out by an independent researcher (i.e. not the therapist). This material is then interpreted from two contrasting standpoints (the concept of 'hermeneutics' can be defined as 'principles of interpretation'). First, the data are analysed in terms of constructing an 'affirmative' argument that the client benefited from therapy, and that the benefit derived from the process of therapy rather than from other factors. Second, the rich case record is analysed from a 'sceptic' position that assembles a reading of the case as a poor outcome, or which attributes any positive changes to factors other than therapy (e.g. the client was trying to please the researcher, or became less depressed because she got a new job). Following the presentation of the affirmative and sceptic cases, rebuttals are prepared from each position. Finally, all of this information (the rich case record, the affirmative and sceptic cases, and the rebuttals) are sent to a set of expert judges, who decide on whether the balance of evidence supports a conclusion that the client was substantially helped as a result of the therapy that he or she had received. Further information on these procedures can be found in Elliott (2001, 2002a), McLeod (2010a) and a set of papers edited by Fishman (2011). The HSCED approach has two major methodological advantages compared to $n=1$ and other methods of analysing case study information. First, HSCED is a flexible approach that makes it possible to incorporate many different kinds of data. Second, the externally verifiable 'adversarial' process through which data are analysed and conclusions are reached provides readers with a great deal of confidence that the findings reported are robust and credible. At the present time, few examples of HSCED studies have been published. Probably the two most impressive studies that have been carried out using this method have been a case of emotion-focused therapy (EFT) for phobic anxiety (Elliott et al., 2009) and a case of transactional analysis (TA) therapy for depression (Widdowson, 2012). These reports are particularly thorough, and include detailed information around the affirmative and sceptic interpretations of the case material, and the grounds on which the expert adjudicators arrived at their decisions. Both of these studies are strategically important in relation to the development of an evidence base for the effectiveness of these therapies. Up until the publication of these cases, there was no properly validated evidence of the effectiveness of EFT for anxiety or TA for depression. The existence of these rigorous case reports therefore provided *prima facie* grounds for justifying investment in further large-scale research into the effectiveness of these therapy approaches with these client groups. In addition, the case reports provided preliminary evidence of the causal factors, within each therapy, that may be responsible for the changes that were observed in the clients who participated.

Qualitative outcome studies

It is possible to use qualitative methods to develop an understanding of the positive and negative effects of therapy that is grounded in client accounts of their experience. Although quantitative methods such as questionnaires and rating scales represent highly efficient ways of collecting standardised comparative data across large numbers of people, these methods run the risk of imposing the ideas and categories of the researcher, and missing important themes that may be highly significant to research participants. By contrast, although qualitative methods are awkward to use with large samples, they are well suited to giving a 'voice' to those who have participated in therapy. In principle, there exists a wide range of qualitative methods that could be used in order to explore therapy outcome, including diaries, projective techniques, participant observation, therapy transcripts, autoethnography, and arts-based techniques. In practice, almost all qualitative outcome research that has been published in recent years has relied on the use of interviews with clients. Most of these studies have interviewed clients only at the end of therapy. However, some researchers have interviewed clients before therapy, and then have used what the person said at that time in a later follow-up interview as a means of reminding the client about how he or she had felt at the start of therapy, in order to facilitate a conversation about what has changed.

The Change Interview

In the main, researchers carrying out qualitative outcome studies have devised their own interview schedules, which reflect the specific areas that are of interest to them. At the present time, the only standard schedule which has been widely adopted is the *change interview*, developed by Elliott et al. (2001). An important feature of the change interview is that it incorporates probe questions that explore the extent to which any changes reported by the client could be seen as arising from events and experiences outside of the actual therapy that was received. It is possible to supplement the change interview schedule with additional questions that may be relevant to the particular research questions being pursued. Instructions for conducting the change interview are available at www.experiential-researchers.org/instruments.html. Examples of studies that have made use of the change interview include Elliott et al. (2009) and Klein and Elliott (2006).

Box 8.5

Qualitative outcome research has proved to be a highly fertile source of insights around the meaning of therapy for clients. Some important ideas have emerged from this line of work:

- Clients possess criteria for evaluating the helpfulness of therapy that are largely different from the criteria used by therapists and therapy researchers (Kuhnlein, 1999; Valkonen et al. 2011).
- Clients who have received different types of therapy report different types of benefit (Nilsson et al., 2007).
- The enduring impact of therapy depends on the capacity of the client to continue to make use of ideas and coping strategies that have been acquired within therapy (Glasman, Finlay and Brock, 2004).
- People who move in and out of therapy at different points in their life evaluate the helpfulness of therapy in relation to their particular needs that predominate on each occasion (McKenna and Todd, 1997).
- A surprisingly high proportion of clients, when allowed to reflect on the helpfulness of therapy in their own terms, report that they have been disappointed by the therapy they have received, or that it has had a negative impact on them (Dale et al., 1998; Howe, 1989, 1996; Morris, 2005).

These themes reflect an understanding of the value of therapy that differs in important ways from the depiction of therapy outcome in quantitative research. The picture that arises from reading qualitative outcome research is one that makes quite modest claims about the effectiveness of therapy for people who may be facing massive life difficulties, and which emphasises the active role of the client rather than the potency of therapeutic techniques. Unfortunately, relatively few qualitative outcome studies have been published. This means that it is not yet possible to carry out a credible analysis of the cumulative findings associated with this area of inquiry. Consequently, the results of qualitative outcome research have had little or no influence on policy and practice. A further difficulty around this type of research is that studies have tended to be conducted with minimal reference to previous studies, thus leading to a somewhat fragmented literature. These methodological issues are discussed in more detail in McLeod (2011: Ch. 13).

Exercise 8.4 Ethical issues in outcome research

It is clear that there are many different ways in which useful and relevant information about the effects of therapy can be collected, analysed and reported. However, there are significant ethical challenges associated with all of these methodologies. Make a list of all of the outcome research approaches that are discussed in this chapter. Beside each approach, make a note of at least two ethical issues that might arise, such as threats to confidentiality, harm to the client, or equality of opportunity for all. (You may find it helpful to consult the section on research ethics on pp. 80–1.) What are the implications of the existence of these ethical issues, and the ways in which they are handled, for the quality of the evidence that has been produced around the effectiveness of counselling and psychotherapy?

Creative arts approaches

The strategies for collecting information about outcome, described in earlier sections of this chapter, have depended on either quantification/ scaling of experience (e.g. filling in a questionnaire) or putting experience into words (e.g. in an interview). It is obvious that there are likely to be important aspects of the experience of therapeutic change that elude either or both of these strategies. There are probably two main limitations of mainstream questionnaire and interview methodologies. First, the person is always in a position of responding to a request/question from another, rather than being in a position of freely engaging in self-expression. Second, questionnaires and interviews are not particularly effective at accessing aspects of experience that are implicit, out of

awareness, or unconscious. An alternative source of outcome information, which addresses these limitations to at least some degree, is to
provide an opportunity for the person to use creativity and art-making
as a means of expressing what therapy has meant to them. The longest-
established approach of this type can be found in the use of *projective
techniques* (also known as *projective tests*). In a projective technique, the
participant is asked to respond to a relatively unstructured, ambiguous
stimulus in an open-ended way. Typical projective techniques are the
Rorschach inkblot test, in which the person is invited to report on what
they see in each of a set of symmetrical inkblots, and the thematic apperception test (TAT), where the person tells or writes imaginative stories in
response to a set of pictures. Other widely used projective tests include
story completion and sentence completion techniques, which involve
writing endings to incomplete sentence or story stems. These and other
projective instruments are described by Semeonoff (1976). The assumption underlying these techniques is that the person will project his or
her characteristic way of thinking and feeling into the way he or she
reacts to the open-ended projective task. For example, in a TAT story, the
respondent may unconsciously invest the hero or heroine of the story
with his or her own personal motives and patterns of behaviour. A person with a strong need for achievement may write stories that all make
reference to winning or doing well. Conversely, a person with a strong
need for sociability may write stories emphasising relationships and
friendships. An important feature of projective techniques is the intention to gain access to fantasy and imagination rather than consciously
processed 'socially desirable' responses.

   Projective techniques have in the past been widely used within clinical
and occupational psychology for such purposes as personality assessment,
clinical diagnosis, and appraisal of managerial potential (Cornelius, 1983)
and in market research (Branthwaite and Lunn, 1983). Projective techniques were extensively used in the early research into client-centred
therapy carried out by Rogers and his colleagues at the University of
Chicago (Rogers and Dymond, 1954). In recent years, however, there has
been increasing scepticism over the validity of these instruments. The use
of projective techniques can be criticised on two grounds. First, the
responses that people make to projective stimuli tend to be affected by the
situation they are in, their mood at the time of testing, and their relationship with the person administering the test. Second, the open-ended and
complex nature of the projective response means that it can often be difficult to interpret the meaning or significance of what the person has said
or written. Both these factors have led many psychologists to question the
reliability of projective techniques, and to the neglect in recent years of
projective methods in counselling and psychotherapy outcome research.
Despite the current lack of interest in projective techniques within the

therapy research community, there is good reason to suppose that they may have a great deal to offer in some research settings. There is good evidence that projective techniques can, if used properly, provide data equal in reliability and validity to any self-report questionnaire (McClelland, 1980, 1981).

An example of an outcome study that made use of a method that sought to draw on the creativity, imagination and implicit knowing of clients can be found in Rodgers (2006). In this study, clients were invited to draw a *life space map* before entering counselling, and again following their final therapy session. Clients were encouraged to use their life space maps to create images of their life at that moment in time, including the people, places and activities that were significant to them. At the follow-up interview, once the second map was drawn, the researcher placed the earlier map beside it and asked clients to talk about what these pictures meant to them in relation to the helpfulness (or otherwise) of the counselling they had received. The majority of participants in this study reported that the opportunity to communicate through imagery and colour allowed them to give expression to aspects of the therapy that were absent in the research questionnaires which they had also been asked to complete during the course of therapy.

There is a growing appreciation within the qualitative research community of the potential value of projective, arts-based and expressive techniques for collecting data (see, for example, Panhofer, 2011). It is probable that more studies of this type will be conducted in future, allowing a more informed appraisal of the strengths and limitations of these approaches.

Box 8.6

Different research methods – different success rates

When interpreting the results of research into the outcomes of counselling and psychotherapy, or considering the implications for policy of this research literature, it is important to keep in mind that different research approaches tend to generate different estimates of the helpfulness of therapy. The highest success rates (around 90 per cent) are found in client satisfaction studies. Next most positive are findings from RCTs, then results from practice-based studies (both around 55–70 per cent good outcomes). Finally, the least positive findings have been reported by qualitative studies (50 per cent good outcomes). How can these varying success rates be understood? At the extremes, it is perhaps easy to see that satisfaction studies tend to reflect some kind of 'halo' effect, or gratitude to the therapist, that is at its peak at the end of therapy. It is also easy to see that in-depth interviews allow clients an opportunity to express any ambivalence they might hold about the therapy they have received. The differences between success rates reported by RCTs and practice-based research have been estimated by Barkham et al. (2008)

to have achieved about 12 per cent better outcomes found in RCTs. It is informative to consider some of the potential reasons for this discrepancy. In RCTs, therapists trained in a specific approach work with clients around tightly defined problems. In naturalistic studies, by contrast, therapists are usually in a situation where they are called upon to adapt their approach to meet the needs of a wide variety of clients, which may be hard to accomplish in all cases. Also, in an RCT, a client is only included in the study if he or she has an initial score within a certain range (i.e. a high enough problem score to allow some improvement, but not too high as to be intractable). In practice-based studies, though, all clients are included, even those who report zero or near-zero problem scores at the outset (probably because of some form of denial or lack of awareness), and who can only get worse (at least, as measured by whatever questionnaire is being used in the study). Samples in practice-based studies may also include clients with extremely high scores who may need longer therapy than is available. Because of the severity and complexity of their difficulties, these clients are unlikely to improve to the extent of being classified as 'recovered' at the end of therapy, even if therapy may have in fact saved their lives. Finally, RCTs create 'special' therapeutic environments where therapists are given additional training, supervision and support, have high expectations for success, and strive to do their best work all the time because they know they are being closely monitored. A further factor that needs to be considered when interpreting the results of practice-based studies is that it is probably this type of research which yields an inflated picture of outcome, due to the fact that clients who benefit from therapy are more likely to complete end-of-therapy questionnaires, whereas clients who do not benefit are more likely to have unplanned endings and thus fail to record end-of-therapy scores. Where is the 'truth' in all this? Is it possible to determine the 'real' effectiveness of therapy? A mature appreciation of the strengths and limitations of different research methods leads to a conclusion that we need to be able to embrace multiple truths. For example, there is an important truth in the finding that 90 per cent of clients are satisfied with the service they have received. These people are not lying, but instead are expressing something significant about what therapy meant for them. Similarly, the fact that more than 65 per cent of clients in therapy RCTs seem to get well reflects a version of reality that has currency in a medical world in which investment in counselling and psychotherapy is balanced against investment in antidepressant medication and other drug treatments on the basis of that particular form of evidence. The most interesting truth, for those who are therapy practitioners, is that the closer a study gets to the everyday lived experience of therapy, the less positive its findings become.

Service-level research into the effectiveness of therapy

The approaches to evaluating the effectiveness of therapy that have been discussed in earlier sections of this chapter have all focused on effectiveness at the level of the individual client. An alternative strategy is to examine effectiveness at the level of the counselling/psychotherapy clinic or service. The issue of 'What makes a good service?' is highly relevant in terms of the quality of provision that is available to users of therapy. For example, there may be good evidence that a particular therapy approach is effective for clients with a particular type of problem. However, in practice that approach will be delivered in the context of some kind of organisational structure, and its 'real-world' effectiveness will depend on the way in which that organisation is managed.

Research into the adequacy of therapy services usually seeks to address four key dimensions of service delivery:

- *Accessibility*: ease of referral (or self-referral); geographical convenience; waiting time to first appointment.
- *Acceptability*: choice of treatment; how much the treatment approach is valued by users; warmth and efficiency of therapists and receptionists; proportion of dropouts from treatment.
- *Appropriateness*: whether the right treatment is provided; skills and qualifications of staff; whether an adequate number of sessions is offered.
- *Effectiveness*: the proportion of clients who recover and stay recovered; value for money.

It is possible to collect data on these factors from a number of sources. For example, client satisfaction questionnaires provide useful information on clients' views of the accessibility and acceptability of a service. Case files can be used to generate information on waiting times, proportion of clients who did not attend, and geographical convenience (postcode analysis). Quality audit procedures can collect data on the training, qualifications and supervision of therapists and the appropriateness of the treatment options that are available. Any important quality issues that can emerge from this kind of study concern the adequacy with which an organisation is able to compile reliable and valid information on its activities; adequacy of documentation can almost be regarded as a further dimension of service quality.

Service-level evaluation of counselling and psychotherapy has only begun to be carried out in recent years. The data generated in the UK by the CORE system (www.coreims.co.uk) has made it possible to establish benchmarks for counselling services in respect of several quality evaluation factors (see, for example, Mullin et al., 2006). Other analyses of therapy services within the NHS have been carried out by Gyani et al. (2011) and the Royal College of Psychiatrists (2011). These studies have identified major differences across similarly funded services in relation to such factors as waiting time and client satisfaction. The existence of wide variation across services seems likely to stimulate further research in future years into the underlying causes of these differences.

Box 8.7

Evaluating the impact of therapy services on communities and organisations

A neglected area of research into the effectiveness of counselling and psycho-therapy concerns the extent to which the provision of adequate therapy services makes a difference to the overall level of mental health and well-being experienced in a community. It seems reasonable to assume that someone with a serious mental health problem will generate stress in those around him or her. Conversely, if that person benefits from therapy, then it may be that those within his or her circle of family, friends and work colleagues may experience enhanced well-being. Exploration of this kind of societal-level outcome has important implications for planning and investment. For example, if a university was to close down (or expand) its counselling service, what would the impact be on student attainment and staff productivity? If a country (e.g. England in the period 2008–2012, through the Improving Access to Psychological Therapies scheme – IAPT) massively increases its resourcing of therapy services, to what extent would that initiative have an effect on welfare expenditure, or even crime rates? There is virtually no evidence around any of these issues. In one study, Reynolds (1997) found that when a workplace counselling service was introduced into one organisation, overall staff well-being was enhanced, even among those who had not attended counselling. However, this study has not been replicated elsewhere. At a broad societal level, the increase in number of trained therapists in the period 1980–2000 has been accompanied by an increase in levels of reported anxiety, depression and other emotional difficulties. Although there are many ways in which this association could be interpreted, it is not a pattern that readily suggests that greater access to counselling and psychotherapy necessarily leads to a populace that is better adjusted and more satisfied with life.

Using outcome data to inform practice: client tracking studies

Up until about 1990, counselling and psychotherapy outcome research was an activity that did not directly impinge on practice. Even when outcome data might have been collected within a therapy clinic or agency, the questionnaires or interviews submitted by clients were not seen by their therapists, and instead were processed by researchers and administrators and published in the form of reports in which individual therapists could not identify their own clients. At that time, most therapy outcome scales were lengthy, protected by copyright, and not readily accessible for practitioners. Outside of the world of CBT, where clients had always been required to provide week-by-week information about the frequency and severity of their problems, very few counsellors and psychotherapists made routine use of measures. All this began to change quite rapidly. Several groups of researchers and practitioners, in different locations, developed brief outcome scales that could be used with clients on a regular basis without eating into scarce therapy time (see Table 8.1, above, for some examples of these scales). Many of these scales were published on the Internet, and were free to use. At the same time, an important conceptual shift occurred, which created a powerful rationale for therapists to integrate the use of such scales into their everyday practice with clients. In a series of studies, Michael Lambert and his colleagues (1989) were able to show that around 10 per cent of clients tended to deteriorate in therapy, and that therapists were generally not very effective in detecting evidence of this kind of negative outcome. They found that if the client completed a brief outcome measure at the start of each session, and information about progress or deterioration was made immediately available to the therapist, then it became possible for practitioners to identify potential poor outcome cases and make necessary adjustments to bring the therapy back on track. The results of controlled studies that compared cases where such feedback was provided, with cases where clients completed scales but feedback was not provided, yielded compelling evidence that this procedure significantly reduced the proportion of poor outcomes. In addition, a further unexpected finding emerged: over all cases (not just those at risk of deteriorating), therapists who had access to outcome feedback used fewer sessions because they had a clearer appreciation of when the client had got better. These findings have been replicated in studies conducted in a number of different places.

A further contribution to this conceptual shift occurred when Scott Miller and his colleagues (2005) began to experiment with making both outcome and process information available to the client as well as to the therapist. The rationale for this stance was a view that it is important to know about what is working in therapy, and what is not working, and to agree ways to do more of the former and less of the latter. This form of practice has been described as one in which brief outcome and process/alliance measures are used as 'conversational tools': opportunities for the client and therapist to reflect on their work together (Sundet, 2009, 2012). A key aspect of this approach has been the argument that the use of such tools empowers the client to become a more active participant in therapy (Cooper and McLeod, 2011).

These developments represent a fundamental shift in the relationship between research and practice in counselling and psychotherapy. Just as doctors are able to engage in routine monitoring of the progress of treatment using stethoscopes, thermometers and blood pressure testing, counsellors and psychotherapists are beginning to be able to accomplish similar possibilities through the use of brief outcome and process measures. Counsellors and psychotherapists have always taken a keen interest in whether their clients are getting better, and are engage with the therapeutic relationship (see, for example, Daniel and McLeod, 2006).

These new tools open up a more explicit client involvement in, and control over, this process. The use of feedback tools has a wide range of implications for practice, which are only beginning to be understood and explored.

The 'Dodo Bird Verdict' and the issue of differential outcomes

Box 8.8

In a well-known scene in *Alice's Adventures in Wonderland*, Lewis Carroll created a scene in which a race was held that ended with the Dodo bird declaring that 'Everyone is a winner and all must have prizes'. In an early, influential review of the findings of controlled studies of the outcome of psychotherapy, Luborsky et al. (1975) used this phrase to sum up their conclusions: most therapy approaches seemed to be equally effective for most conditions. The 'Dodo Bird Verdict' has continued to serve as a reasonable characterisation of the conclusions that can be drawn from therapy outcome research, even up to the present time. The repeated confirmation, in research, that all therapies are broadly equivalent in effectiveness, makes little sense to most practitioners. How can it be that, say, brief solution-focused therapy and long-term psycho-dynamic psychotherapy produce the same results? To understand this issue, it is necessary to take account of the methodology that lies behind the studies which have been analysed by Luborsky et al. (1975) and later generations of reviewers. Almost all of the studies estimated change on the basis of pre- and post-therapy self-report questionnaire measures. Then the overall magnitude of change was aggregated across studies using the statistical technique of meta-analysis of effect sizes. Both of these procedures have the consequence of reducing complex data (i.e. measures of anxiety, depression, interpersonal functioning, etc.) to a single evaluative dimension ('How good was the therapy?'). There are very few studies that have specifically tried to examine differential outcomes. Nilsson et al. (2007) interviewed clients who had received either CBT or psychodynamic therapy. In a careful qualitative analysis of this interview material, they found that clients in each group seemed equally satisfied with their therapy (the Dodo Bird Verdict), but that they reported contrasting patterns of learning. The CBT clients had become better at self-management of emotions, while the psychodynamic clients had become better at managing relationships.

The politics of therapy outcome research

It is comforting to envisage scientists as comprising a group of people who have dedicated their lives to the pursuit of truth, wherever it might lead them. The reality is somewhat different. There are some areas of scientific inquiry, such as finding a cure for cancer, that are politically neutral. There are other areas, such as climate change, that lie at the heart of current debates about the future of society. Political pressure on the conduct of science may take the form of influence on the ideas, attitudes and biases of individual researchers, or can consist of various types of 'rewards' for arriving at the 'right' answer or asking the 'right' questions. It is clear that each of these forms of political influence exists within the field of counselling and psychotherapy outcome research. There is a lot at stake in being able to demonstrate that one approach to therapy is more effective than another. As a consequence, politics probably plays a greater role in outcome research than it does in any other area of therapy research.

The micro-politics of therapy research focuses on the ways in which research findings are shaped by the expectations and prejudices of the researcher. The idea that the beliefs of the researcher can influence his or her results has been documented on many occasions within psychology, over several decades (see, for example, Rosenthal and Rosnow, 2009; Rosenthal and Rubin, 1978) and in the well-known studies that show that students who are liked by their teacher do better than students who are less popular (the 'Pygmalion effect'); and people work harder when they are being observed by researchers (the 'Hawthorne effect'). This source of influence does not arise from conscious deceit on the part of investigators, but instead seems to be associated with a myriad of subtle, unconscious ways in which the responses of research subjects or partici-pants can be nudged in a particular direction. For example, a researcher running an experiment might unwittingly smile more, or talk more warmly, to some participants than others. Within therapy outcome research, the most obvious potential for researcher bias to influence research findings occurs in the area of qualitative research. In the con-text of a research interview, for instance, there are many subtle ways in which the interviewer might convey interest or approval of certain informant statements or themes, and disapproval of others. Competent qualitative researchers are well aware of such sources of bias, and have developed a number of strategies for dealing with it (such as inviting independent auditors to scrutinise their interview transcripts and ana-lysis). In fact, the clearest evidence of researcher bias in therapy outcome studies has been found in RCT studies. Luborsky et al. (1999) analysed the professional background and affiliations of the authors of therapy RCTs that compared the effectiveness of different approaches to therapy (e.g. psychodynamic vs. CBT). This investigation found a strong associa-tion between the professional allegiance of researchers and the findings reported in their research. For example, in studies that compared psy-chodynamic psychotherapy and CBT, those that were instigated and managed by researchers who identified with CBT found that CBT was more effective. By contrast, researchers who identified with psychody-namic ideas found that psychodynamic psychotherapy was more effec-tive. The phenomenon of the 'researcher allegiance effect' has continued to represent a challenge to the counselling and psychotherapy research community (Berman and Reich, 2010; Budge et al., 2010; Leykin and DeRubeis, 2009; McLeod, B., 2009). The logic of the controlled trial research design depends on the existence of 'equipoise' in the minds of researchers – an openness to whatever answer emerges from the data. It seems clear that equipoise is hard to achieve in the context of a psychotherapy research study in which there are multiple ways in which attitudes and expectations can be subtly conveyed to clients and therapists. Obviously, one answer is to require therapy trials to be designed and managed by groups of researchers who reflect different approaches. In practice, this solution is hard to implement, because it adds a level of inter-organisation or inter-institution collaboration to a research task that is already highly demanding.

The model of consumer research – an explicitly non-partisan approach to deciding whether stuff works and is good value for money

Box 8.9

There are many areas of contemporary life in which the evaluation of products and services is carried out by organisations that are completely independent of manufacturers or service providers. For example, anyone buying a car is likely to give much more weight to reports compiled by *Which?*, the AA and the European Safety Commission, or even motoring magazines, rather than glossy brochures emanating from motor manufacturers. Within the public service sector, independent inspections of schools, hospitals, prisons and care homes are made by independent inspectors. By contrast, in the field of counselling, psychotherapy and mental health, the majority of studies of the effectiveness of treatment approaches are carried out by individuals and organisations that have a vested interest in promoting a particular drug or type of therapy. It may be time to shift the balance. It is probable that studies of the effectiveness of therapy conducted by consumer groups (e.g. Seligman, 1995) or independent research institutes would be more likely to focus on questions relating to actual benefit experienced by service users, and less likely to perpetuate factional conflict between adherents of competing schools of therapy.

The macro-politics of counselling and psychotherapy outcome research refers to the ways in which funding is made available for certain types of research rather than others, papers come to be published in high-status journals, and research-based policy recommendations and clinical guidelines are formulated and disseminated. The existence of political factors in relation to these activities is often denied by those who hold power and exert influence in these spheres, on the basis that anyone can bid for a research grant, papers are grant bids that are anonymously reviewed, anyone can apply to serve on a guidelines committee, and so on. However, while it is true that these democratic and transparent structures are in place, it is also true that research funding is much more likely to be awarded to those working in elite universities, and that these people tend to 'know the ropes' in terms of where and how to get papers published and so forth. There are major areas of counselling and psychotherapy training and provision that have no connection at all with universities or other state institutions, and as a result are not operating in the same research league as therapy approaches that can draw on the efforts of academic researchers who are based in university departments of psychology and psychiatry. There is little or no discussion of these issues in the counselling and psychotherapy professional or research literature (although Pearson and Coomber, 2010, give a glimpse of what is possible), but it is not hard to verify the institutional and organisational politics of therapy research – all that is necessary is to access any one of the various NICE guidelines for psychological therapy and make a list of who compiled the guidelines, who did the research that was cited in the guidelines, where they all work, and which therapy approaches they represent.

A further, and less overt, political dimension of the counselling and psychotherapy outcome literature concerns the argument that RCTs are particularly valuable because they represent the most rigorous and conservative estimate of the effectiveness of therapy (see, for example, Wessely, 2006). The basis of this argument lies in decades of medical research, where it has repeatedly been found that non-randomised studies, such as naturalistic practice-based follow-up studies of patients, tend to overestimate the effect of treatments because they allow sources of bias to creep in, such as selective allocation of patients to the treatment that their doctor believes would be better for them, or screening outpatients who might not do well with an exciting new technique or drug (Concato et al., 2000; Kunz and Oxman, 1998; Schulz et al., 1995). The implication from medical research, therefore, is that to be really sure that a treatment is effective (or to know the degree to which it is effective – the effect size), it is essential to subject that treatment to a carefully controlled trial. In the field of counselling and psychotherapy, however, this pattern is not found (see Box 8.6 above) – RCTs generally yield *higher* effect sizes than other methodologies. It is notable here that the closer the methodology gets to the voice and experience of the user/consumer of therapy, the less positive is the picture of effectiveness that emerges. A political fault-line can be seen to exist here that does not cut across sub-groups within the counselling and psychotherapy profession, but between the profession (which has an interest in presenting therapy as a good thing) and the general public (who are less convinced – see Anderson and Brownlie, 2011).

This brief discussion of the micro- and macro-politics of counselling and psychotherapy outcome research can do no more than act as a reminder of the underlying political nature of any attempt to establish a collective consensus around what counts as 'knowledge' (see Chapter 3 for further elaboration of these themes). It is certainly the case that there is a political dimension to all therapy research. But the stakes are higher in outcome research, because of the direct connection between research, livelihood and status.

Learning from medical research: the MRC guidelines for evaluating the effectiveness of complex interventions

Box 8.10

Some medical research addresses questions around the efficacy of small-scale changes to treatment intervention, for example looking at whether drug X is more effective than drug Y for the treatment of a particular condition. In such a study, all other factors relating to the diagnosis and selection of patients, and the administration of the drug, are held constant, which makes it possible to concentrate on measuring very specific health outcomes associated with the medication that is being studied. By contrast, other medical research addresses the efficacy of highly complex interventions, such as the introduction of a new interdisciplinary team approach to managing a long-term health condition. The Medical Research Council, the lead government funding body for medical research in the UK, have published guidelines for how to evaluate the effectiveness of complex interventions (Craig et al., 2008). These guidelines suggest that simply carrying out a randomised trial does not provide a reliable means of generating useful evidence for the effectiveness of complex interventions. Instead, what is required is the planned deployment of a range of research approaches, informed by theoretical analysis and preliminary research into the component elements of the intervention. Counselling and psychotherapy are complex interventions that typically involve multiple sequences of therapeutic interaction over several hours of face-to-face contact. The MRC guidelines (available on-line at www.mrc.ac.uk/complexinterventionsguidance) represent a valuable source of information for anyone seeking to develop a strategic perspective on therapy outcome research.

Conclusions

The fact that this is the longest chapter in the book reflects both the complexity of the challenge that is involved in investigating the outcomes of counselling and psychotherapy and the massive practical implications of this area of research. The question of outcome has been, and probably always will remain, a major preoccupation of those who engage in research into counselling and psychotherapy. This is an area of research that has been dominated by medical model assumptions and randomised controlled trials (RCTs). However, several examples have been provided in this chapter of approaches to outcome evaluation that more fully embody the values and practices of counselling and psychotherapy. We have to learn to live with randomised trials and cost-effectiveness studies because they reflect a primary mode of operation of modern bureaucratic forms of governance and decision-making. But it is essential for counsellors and psychotherapists to learn how to deconstruct and critique these forms, point out their limitations in relation to our area of activity, and be able to offer an alternative, practice-focused perspective on evaluating the outcomes of counselling.

The message of this chapter is that an understanding of the outcomes of counselling and psychotherapy is crucially important for counsellors and psychotherapists (and for those who pay for their services), but that doing justice to this topic presents a major challenge for researchers because of the complexity of the processes and phenomena that are being investigated. There is no single methodology (e.g. randomised trials, case studies, qualitative interviews) that can provide the answer. Each of these methodologies has its own distinctive strengths, as well as its limitations. True progress in research into the effectiveness of therapy is not assisted by the adoption of fixed positions around the pros and cons of various methodologies. Instead, as in other areas of therapy research, the further development of a methodologically pluralist stance, which acknowledges and embraces the unique (but partial) contribution that can be made by many different sources of knowing (including personal knowing and theoretical understanding).

Exercise 8.5 Designing an outcome evaluation system

Imagine that you have been asked to construct an outcome evaluation system for a counselling/psychotherapy agency. Given the limited practical resources that are likely to be available, what would you recommend?

9

Investigating the process of therapy

The previous chapter discussed the issues associated with research into the effectiveness of counselling and psychotherapy. Outcome studies have demonstrated that therapy can be beneficial, at least for the majority of clients. However, what is less clear, much of the time, is *how* and *why* it is beneficial. In response to these issues, the focus of much therapy research has aimed at identifying the *processes* within the therapy hour that were associated with good client progress. This area of research can be regarded as a journey into the interior of therapy. Over the last 70 years, therapy researchers have generated a wide range of approaches and techniques for investigating process issues, and their findings have changed the shape of therapy practice.

There are a number of substantial difficulties facing any researcher intending to carry out a process study. First, it is necessary to arrive at a working definition or understanding of 'therapy process'. The counselling and psychotherapy literature contains many diverse ideas about the nature of process (see Elliott, 1991; McLeod, 2009). For some writers, a process is a general condition which exists in a therapeutic relationship, for example an emotional climate of acceptance and warmth. For other writers a process consists of a sequence of behaviours or actions engaged in by either the counsellor or the client, or both together. Some researchers have viewed process in terms of aspects of the experience of either the client or the counsellor. Yet others have adopted a definition of process that encompasses contractual aspects of therapy such as the frequency, length or number of sessions. The complexity of the process of therapy means that there are many interesting and important aspects of process that can be investigated. Table 9.1 offers an (incomplete) list of process factors that have been studied in therapy research.

Table 9.1   Process variables that have been investigated in psychotherapy research studies

Activating client resources	Metaphoric language
Authenticity/congruence	Reflection/clarification
Case formulation	Relational depth
Client expectations and preferences	Scheduling (weekly vs. other)
Client role preparation	Stage of assimilation of problem
Client self-exploration	Stages of change
Client suitability	Therapeutic alliance
Contracting	Therapist affirmation of client
Emotional expression	Therapist caring
Empathy	Therapist self-disclosure
Experiential confrontation	Therapist skill
Externalising the problem	Therapist support
Fees	Therapist understanding
Focus on life problems and core personal relationships	Therapist warmth
Focusing on here-and-now	Things not said
Goal consensus	Time-limited vs. unlimited
Homework compliance	Treatment duration
Innovative moments	Use of feedback
Interpretation	Use of first-person language
	Use of Socratic questioning

Box 9.1

The complexity of therapy process

Elliott (1991) suggests that it is useful to think in terms of four levels of therapy process, associated with different timescales:

- *micro-processes*, such as a speaking turn or a non-verbal gesture, may last from a few seconds to one or two minutes in length;
- a therapeutic episode or *event*, such as 'making sense of why I got so angry yesterday', may last for several minutes;
- a whole counselling *session* may represent an important process unit, for example the process of agreeing a contract in the first session;
- the process taking place over the entire *course of treatment* may be of interest, for example in terms of models of stages in treatment (beginning–middle–end).

In addition to these different time units, the counselling process at any moment can be explored in terms of either *individual* processes (what either the counsellor or client is thinking/feeling/doing) or in terms of dyadic or relational processes (e.g. interaction patterns such as how the client responded to the therapist's statement). An alternative, 9-level model of classification of therapy process can be found in Orlinsky et al. (2004).

Exercise 9.1 Reflecting on your own experience of the process of therapy

Take a few minutes to think about your own involvement in therapy, as a practitioner and as a client. Which processes have been particularly significant for
you, in terms of making a contribution to good outcomes? Which processes
are central to the theoretical model of therapy that you espouse? In what ways
have research findings informed your understanding and competence in
respect of these processes? What kind of research could be conducted that
would deepen or extend your understanding and competence?

Another set of problems for the process researcher arises from the challenge
of gathering valid and relevant data on what takes place during a therapy
session. However process is understood or defined, there is general
agreement that it comprises a highly complex and elusive set of phenomena,
which are difficult to observe or measure. Finally, there are issues arising
from the requirement to collect this information ethically. In comparison
with outcome research, where in principle all the research data can be
gathered outside of sessions, in process studies it may be necessary to
intrude into the on-going flow of the therapeutic work between client and
counsellor. With this intrusion comes the danger of harming the client.

The purpose of this chapter is to review the various research strategies
that have been employed in therapy process research. This discussion of
the methods used in process studies will be followed by an exploration
of some of the fundamental methodological issues associated with the
use of these techniques. For reasons of space, it is not possible to provide a comprehensive account of the entire field of therapy process
research. Instead, some key topics within the field are examined,
selected to illustrate the nature and contribution of therapy process
research as a whole.

Suggested further reading

Sources of information about how the findings of process can be
used to enhance the effectiveness of therapy provided for clients:

Tryon, G.S. (ed.) (2002). *Counselling Based on Process Research:
Applying What We Know.* Boston, MA: Allyn and Bacon.

A review of the main conclusions that can be drawn from process research:

Cooper, M. (2008). *Essential Research Findings in Counselling and
Psychotherapy: The Facts Are Friendly.* London: Sage.

Gaining access to the interior of therapy: tools and methods

The multifaceted nature of therapy process has meant that researchers have needed to devise a wide range of methods of gathering information about what happens during therapy sessions. This section presents an overview of some of the main techniques that have been developed.

Qualitative, open-ended descriptions of the experience of therapy

An important area of process research has consisted of open-ended *client accounts* of their experiences during therapy. Rogers (1951) contains a chapter on 'the relationship as experienced by the client' which draws on diaries kept by clients. Axline (1950), Fitts (1965) and Lipkin (1948) invited clients to write descriptions of their experiences. Other researchers have elicited open-ended accounts of process from clients through in-depth interviews (Maluccio, 1979; Mayer and Timms, 1970). All of these account-gathering studies have invited clients (and in some instances therapists) to describe the whole of their experience in therapy. Bachelor (1988) gathered more focused, briefer descriptions from clients of specific episodes of 'feeling understood'. Lietaer (1992) used open-ended questionnaires to compile client accounts of what they found helpful and hindering in counselling. Berzon et al. (1963) and Bloch et al. (1979) used an open-ended questionnaire to elicit from participants their descriptions of the 'most important event' in group therapy. Llewelyn et al. (1988) adopted a similar approach in asking clients in individual therapy to write about 'helpful aspects' of sessions. Martin and Stelmazonek (1988) invited clients to recall the most memorable images or events from sessions. Each of these strategies for collecting client and therapist accounts or descriptions of their experience of the process of therapy have continued to be used in current research. More recent examples of client experience studies are provided in later sections of this chapter.

The distinctive characteristic of the account-gathering approach for investigating process is that it yields rich descriptive data that are clearly authentic and stimulating. However, the stories that clients and counsellors tell about their experiences of therapeutic process are complex and multi-layered. It can therefore be difficult to make sense of this material, and to organise it in terms of themes and processes. Another limitation of this kind of account-gathering is that informants undoubtedly forget at least some of what happened during sessions, and may to some extent offer the researcher a reconstruction of the process based on what they now believe must have happened, rather than a direct description. In addition, what emerges from the interview must always be regarded as, at least to some extent, a 'co-construction' which draws on both informant and interviewer perceptions of the topic.

Observational methods

A research strategy that overcomes many of the problems of the accounts technique is *observation* of therapy sessions. For research purposes, observation means recording on either video or audio tape. The earliest recordings (on acetate discs) of therapy sessions were made by Frank Robinson and Carl Rogers at Ohio State University in the 1940s (see Hill and Corbett, 1993; Rogers, 1942). In this research, transcripts were made of clients and counsellor statements, and various methods were developed for categorising these verbal events. In more recent times, transcripts have been supplemented by coding done by trained raters who either watch or listen to the actual tape, thus preventing loss of crucial information about such non-verbal dimensions as voice quality, posture and gaze. There are now available a wide range of tools for carrying out ratings of process variables based on session tapes. Some of the most widely used of these instruments are listed in Box 9.2. The application of this approach involves constructing a coding manual, training raters and monitoring inter-rater reliability. Hill (1991) and Lepper and Riding (2006) provide excellent guidelines around the practical issues involved in this type of investigation. Another perspective on the analysis of session tapes has been taken by Hill (2012), Mahrer et al. (1986) and Schielke et al. (2009), who advocate the use of teams of observers, each offering his or her interpretation of the process material.

The main advantage of observation as a means of gathering information about process is that it enables the researcher to glean standardised, quantitative data. Observational data in the form of audio or video recordings can be readily used to analyse *sequences* of behaviour: it becomes possible to determine what behaviour or linguistic patterns or events are preceded, or followed, by other behaviours and events. A valuable aspect of observational data, for some purposes, is that it does not involve the need to take account of the ability of the client or therapist to be an accurate reporter of his or her own intentions and actions. However, a weakness of observational material is that it gives little or no access to the internal processes occurring in either client or counsellor.

Box 9.2

Observational measures of therapy process

Accurate Empathy Scale: A 9-point scale, applied by trained observers to tape segments. Similar scales for non-possessive warmth and genuineness. (Truax and Carkhuff, 1967)

Working Alliance Inventory (WAI): Observer form. Scales: working alliance factors of goals, tasks and bond. (Horvath and Greenberg, 1986, 1989)

Experiencing Scale (EXP): 7-point scale, applied by trained observers to 2–8-minute tape segments, transcripts or written materials. Measures depth of experiencing in client, counsellor or group. (Klein et al., 1986)

Client and Therapist Vocal Quality: Coding made by trained observers. Each client/therapist statement is coded. Four categories of vocal pattern: focused, externalising, limited, emotional. (Rice, 1992; Rice and Kerr, 1986)

Client Perceptual Processing: Trained judges rate seven categories of perceptual processing, using both transcript and audiotape. (Toukmanian, 1986, 1992)

Verbal Response Modes: Trained judges rate 14 categories of verbal behaviour, using transcripts of whole sessions. (Hill, 1986)

Vanderbilt Psychotherapy Process Scale (VPPS): Eighty Likert-scaled items used by trained raters. Scales: patient exploration, therapist exploration, patient psychic distress, patient participation, patient hostility, patient dependency, therapist warmth and friendliness, and negative therapist attitude. (Suh et al., 1986)

Narrative Process Coding Scheme (NPCS): Trained judges code therapy transcripts in terms of topic shifts, and internal, external and reflexive modes of narrative processing. (Angus et al., 1999)

Questionnaire measures of process variables

A method that retains the advantages of structure and quantification associated with coding of observational data, while nevertheless including the actual experiences of clients or their therapists, involves the use of *questionnaires* or *rating scales*. There are a number of questionnaires assessing process variables that clients or counsellors can complete at the end of sessions, or periodically throughout a course of treatment. Some of these process instruments are described in Box 9.3. These scales can be completed in a few minutes, and are convenient for both researcher and research participant. However, it is important to note that these tools can only give access to process factors operating over a whole session (or several sessions); they are not applicable for the study of discrete episodes or events (e.g. a moment of insight, or a single powerful empathic reflection) within single sessions.

Questionnaire-based therapy process measures

Box 9.3

Working Alliance Inventory (WAI): Client and therapist forms. Sub-scales: work-ing alliance factors of goals, tasks and bond. (Hatcher and Gillaspy, 2006; Horvath and Greenberg, 1986, 1989)

Barrett-Lennard Relationship Inventory (BLRI): Client and therapist forms. Sub-scales: level of regard, congruence, empathic understanding, unconditionality of regard. (Barrett-Lennard, 1986)

Therapy Session Report: Client and therapist forms. Sub-scales include: topic and concerns in session, affective quality of session, relatedness, goal attain-ment, evaluation of session. (Orlinsky and Howard, 1975, 1986)

Session Evaluation Questionnaire (SEQ): Client and therapist forms. Sub-scales: depth, smoothness, positivity, arousal. (Stiles, 1980; Stiles and Snow, 1984; Stiles et al., 2002)

Agnew Relationship Measure (ARM): Client and therapist forms; 5, 10 or 28 items, rated on 7-point scale. Sub-scales: bond, confidence, partnership, open-ness, client initiative. (Agnew-Davies et al., 1998; Cahill et al., 2012)

Session Rating Scale (SRS): Client form. Four-item visual analogue measure of client satisfaction with the process of therapy. (Duncan et al., 2003; Miller et al., 2005)

Exercise 9.2 Exploring the use of process instruments in action

Many of the scales listed in Boxes 9.2 and 9.3 are available on-line. To gain some first-hand experience of these instruments, download some that are of special interest to you, or are accessible, and try them out in simulated con-ditions. For example, imagine that you are a client who has just finished a therapy session; complete a process scale that asks you about your experi-ence during that session. Alternatively, watch a section of a therapy video, such as the Carl Rogers *Gloria* tape (available on YouTube), and use an observer rating scale to quantify aspects of the process. As you are using the scales, be mindful of your own reactions to them – do they seem to capture your experience, or what you are observing, in a true fashion? This exercise is particularly suited for use in a group, where the varying reactions of different group members can be compared and discussed.

Interpersonal process recall

A limitation of all the process research strategies reviewed so far is that none of them readily allows access to the flow of *covert* processes taking place in the exchange between client and counsellor. It could be argued that, for all their value, account-gathering, observations and questionnaires can never deliver anything better than a fuzzy picture of therapeutic process. The development of a means of obtaining a sharper and clearer image of the interior of therapy has relied mainly on the application and adaptation of a technique known as *interpersonal process recall* (IPR). Kagan and his colleagues evolved IPR in the 1960s primarily as an approach to training counselling skills (Barker, 1985; Kagan, 1980, 1984; Kagan et al., 1963). At the heart of the IPR method is the recall interview. An audio or video tape is made of a counselling session. Soon after the end of the session, a recall interview is carried out with one of the therapy participants (client or counsellor) in which they are invited to respond to a structured set of questions about what they were experiencing at different points on the tape. The recording is played back to the participant, who will usually be in charge of the stop–go controls of the tape. Whenever the person decides that something significant is happening on the tape, he or she pauses the playback and explores what he or she was thinking and feeling at that point during the original session. The assumption is that if the recall interview is carried out within a few hours of the therapy session, it will be possible by this method to re-stimulate the actual experience the person had during the session. In the context of training, the purpose of the exercise is to help the trainee counsellor to be more aware of the richness and diversity of his or her reactions to the client, and to become more skilled and confident in drawing on these reactions during therapeutic work. The distinctive merits of the IPR method are that it slows down the process of interaction, thus allowing informants to unfold more of their experience and awareness than they would normally be capable of disclosing, and that the skill and presence of the interviewer enables the informant to feel safe enough to be open in acknowledging all facets of the process.

It can readily be seen that IPR represents a unique and invaluable tool for process research. Elliott has suggested that:

> [IPR] allows the researcher to gather information on the moment-to-moment perceptions, intentions and reactions of clients and therapists during therapy sessions – subjective impressions which are missing from even the best transcriptions or recordings. (1986: 505)

The application of IPR in research situations allows the investigator to gather fine-grained descriptions or moment-by-moment ratings of critical episodes within the therapy hour. The programme of research carried out by Rennie (1990) and his associates exemplifies a particularly influential use of IPR interviews to explore the client experience of individual sessions of therapy. In this research, the client reviews the whole of the tape of a therapy hour, giving as comprehensive an account as possible of what he or she was thinking and feeling during that session. The transcript of this recall interview is then subjected to a *grounded theory* analysis (Rennie et al., 1988). This technique, described in more detail in Chapter 6, involves breaking up the text into separate 'meaning units' which are categorised in terms of meanings that are grounded as closely as possible in the experiences of the informant. The researcher then reviews this set of categories in order to conceptualise more abstract, higher-level categories and eventually to construct a model or theory of the phenomenon that is firmly 'grounded' in actual experience. The findings of this research programme have emerged as a series of papers on fundamental themes in the experience of being a client: reflexivity (Rennie, 1992) and deference (Rennie, 1994a). Angus and Rennie (1988, 1989) have applied this app-roach to investigating the ways in which clients experience the use of metaphor in therapy. Elliott et al. (1982) used IPR to examine the perceived helpfulness of different kinds of therapist interventions. Angus and Rennie (1988, 1989) have employed the method to explore the meaning for clients of metaphors that emerge during therapy. Hill (1989) has utilised IPR as part of a battery of techniques included in a series of intensive case studies. IPR was also used by Moerman and McLeod (2006) in a study of the experiences of clients receiving counselling for alcohol problems.

   The main disadvantage of IPR methodology is that it can be highly time-consuming and demanding for both researchers and informants. To address this problem, Elliott has devised a form of IPR known as *brief structured recall* (Elliott and Shapiro, 1988), in which the informant selects only one or two events for intensive analysis (e.g. the most help-ful event), rather than working through the whole tape. Another diffi-culty with IPR studies is that it is not possible to know whether the informant is in fact recalling what actually happened, or is to a greater or lesser extent imposing a retrospective gloss on what is being shown or heard on the tape. Normally, participants are given careful instructions to engage in the former rather than the latter type of activity.

Suggested further reading

Larsen, D., Flesaker, K. and Stege, R. (2008). Qualitative inter-viewing using interpersonal process recall: Investigating internal experiences during professional–client conversation. *International Journal of Qualitative Methods*, 7, 18–37. (A useful review of the pros and cons of IPR, and how it can be adapted for different research purposes.)

Self-monitoring

A further approach to gathering data about process has been on-line live *self-monitoring*. In a study of empathy, Barkham and Shapiro (1986) asked clients to press a concealed button whenever they felt that the counsellor was understanding them well. The output from the button was fed into a computer record. This technique has the strength of providing direct recording of process factors at the time they are occurring. However, it is likely that many counsellors and clients would find this approach unacceptably intrusive. This type of technique has not been widely used in process research.

Using a case study approach to track the unfolding of therapy processes

A case study approach represents a powerful technique for investigating the process of therapy. There are three reasons why case study methodology is particularly appropriate. First, there are many important therapeutic processes that occur over the course of several sessions, with influential process theories that are associated with these factors. Second, it is clear that different therapy processes are inevitably mutually interdependent and linked together. For example, client expression of emotion probably makes it easier for a therapist to respond empathically, whereas minimal client emotionality can give a therapist insufficient material from which to base an effective empathic reflection. Third, there may not be a linear relationship between different process factors, and between process factors and eventual outcome. For instance, very high or very low levels of therapist self-disclosure may not lead to good outcomes, because in the former situation the client may experience the therapist as acting out of role (e.g. acting like a client), and in the latter situation the client may have a sense of the therapist as distanced and emotionally disengaged. It seems likely, therefore, that moderate levels of therapist will be found to be most productive. This kind of complex causal relationship is more readily investigated within a case study, where multiple sources of information, over time, can be examined.

   Good examples of the use of a case study approach to analyse the process of therapy can be found in the work of Clara Hill (1989; Hill et al., 2008; Kasper et al., 2008) and Bill Stiles (2002, 2005, 2007; Stiles et al., 1991, 1992). Hill (1989) published a book-length analysis of the therapy process within eight cases, exploring the role of specific techniques used by each therapist against the significance of common therapeutic factors. Hill et al. (2008) and Kasper et al. (2008) examined the effect of therapist here-and-now immediacy as a process factor in two contrasting cases – one in which the therapist displayed a great deal of immediacy, the other with lower levels of this type of intervention.

Suggested further reading

McLeod, J. (2010). *Case Study Research in Counselling and Psycho-therapy*. London: Sage. (A comprehensive discussion of how methods of systematic case study research can be used to inves-tigate the process and outcomes of therapy.)

In conclusion, it can be seen that there are a number of strategies for investigating processes in therapy sessions. Each of these strategies has something to offer, but all have their limitations. As in other areas of therapy research, the diversity of approaches and instruments gives the impression of fragmentation and incoherence. In the field of process research, such coherence as exists has centred around a number of thematic programmes of research. In the following section, the use of different methodologies in therapy process research is illustrated through discussion of research into the therapeutic relationship.

Exercise 9.3 Exploring the potential of different strategies for collecting information on the process of therapy

Identify one aspect of the process of therapy (e.g. one of the items in Table 9.1) that you might be interested in investigating by carrying out a research study. Imaginatively consider how that process variable might be explored using each of the methods outlined in the preceding sections of this chapter (client/therapist qualitative accounts, observer ratings, questionnaires and so on). List the strengths and weaknesses of each method, in respect of your research goals. In what ways do different methods highlight certain facets of the process in which you are interested, but conceal other facets? What are the implications of your conclusions for the conduct of therapy process research?

Research into the therapeutic relationship: developing practical knowledge

The history and development of research into the therapeutic relation-ship provides a basis for appreciating the way that different research strategies, and different research teams, can combine to generate research evidence that has important implication for practice. Since the 1950s, a large number of distinct therapy approaches have emerged, and an even larger number of therapy techniques and interventions have been devised. At the same time as these developments, an alternative line of argument has been promulgated within the therapy world, asserting that at the heart of therapy for any client is a process of forming a relationship with a caring and empathic therapist, and engaging in emotional learning in and through that relationship. In an evidence-based professional context, it is necessary to offer credible research evidence that demonstrates how therapeutic relationships operate, and why they have a positive impact. The following sections of this chapter track the story of that research.

Facilitative conditions: the client-centred research programme

The single most important programme of research into therapeutic process has been the series of studies on aspects of client-centred counselling and psychotherapy carried out by Rogers and his colleagues. This series of studies is significant for two reasons. First, it pioneered many research methods that have subsequently been widely adopted. Second, it used research to test and develop theory in a systematic manner. The major research publications from this programme were books by Rogers and Dymond (1954) and Rogers et al. (1967). Summaries of the aims and scope of this body of work can be found in Barrett-Lennard (1979), Lietaer (1990) and McLeod (2002).

Box 9.4

Stages in the development of research into client-centred therapy

Talk by Rogers at the University of Minnesota in December 1940 on 'Newer concepts of psychotherapy', later to appear as Chapter 2 of *Counseling and Psychotherapy* (Rogers, 1942).

1940–45: Early research studies at the University of Ohio, mainly based on coding and analysis of transcripts of therapy sessions.

1945–57: Research group at the University of Chicago Counseling Center constructs a distinctive client-centred research model. Methods include: Q-sort, TAT, Rorschach, questionnaires, case studies. Research explores links between process (e.g. congruence between client self and ideal self as assessed by Q-sort) and outcomes. Publication in 1957 of 'Necessary and sufficient conditions' paper.

1957–65: Research group at University of Wisconsin carried out large-scale project on process and outcomes of client-centred therapy with hospitalised schizophrenic patients. New methods include rating scales to assess process variables such as empathy, acceptance, congruence and experiencing.

1965–1980: No strong institutional base for client-centred research. Continuing research on core conditions (e.g. Barrett-Lennard, 1986) and experiencing (e.g. Klein et al., 1986). Research mainly into client-centred and person-centred concepts rather than therapy.

Resurgence of research into person-centred and experiential therapy (Cain and Seeman, 2002; Elliott, 2002b; Greenberg et al., 1998; Cooper et al., 2010) using a range of qualitative, quantitative and case study methodologies.

The first phase of the programme of research into client-centred therapy was mainly concerned with describing process variables such as 'non-directiveness' and 'self-acceptance' in terms of client and counsellor behaviours and actions. The second phase, centred on the Rogers and Dymond (1954) book, explored the relationship between process and outcome, and continued to develop new techniques, such as the Q-sort, that could be used for this purpose. These first two phases depict a path that has been followed by most subsequent process researchers. The next phase in the client-centred programme represents a stage of development that has been achieved by few other process researchers. In 1957 Rogers integrated the findings from the work done up to that point into an explicit theoretical model that made powerful predictions about the links between process and outcome. This model postulated certain 'necessary and sufficient conditions' (subsequently labelled 'core conditions') for positive personality change in clients. Rogers wrote that:

1 For constructive personality change to occur, it is necessary that these conditions exist and continue to exist over time – two persons in psychological contact.
2 The first, whom we shall term the client, is in a state of incongruence, being vulnerable and anxious.
3 The second person, whom we shall term the therapist, is congruent or integrated in the relationship.
4 The therapist experiences unconditional positive regard for the client.
5 The therapist experiences an empathic understanding of the client's internal frame of reference, and endeavours to communicate this to the client. The communication to the client of the therapist's empathic understanding and unconditional positive regard is to a minimal extent achieved.

No other conditions are necessary. If these six conditions exist, and continue over a period of time, this is sufficient. The process of constructive personality change will follow. (Rogers, 1957: 95)

This theory acted as a catalyst for a substantial number of studies designed to test its predictions. However, there turned out to be major methodological difficulties involved in assembling a combination of clients, therapists and research instruments appropriate to testing the theory. For example, the instruments designed to assess levels of therapist empathy and acceptance revealed that most therapists exhibited only moderate levels of these qualities. A more satisfactory test of the theory would have been to compare groups of therapists that were either high or low in facilitative conditions, but this was not possible for practical and ethical reasons. Several studies assessed the conditions, but not from the perspective of the client. Other researchers found that observers rating therapy tapes on the conditions found it hard to differentiate between congruence, empathy and acceptance, but appeared to be basing their ratings on their image of a 'good therapist'. The result of all this has been that the theory has been neither unequivocally supported nor rejected, even after several major research projects devoted to it (Cramer, 1992). Watson (1984), for example, comes to the conclusion that the research has not been rigorous enough to test the theory properly, so no judgement can be made on whether it is true or not. Patterson (1984), while acknowledging these methodological problems, nevertheless argues that the trend of results has been in favour of the facilitative conditions model.

The story of the client-centred research programme, and particularly the research into facilitative conditions, illustrates some fundamental issues about process research. It is relatively easy to describe process phenomena that appear to make a significant contribution to outcome and are acknowledged by clinicians as interesting and worthy of research. It is harder, but possible, to devise instruments for measuring these phenomena. However, it is extremely difficult to construct a theory that will allow the interactions between these phenomena to be understood. Finally, even if such a theory is constructed, it is almost impossible to test it adequately.

Suggested further reading

Sachse, R. and Elliott, R. (2002). Process-outcome research on humanistic therapy variables. In D.J. Cain and J. Seeman (eds.), *Humanistic Psychotherapies: Handbook of Research and Practice*. Washington, DC: American Psychological Association. (A straightforward, practical summary of some of the practical implications of process research conducted within the person-centred approach.)

Later developments in process research into the 'core conditions'

In the post-Rogers era, research in client-centred/person-centred process factors such as empathy, acceptance and congruence has largely steered clear of any attempt to address 'big theory' questions such as the 'necessary and sufficient conditions' hypothesis. Instead, the recent efforts of person-centred process researchers have focused on revisiting, dismantling and redefining basic concepts such as empathy (Barrett-Lennard, 1981; Bohart and Greenberg, 1997) and congruence (Grafanaki, 2001; Schnellbacher and Leijssen, 2008). An important strand of inquiry has developed a conception of therapist 'presence' as a fresh way of making sense of the older client-centred notion of 'congruence' (Geller and Greenberg, 2002; Geller et al., 2010). Another strand has concentrated on defining, describing and measuring the quality of *relational depth*, which can be understood as a process in which high levels of mutual client–therapist acceptance, empathy and congruence are achieved (Cooper, 2005; Knox, 2008; Knox and Cooper, 2010, 2011; McMillan and McLeod, 2006). A further strand has sought to develop an appreciation of the client as an active agent in the process of therapy (Bohart and Tallman, 2010; Rennie, 2000, 2001) – an idea that was implicit in the 'necessary and sufficient conditions' model but not studied in detail in the earlier stages of the person-centred research programme. These recent research studies have used a combination of qualitative interviews and questionnaire measures.

Research into the working alliance

The debate over the status of the facilitative conditions model has largely died away. Practitioners within the person-centred approach, and trained in other approaches, continue to find the 'core conditions' theory useful in guiding their work with clients. However, the counselling and psychotherapy process research community has, on the whole, moved on to other concerns. The main ideas of the facilitative conditions model have been assimilated into the *working alliance* theory developed by Bordin (1979) and Horvath and Greenberg (1986). The starting point for this area of research was the theoretical statement by Bordin (1979), drawing on psychoanalytic theory (and not referencing Carl Rogers), that an effective client–therapist relationship was based on three qualities: a strong emotional *bond* between therapist and client, and a satisfactory level of agreement between therapist and client around the *goals* and *tasks* of therapy (i.e. the practicalities of how they were going to work together). The attraction of this formulation, for many counsellors and psychotherapists, was that it represented a set of ideas that acknowledged the reality of the psychoanalytic concept of unconscious transference, but carved out a space for thinking about the more conscious, rationally based aspects of the relationship. In addition, the notions of goals and tasks made sense to cognitive and cognitive-behavioural practitioners. The image of therapist and client as 'allies' who were working together in a battle to overcome the client's depression or anxiety represented a powerful metaphor that was intuitively appealing. Finally, Bordin's model retained the spirit of the Rogerian approach to the relationship, but without getting bogged down in arguments about whether certain relationships were 'necessary' or 'sufficient'. The working alliance therefore supplied a theoretical framework within which a new wave of research into relationship aspects of the process of therapy could proceed. This area of research was given a further impetus by the development of the client-friendly *working alliance inventory* (Hatcher and Gillaspy, 2006; Horvath and Greenberg, 1986, 1989), a questionnaire measure of bond, goal and task dimensions of the relationship. Over the years, other similar measures have also been developed (see Box 9.3 and Hatcher, 2010).

Several hundred research studies have been carried out using the working alliance inventory and other similar measures. These studies have consistently demonstrated three key findings that have major implications for practice:

- the strength of the therapeutic alliance is associated with good outcome;
- in most good outcome cases, a productive therapeutic relationship is established by around the third session;
- the therapeutic alliance plays a significant role in all forms of therapy, even approaches that do not have a specific relational focus such as CBT.

An important area of further research into the alliance that builds on these findings consists of studies that explore the process which occurs when a client and therapist have difficulty in forming an alliance, or experience a rupture in their relationship (Eubanks-Carter et al., 2010). This area of research has made use of a range of methodologies, including qualitative interview-based studies and randomised controlled trials. Systematic case study analyses of processes of alliance formation and repair over the whole course of therapy have been conducted by Michel et al. (2011) and Råbu et al. (2011). Another line of research that has emerged from the working alliance paradigm comprises studies that have examined the impact of training for therapists in becoming more aware of the dynamics of the client–therapist relationship and acquiring skills in promoting effective alliances with clients (Binder and Henry, 2010; Crits-Christoph et al., 2010; Muran et al., 2010).

Other domains of research into the process of the client–therapist
relationship

At the end of three decades of research into the therapeutic alliance,
some key figures within this research community have suggested that
the concept of the alliance may have outlived its usefulness (Safran and
Muran, 2006). Certainly, recent years have seen the publication of
research into an ever-widening range of aspects of the therapeutic relationship. Among the topics that have received attention have been
therapist and client self-disclosure (Farber, 2006; Hill and Knox, 2001),
the process of therapist responsiveness to client anger (Dalenberg, 2004),
client internalisation of an image of their therapist (Knox et al., 1999;
Wachholz and Stuhr, 1999), therapist qualities that influence the therapeutic alliance (Hersoug et al., 2009), the endings phase of therapy
(Etherington and Bridges, 2011; Knox et al., 2011) and even the relational significance of tummy-rumbling (King, 2011; Sussman, 2001).
There have been several qualitative studies that have interviewed clients
around their experience of the therapeutic relationship as a whole,
rather than focusing on a specific relationship factor (Bachelor, 1995;
Bedi et al., 2005; Levitt et al., 2006; Ward, 2005). Taken together, these
studies are beginning to contribute to the accumulation of ideas and
observations that extend and transcend the working alliance perspective
on the therapeutic relationship, and will inevitably over time lead to the
emergence of a new theory.

Suggested further reading

The ultimate test of research into the characteristics of facilitative
therapeutic relationships is whether it can be used to enhance practice. These sources explore that issue from a range of perspectives:

Agnew-Davies, R. (1999). Learning from research into the counselling relationship. In C. Feltham (ed.), *Understanding the
Counselling Relationship*. London: Sage.

Muran, J.C. and Barber, J.P. (eds.) (2010). *The Therapeutic
Alliance: An Evidence-based Approach to Practice*, 2nd edn. New
York: Guilford Press.

Norcross, J.C. (ed.) (2011). *Psychotherapy Relationships that
Work: Evidence-based Responsiveness*, 2nd edn. New York: Oxford
University Press.

Exercise 9.4 Your own personal curiosity about the
therapeutic relationship

Take a few moments to reflect on your involvement in therapeutic relationships, as a provider and recipient of therapy, and perhaps also as a friend or
family member of someone receiving therapy. What has struck you as particularly important in these relationships, in terms of negative as well as
positive experiences? To what extent does working alliance theory and
research help you to make sense of these experiences? What other
research questions or directions do you believe might be valuable?

Other major areas of therapy process research

This section summarises the diverse range of methodological approaches
that have been used by counselling and psychotherapy researchers to
explore other major aspects of the process of therapy: helpfulness of
therapeutic communication, the nature of significant events in therapy,
helpful factors in therapy, assimilation of problematic experiences, and
the operation of unconscious processes within therapy.

Helpfulness of therapeutic communication

Following on from at least one of the major lines of inquiry opened up
by the client-centred research programme, a number of investigators
have developed methods of examining the types of communication that
therapists use with clients. Behind this research is an assumption that
some types of communication, or therapist intention, may lead to good
outcomes while other types may in fact hinder clients. The approach that
has been taken in these studies has been to develop a list or taxonomy of
relevant therapist behaviour and then, using a modified recall interview,
to ask the client to rate the helpfulness of therapist responses contained
within segments of each session. An alternative approach has been to
carry out ratings on segments of therapy tapes, without involving the
actual therapy participants (Stiles, 1986). In a review of the literature in
this area, Elliott et al. (1987) have identified more than 20 different systems for classifying counsellor behaviour or response modes. The
response modes that appear in most of these systems are questioning,
advising, giving information, minimal responding, reflecting, interpretation, self-disclosure, reassurance, confrontation and acknowledgement.
The validity of these categories is supported through demonstration that
therapists using different approaches exhibit different profiles of verbal behaviour (Hill, 1986). In subsequent work on this topic, Hill and

O'Grady (1985), Hill et al. (1988) and Martin et al. (1989) argued that it was more appropriate to assess therapist *intentions* rather than their behaviour or response mode. Hill and O'Grady (1985) developed a list of 19 therapist intentions: set limits, get information, give information, support, focus, clarify, convey hope, facilitate emotional catharsis, identify maladaptive cognitions, give feedback on behaviour, encourage self-control, work with feelings, encourage insight, promote change, reinforce change, overcome resistance, challenge, resolve problems in the therapeutic relationship, and deal with therapist needs. More recently, some researchers have conducted fine-grained analyses of the conversational strategies used by therapists and clients during sessions, based on *conversation analysis* of session recordings (Peräkylä et al., 2011). Research into counsellor response modes, intentions and conversational strategies has an immediate relevance to anyone involved in counsellor training. Hill (1986) and Stiles (1986) describe their initial interest in this area of research as growing out of their own experiences in training and their later work as trainers.

Events, tasks and good moments

The research carried out within the client-centred programme, and the studies of therapist responses and intentions, have mainly the relationship between global measures (whole session or segments sampled from a whole session) of a process variable such as empathy, and associated ratings of helpfulness or satisfaction. An alternative has been studying the micro-processes that occur within specific change *events*. Elliott and Shapiro suggest that

> significant therapy events are portions of therapy sessions (generally 4–8 minutes in length) in which clients experience a meaningful degree of help or change ... We see significant events as windows into the process of change in psychotherapy ... instead of taking random samples from therapy sessions, we look where the 'action' is most likely to be ... significant events represent important general therapeutic factors but in more concentrated form. (1992: 164)

These researchers have developed a style of process research that has been labelled the 'events paradigm'.

Some of the most influential events research has been produced by the research team led by Robert Elliott (1986). The basis for their work has been the application of IPR methods to the *comprehensive process analysis* (CPA) of helpful events. The aim of CPA is to develop an understanding of significant events in a way that takes account of the *context* within which the event takes place (e.g. the therapeutic alliance, the general coping style of the client), the important features of the *event* itself (e.g. counsellor response mode and client reaction), and the *impact* of the event in terms of outcomes such as insight or decreased anxiety. Elliott (1984) has described his approach as a 'discovery-oriented' method, a way of enlisting therapists and clients as 'guides' to the 'uncharted territory' of change events in counselling and psychotherapy. For Elliott (1984), the fundamental research question is: 'What would we find out if we asked clients and therapists to point to significant moments of psychological change in psychotherapy?' His assumption is that if researchers can supply participants in therapy with the means of describing in close detail what goes on before, during and after these change events, then powerful models can be generated that can be applied to make therapy more effective.

In the studies carried out by the Elliott team, a video recording is made of a therapy session. Following the session, the client participates in a modified version of IPR, known as *brief structured recall*, which involves identifying the most helpful event in the sessions, tracking through the tape to find the event, and then engaging in a CPA interview, which consists of answering a number of questions about the meaning and impact of that event as that section of the tape is being replayed. Subsequently, the therapist is played the identified event and participates in a similar CPA inquiry interview. At some time following the client and therapist interviews, which need to be carried out immediately after the therapy session, a group of observers carry out a parallel CPA exploration of the event. The actual CPA inquiry always begins with an *expansion* of the event. In this phase, the client, therapist or observers 'spell out' their sense of the implicit meanings or what is said 'between the lines'. Having established this expanded version of the event, the research participants answer questions (quantitative and qualitative) concerning context, event structure and impact. Finally, the client and therapists are replayed the identified event later, to enable delayed or undisclosed feelings about the event to be included in the data.

Having amassed this material, which is all carefully transcribed, the research team then collates the data into client, therapist and observer *versions* of the event. The similarities and differences between these versions are identified, and the areas of greatest discrepancy analysed in further detail. The outcome of this process is the construction of a *consensus version* of the event. Elliott and Shapiro describe the data analysis as an 'iterative, cyclical process' (1992: 173) involving considerable dialogue between the members of the research group. Detailed accounts of this methodology are available in Elliott (1984, 1986) and Elliott and Shapiro (1992). The products of this approach can be seen in Elliott (1983) and Elliott and Shapiro (1992).

Greenberg (1984, 1992) and Rice (1992; Rice and Saperia, 1984) have approached the investigation of change events from the point of view of *task analysis*. Rice and Saperia suggest that

> successful psychotherapy can be viewed as involving the resolution of a series of affective tasks ... One of the things that distinguishes the experienced therapist from the beginner is the ability to recognize certain kinds of client statements as 'markers' signifying that there is an affective task that needs to be worked on and that the client is ready to work with it. Experienced therapists also have some general, often implicit, guidelines, derived from theory and extensive clinical observation, for working with different kinds of affective tasks. (1984: 29)

A distinctive feature of task analysis studies has been a rigorous focusing on the experience of the *client*: 'The client is the one in whom change takes place; the therapist's job is to facilitate the process of client change' (Rice and Greenberg, 1984: 23). The assumptions that drive task analysis research are that the identification of task sequences associated with successfully working through different types of 'stuck' or problematic feeling states will be of great practical value as well as being instrumental in the creation of new theory.

The research strategy used in task analysis studies has been to begin with a therapist-defined 'recurring event' that appears to be productive in terms of its potential as a vehicle for client change and development. The implicit cognitive map that the therapist uses to make sense of this type of event is elicited from him or her by the investigator. A particularly important element in this 'map' will be the 'markers', in terms of patterns of client behaviour and expressed feeling, that indicate the beginning of an event. Other elements that are identified at this point are the intentions and operations carried out by the therapist during such an event, the resulting client process, and the indicators of the final resolution of the event. These elements constitute an initial, therapist-defined model of the task. The next stage in task analysis is to verify the existence of this event by asking clients who have to complete post-session questionnaires.

Having identified a recurring event that appears worthy of further intensive investigation, the researcher now goes on to construct a *performance diagram* of the sequence of client tasks that comprise the event. Greenberg (1992) describes this step as a 'rational analysis' or 'thought experiment', in which the researcher tries out in imagination various task sequences before arriving at one that appears to provide an appropriate framework for understanding the actual task performance of the client. The researcher then finds ways of measuring as many aspects of the performance diagram as possible through standard techniques and scales. This diagram is then applied to the intensive analysis of a series of actual events, thereby expanding and making corrections to that model. This intensive analysis is based around an IPR recall interview focusing on the event, supplemented by any appropriate test and rating data. As the model becomes more explicit, hypotheses can be derived from it and tested against the data. The final stage of the task analysis process is to gather data relating successful task completion to outcome measures.

The task analysis approach to process research can be likened to carrying out a multi-stage research programme, encompassing rational analysis, model-building, verification and evaluation on a single type of recurring therapeutic event. This research strategy has resulted in the publication of a manual of process-experiential therapy (Greenberg et al., 1993), which includes guidelines for working with clients in relation to six key therapeutic tasks:

1 Systematic evocative unfolding at a marker of a problematic reaction point.
2 Experiential focusing for an unclear felt sense.
3 Two-chair dialogue at a self-evaluative split.
4 Two-chair enactment for self-interruptive split.
5 Empty-chair work to resolve emotional 'unfinished business'.
6 Empathic affirmation at a marker of intense vulnerability.

The work of Greenberg et al. (1993) demonstrates how process research can contribute to the construction of an effective, research-informed approach to therapy. Their research programme also illustrates one of the ways in which the original Rogerian 'conditions' of empathy, acceptance and congruence have influenced a later generation of researchers: for Greenberg and his colleagues, the 'core conditions' are viewed as essential elements within longer task sequences.

A third approach to the investigation of significant events in therapy has been pioneered by Mahrer (Mahrer and Nadler, 1986; Mahrer et al., 1986; Mahrer et al., 1987). The aim of this research programme has been to identify the therapist operations that contribute to the creation of *good moments* in therapy. Mahrer and Nadler propose that 'it is axiomatic that there are identifiable moments when clients manifest good therapeutic process, good movement, improvement, progress or change' (1986: 10). Using this broad definition of the 'good moment' in psychotherapy sessions, Mahrer and Nadler (1986) carried out an extensive review of the theoretical and research literature, and arrived at a set of 12 categories of observable change points (providing meaningful information about self, exploring feelings, emergence of previously warded-off material, expression of insight and understanding, communicating expressively, manifesting a good working relationship with the therapist,

expressing strong feelings towards the therapist, expressing strong feelings in extra-therapy contexts, manifesting a qualitatively altered personality state, undergoing new extra-therapy behaviours, reporting
changes in target behaviour, expressing a general state of well-being).
They then constructed a coding manual and instructions so that judges
could reliably define these moments in audio tapes and transcripts of
therapy sessions. A distinctive feature of the research strategy adopted by
Mahrer and his colleagues has been the explicit use of a group of expert
therapists as observers of process (Mahrer et al., 1986), on the basis that
only clinically sophisticated judges would be able to understand the
significance of good moments.

The procedure followed by this research group can be illustrated by
the study by Mahrer et al. (1986). The research team began by selecting an audio tape (contributed by a practitioner from an on-going
case) of an hour of therapy that appeared to represent a 'good' session.
Each of the 11 members of the research group took four categories,
and initially coded every client statement that qualified as meeting
the definition of one of their categories. Following this, all 11 judges
reviewed these provisional codings, and examples that were agreed by
70 per cent (eight members) of the team were accepted and retained.
Then the judges reviewed the data yet again, and classified some of the
statements as examples of 'very good' moments. This data provided a
picture of the type of 'good moment' prevalent in this therapy dyad.
In order to generate some hypotheses concerning what the therapist
and client did to bring about these good moments, each of the judges
independently generated a set of hypotheses that might account for
each cluster of moments. The research team discussed these hypotheses and arrived at a consensus account.

The work of Elliott, Greenberg, Rice and Mahrer represent different
approaches to investigating the incidence, form and sequencing of
helpful events in therapy sessions. These researchers may have contrasting ideas of how best to identify and make sense of an 'event' but all are
engaged in trying to understand, with as much depth and detail as possible, the micro-processes that are the primary vehicles of therapeutic
change.

Helpful and unhelpful factors in therapy

An underlying theme that runs through a great deal of research on the
process of counselling and psychotherapy is the search to identify
aspects of therapy that clients experience as helpful or hindering. In
one of the earliest studies of this type, Lietaer (1992) asked clients to
provide written descriptions of what they had found most and least

helpful in each session. Llewelyn et al. (1988) developed an open-ended report instrument, the *helpful aspects of therapy* (HAT) form, which invited clients to write a brief description and rating of the most and least helpful events within a session. Paulson et al. (2001) specifically asked clients to describe what their therapist had done that was particularly unhelpful for them. A useful review of this area of research can be found in Timulak (2007).

Assimilation of problematic experiences

The *assimilation model*, devised by Stiles and his associates (Stiles et al., 1991, 1992; Barkham et al., 1996; Honos-Webb et al., 1998, 1999; Stiles, 1991, 2001, 2002, 2005), has been a highly productive and influential area of therapy process research. The model considers therapeutic change as proceeding through a series of stages (see Table 9.2) that relate to a process of coming to terms with *problematic experiences*.

Table 9.2   Stages in the assimilation of a problematic experience

0   *Warded off*. Client is unaware of the problem; the problematic voice is silent or dissociated. Affect may be minimal, reflecting successful avoidance.

1   *Unwanted thoughts*. Client prefers not to think about the experience; topics are raised by therapist or external circumstances. Affect involves strong but unfocused negative feelings; their connection with the content may be unclear. Problematic voices emerge in response to therapist interventions or external circumstances and are suppressed or avoided.

2   *Vague awareness*. Client is aware of a problematic experience but cannot formulate the problem clearly. Affect includes acute psychological pain or panic associated with the problematic experience. Problematic voice emerges into sustained awareness.

3   *Problem statement/clarification*. Content includes a clear statement of the problem – something that could be or is being worked on. Opposing voices are differentiated and can talk about each other. Affect is negative but manageable, not panicky.

4   *Understanding/insight*. The problematic experience is formulated and understood in some way. Voices reach an understanding with each other (a meaning bridge). Affect may be mixed, with some unpleasant recognitions but also some pleasant surprise of the 'A-ha' sort.

5   *Application/working through*. The understanding is used to work on a problem. Voices work together to address problems of living. Affective tone is positive, business-like, optimistic.

6   *Problem solution*. Client achieves a successful solution for a specific problem. Voices can be used flexibly. Affect is positive, satisfied, proud of accomplishment.

7   *Mastery*. Client automatically generalises solutions. Voices are fully integrated, serving as resources in new situations. Affect is positive or neutral (i.e. this is no longer something to get excited about).

Source: Stiles, 2002

The programme of research into the assimilation model has adopted a sequential case study approach. In essence, the model is tested in relation to cases – the task of the research team is to determine whether the model offers an adequate account of the change process that is observed within a case, or whether adjustments and modifications need to be made to the model. Stiles (2003, 2005, 2007) describes this as a 'theory-building' approach to case study research. Examples of how the assimilation model has evolved through application to individual cases can be found in Brinegar et al. (2006), Honos-Webb et al. (1998, 1999, 2006) and Stiles et al. (1990, 1992).

The operation of unconscious processes within therapy

Some of the most powerful and clinically relevant ideas about therapy process have been developed within the psychoanalytic or psychodynamic tradition. The therapeutic processes originally identified by Freud and his colleagues included transference, counter-transference, interpretation, free association and resistance. However, the study of these processes presents unique methodological problems for researchers. From the point of view of psychodynamic theory it is impossible to understand and observe phenomena associated with, say, transference, without having had many years of clinical training. Some psychodynamic therapists would even argue that only the therapist who is actually there with the client can really know whether transference is occurring. Psychodynamic commentators would also suggest that the operation of defence mechanisms makes the client an unreliable source of information about process. The point is that, to carry out credible research into psychodynamic concepts and processes, it is necessary to find ways of gathering data that are consistent with the underlying psychodynamic theory. Interviewing clients, using minimally trained raters, or employing IPR techniques is simply not appropriate in this field of counselling research.

Researchers carrying out studies of psychodynamic processes have generally used expert clinicians to make sophisticated judgements about therapy transcripts. For example, in their research on transference reactions, Luborsky et al. (1986) developed an instrument known as the *core conflictual relationship theme method* (CCRT). In this technique, transcripts of therapy sessions are obtained, and narrative episodes describing relationships with significant others are extracted by trained judges. These relationship episode segments are then passed on to another group of judges, who have the task of identifying the three components of a CCRT within each narrative. These are:

(a) the main wishes, needs or impulses that the client exhibits toward the other person in the story; (b) the responses of the other person; and (c) the responses of the self. An example of such a relationship narrative told to a therapist by a client might be: (a) I want to be free of an unwanted visitor, but (b) he wouldn't understand, he would be insulted, and (c) I feel hassled, resentful, compelled to suffer his presence. (Luborsky et al., 1986: 42)

What the research team are attempting to do is to reduce these everyday life narratives told by clients to their core meanings. So, if the example given was taken out of the specific context of the unwanted visitor, it might be formulated as: (a) I wish to be free of obligations; but (b) other people do not respond; so (c) I comply. Using this technique, Luborsky et al. (1986) have been able to show strong similarities in the core relationship themes that clients produce about significant others, about their relationship with the therapist, and in response to an invitation to share a memory of an early interaction with a parent figure. In other words, it would appear that people unconsciously create patterns and themes in their relationships based on early childhood experience, which they then project onto all new people they meet, including their therapist. This is strong evidence in support of the Freudian concept of transference. Further examples of CCRT research can be found in Barber et al. (1995), Crits-Christoph et al. (1988), Luborsky et al. (1992) and Stiglera et al. (2007).

Suggested further reading

An accessible account of how the CCRT analysis system works and what it can accomplish can found in:

Luborsky, L., Popp, C., Luborsky, E. and Mark, D. (1994). The core conflictual relationship theme. *Psychotherapy Research*, 4, 172–183.

Sampson and Weiss (1986) and their colleagues at the Mount Zion Medical Center in San Francisco have investigated another aspect of unconscious process in therapy. Their view is that in childhood people can develop frightening and constricting 'pathogenic beliefs' that interfere with their ability to enjoy life. In adulthood, the individual has a strong desire to change these beliefs. If such a person enters therapy, the safe relationship with the therapist offers an opportunity to test out these beliefs and learn how to change them:

[T]he patient enters therapy with certain unconscious and conscious goals and with the primary purpose of solving problems and achieving these goals. The obstacles to achieving these goals are the patient's pathogenic beliefs which suggest that the pursuit of these goals *will endanger oneself and/or someone else*. One of the patient's primary efforts in therapy is to disconfirm pathogenic beliefs by testing them in the relationship with the therapist. The therapist's function, according to this theory, is to help the patient understand the nature and ramifications of his or her unconscious pathogenic beliefs by interpretation and by allowing the patient to test them in the therapeutic relationship. (Curtis et al., 1988: 257, emphasis added)

The key to this process is the unconscious 'plan' that the client brings to the therapeutic situation. The research carried out by the Mount Zion group has looked at how to arrive at a definition or formulation of this 'plan', and then examine the extent to which successful psychodynamic therapists deal effectively with the demands and challenges that the plan imposes on them. Each case plan formulation is arrived at by a team of three to five experienced therapists who work with transcripts of an intake interview and the first two therapy sessions. They seek to achieve agreement on four elements of the client's plan: goals, obstructions, tests and insights. An example of a plan formulation is given in Box 9.5. In subsequent sessions, which are also transcribed, the researchers rate the extent to which interpretations made by the therapist are compatible with the plan formulation, and they look at the relationship between the ratio of plan compatible/incompatible interpretations and good or poor outcomes (Silberschatz et al., 1986, 1989).

The formulation of a client's unconscious 'plan' (Curtis et al., 1988)

Box 9.5

Goals

- To work towards ending her relationship with partner.
- To feel less responsible for her mother and exert more control over this relationship.
- To allow herself sexual gratification in a relationship with a man.
- To develop a meaningful and mutually satisfying relationship with a man.

Obstructions

- She believes that she is capable of seriously harming others if she does not carefully tend to them.
- She believes that she is being disloyal to and thus hurtful of her mother if she expresses sexual pleasure in a satisfying relationship.

(Continued)

(Continued)

- She believes that she would be disloyal and abandoning of her mother if she developed new relationships.
- She believes that she is responsible for the difficulties of those less fortunate than herself.

Insights

- To become aware of the degree to which she has complied with her mother's expectation that she assume a caretaking, self-renunciating role.
- To become aware that she inhibits herself from developing and enjoying relationships with others because she feels guilty allowing herself more than her mother has.
- To become aware that her professional isolation represents an identification with her mother.
- To become aware that she has felt angry and resentful towards her father for not shielding her from her mother's influence.

Tests

- She will disagree with the therapist to see if he is critical of her or is hurt or upset by her defiance.
- She will act as if the pursuit of a goal is a selfish or otherwise undesirable action to test whether the therapist wants her to hold herself back.
- She will boast about an accomplishment to see if the therapist is bothered by her self-assurance and success.
- She will exaggerate her occupational strivings (e.g. appear 'ruthless') to see if the therapist approves of her legitimate professional aspirations.

Another influential line of psychodynamically oriented process research has explored the ways in which Bowlby's theory of attachment can be used to understand the dynamics of the relationship between client and therapist. Several research studies (Eames and Roth, 2000; Hardy et al., 1998; Kivlighan et al., 1998; Rubino et al., 2000) have provided convincing evidence for the role of both client and therapist attachment style in shaping the process of therapy. Much of this research has made use of the *adult attachment interview* (AAI), a standardised method for assessing patterns of attachment (Hesse, 1999; Main, 1991). The AAI consists of a 15-item clinical interview, which normally takes around two hours to complete. The questions asked in the interview are intended to 'surprise the unconscious': the person will find himself or herself saying things, or contradicting themselves, in ways that are beyond their conscious control. For participants, the interview is similar to a therapy session, in that they are invited to talk openly, and at length, about childhood experiences and memories which may be quite painful. Analysis of the interview depends less on the content of what the person says, but is largely derived from the style or manner in which the person tells the story of their early life. Detailed protocols have been prepared for reliably analysing AAI material. As with CCRT and plan analysis, the AAI represents a research tool which is designed to access unconscious processes. Several research groups have generated alternative interview schedules and questionnaires that examine different aspects of the attachment process: at least 29 such measures are now available (Ravitz et al., 2010).

An important recent programme of research into the process of psychodynamic and psychoanalytic psychotherapy has been developed by Andrzej Werbart and colleagues in Sweden (Lilliengren and Werbart, 2005, 2010; Philips et al., 2005, 2007a, 2007b; von Below et al., 2010; Werbart and Levander, 2006). These researchers have used interviews before therapy and at follow-up to explore client (and therapist) experiences of what has been helpful and hindering in therapy. Specifically, these studies have focused on the different types of 'private theories' of change and cure that are held by clients, and on the ways in which these ideas unconsciously shape the client's participation in therapy and satisfaction with the outcomes of therapy. For example, a study reported in Werbart and Levander (2006) considered the role of 'private theories' in two cases of psychoanalytic psychotherapy. In both cases, the therapist and client possessed a utopian goal of attaining far-reaching personality change and psychological 'rebirth', but in the end had to settle for a more limited kind of cure based on finding new solutions to old problems. The findings of this study contribute to an enhanced understanding of the role of private theories within the transference and countertransference that took place between client and therapist. It also draws attention to the meaning of the sense of disappointment that was reported by clients and therapists at the conclusion of these therapies – a disappointment that could be regarded as reflecting a process of mourning for the abandonment of utopian personal theories. In methodological terms, this set of studies is notable both for the development and application of a highly effective interview schedule designed to elicit narrative accounts of what occurred in therapy, and a particularly thorough approach to analysis of the data that were collected.

The studies discussed in this section illustrate some of the ways in which unconscious processes in therapy can be investigated, using a combination of qualitative and quantitative approaches. These programmes of research have made a major contribution to the construction of an evidence base for psychodynamic and psychoanalytic counselling and psychotherapy, and have also been of value in relation to training and supervision.

Suggested further reading

Additional examples of psychodynamic process research can be found in:

Levy, R. and Ablon, S. (eds.) (2009). *Handbook of Evidence-Based Psychodynamic Psychotherapy: Bridging the Gap between Science and Practice*. New York: Humana Press.

Conclusions

The studies already covered in this chapter have been selected to give a sense of the diversity of research into process factors in counselling and psychotherapy. For reasons of space and clarity, many other interesting and significant avenues of process research have been omitted. Among the many other process issues that have been investigated are studies of therapist errors (Sachs, 1983), the use of language (Russell, 1989), the experience of cultural difference (Thompson and Jenal, 1994; Tuckwell, 2001; Ward, 2005), the operation of transition objects (Arthern and Madill, 1999), and the significance of psychoperistalsis/tummy rumbling (King, 2011; Sussman, 2001).

It is clear that the study of therapy process presents considerable methodological challenges, and that the design of a process study inevitably involves a trade-off between capturing data on some aspects of process while at the same time losing data on other aspects. For example, studies of therapy process have employed quite different units of analysis: the whole of treatment, single sessions, significant (5–10 minutes) segments of sessions (events), and micro-segments (e.g. therapist or client statements). It is clear that there is no one 'right' unit of analysis. Researchers adopting different unit lengths have all produced valuable results. A further fundamental dilemma in process research concerns the choice of observer perspective. Spence (1982) has made the case that the actual participants in the therapy dyad, the counsellor and client, possess a 'privileged competence', an intimate knowledge of the process that no one else can ever fully appreciate. Spence (1986) goes further in suggesting that any attempt on the part of the therapist or client to explain his or her experience of the process to a third party will inevitably result in a 'smoothing' of that experience. The earliest process studies, carried out by Rogers and Dymond (1954), came to the conclusion that therapists, clients and outside observers had quite different perspectives on process and outcome. Although these perspectives overlap and are in agreement on many occasions, there are also significant areas of disagreement. Process researchers have attempted to resolve these issues of perspective in a number of ways. The use of IPR methods, for example, can be seen as a determined effort to retrieve as much as possible of the privileged data that Spence (1982) would suggest were inevitably smoothed away immediately the therapy hour finishes. Some researchers, such as Elliott (1986), have taken up the challenge of integrating client, counsellor and observer perspectives in a single version. Others, such as Rennie (1990), have constructed a rationale for concentrating solely on the experience of the client.

A final area of challenge in relation to investigations of the process of counselling and psychotherapy concerns the role of theory. There are two key issues around the task of making links between process research and theoretical models of therapy. First, there is no comprehensive theory of the process of therapy that has broad acceptance within the field. As a consequence, it is difficult to see how different strands of process research might fit together. It is as though there are many phenomena and observations in search of theory. Second, the actual conduct of process research tends to lead in the direction of findings and conclusions that do not readily fit into any single theoretical framework. For example, although the research carried out by Werbart and colleagues is explicitly psychoanalytic in orientation, their findings can be readily interpreted from a cognitive perspective (or other perspectives). This realisation has led some researchers, such as the assimilation model group, or those who have studied helpful events, to seek to develop models that are intentionally trans-theoretical. In order to get the best value from the large number of process studies that have been published, what is perhaps required now is further attention to how best to integrate these studies into a general theoretical framework.

Suggested further reading

Further information on what is involved in doing therapy process research can be found in:

Greenberg, L.S. and Pinsof, W.M. (eds.) (1986). *The Psychotherapeutic Process: A Research Handbook*. New York: Guilford Press.

Lepper, G. and Riding, N. (2006). *Researching the Psychotherapy Process: A Practical Guide to Transcript-based Methods*. Basingstoke: Palgrave Macmillan.

Toukmanian, S.G. and Rennie, D.L. (eds.) (1992). *Psychotherapy Process Research: Paradigmatic and Narrative Approaches*. London: Sage.

Critical issues in research on counselling and psychotherapy: continuing the conversation

Previous chapters have provided an overview of the state of contemporary research on the processes and outcomes of counselling and psychotherapy, and an outline of some of the main ideas and skills that underpin the counselling and psychotherapy research literature, for example in fields such as philosophy of science, quantitative methods, and qualitative inquiry. The present chapter represents an invitation to reflect on this material by considering some of the questions that counselling and psychotherapy students and practitioners tend to ask about research. These are all questions that I have been asked myself, during workshops and lectures that I have given. The answers, below, consist of things that I have said in response to these questions, or things that I wished I had said. Written down, as they are here, these questions and responses cannot convey the passion that can accompany such discussions, or the way in which the ensuing flow of dialogue can open up further possibilities on both sides. Nevertheless, I hope that by adopting a dialogical approach to these issues readers will be encouraged to identify their own position in relation to each question, and formulate their own responses. The chapter does not include self-reflection exercises: it is intended that a question-and-response sequence will have the potential to function as a starting point for self-reflection and/or group discussion.

How has research informed your practice? What are the research studies that have made a difference to the way that you work as a therapist?

There are many ways in which research findings have influenced the way I work as a counsellor. I have always practised in situations in which I have seen clients reflecting a wide range of presenting problems. As a result, at least up to now, I have not been particularly interested in research into the outcome and process of therapy with specific client groups. My use of the research literature has therefore been largely focused on ideas that apply to a wide spectrum of clients. Although my primary training was in person-centred (client-centred) counselling, it always seemed to me that the research literature suggested that many different therapy approaches were potentially effective. This research finding has encouraged me to remain open to different ideas, and to want to learn more about different therapy theories and techniques. In recent years, I have become particularly interested in the relevance of client preferences in relation to what will or will not be helpful for them (see McLeod, 2012), and I have been motivated to develop ways in which I can find out what my clients want, and adapt my own therapeutic style to 'meet them half way'. This way of working has also been informed by reading about research into client perceptions of therapist self-disclosure (summarised in Farber, 2006), which has helped me to be more confident in sharing my own ideas and experiences with clients on the basis that one way to help a client to identify what might work for them is for me to be as open as possible about what I have to offer. For many years I have found great meaning in the research by David Rennie into the client's experience of therapy, in particular his vivid demonstration of the power of client deference (Rennie, 1994a). What I learned from this was that I need to work hard to create structures through which my clients can be empowered to let me know about how the therapy is going for them. This insight has, in turn, led to an appreciation of the practical value of research into the use of client feedback and tracking instruments that can be used as part of routine practice (Lambert, 2007). Research by Dreier (2000, 2008) and Mackrill (2008a) has reminded me that it is important to keep in mind that the client's life is lived out there in a real world, which is likely to have a much bigger influence on their feelings and decisions than any intervention I might seek to make. In a different light, the work of Fluckiger and Holtforth (2008) introduced me to a valuable means of focusing on client strengths and resources. These are just a few of the many ways in which the products of research have helped me to become a better counsellor. Clearly, I have been drawn to these research studies because they speak to a pre-existing sense or interest that I have, in the issues that they have addressed. These research studies have helped me to think through, and make sense of, aspects of the practice of therapy that seemed important but which I did not fully understand. They have also, because I have been convinced of the validity of their conclusions, given me the courage to try out and persevere with new ways of working. I do not make any assumption that this set of research influences will necessarily be relevant for other therapists. Each of us has our own starting point, and awareness of different aspects of the role of therapist that are straightforward for us, or are opaque and problematic. Fortunately, the counselling and psychotherapy literature covers a lot of territory, which makes it possible to undertake many different types of journey.

*I came into counselling to work with **people**: why on earth should I bother with research?*

The work of counselling draws on several different types of knowledge. It requires self-knowledge (an appreciation of personal strengths and vulnerabilities), practical knowledge (a capacity to reflect on practice), theoretical knowledge (an ability to use concepts to make sense of complex phenomena), and cultural knowledge (an understanding of the cultural factors that shape personal lives). Research is another source of knowledge. Research consists of the best efforts of many people to ask questions about how therapy works. The kind of knowledge that is made available through an involvement in research overlaps with other sources of knowledge, such as practical knowledge, but offers a unique perspective that is based on standing back from what is happening and looking for patterns. It takes time and effort to learn about research. The same could be said for learning to make best use of other sources of knowledge, such as personal therapy, supervision and theory. The question 'Why on earth should I bother with research?' might equally well be applied to these other areas: 'Why should I bother about supervision, personal therapy or reading about theory?' All of the approaches to therapy that are widely used at the present time have evolved their own tradition of research that is consistent with their core values and assumptions. In all these approaches, there are major challenges around integrating research knowledge with the understandings that arise from practice and self-exploration. It is through seeking to resolve these creative tensions that a community of practice is able to renew itself in order to meet fresh challenges and avoid becoming locked in dogma.

Many studies rely on questionnaire data – how do we know whether the client is being truthful, or merely trying to please his or her therapist?

The problems with self-report questionnaires go way beyond these issues. There is also the issue of the level of the person's awareness around the thing that is being asked, the extent to which questions shape answers, and the areas that are not covered at all in the questionnaire. Some of these issues are explored in McLeod (2001b). I believe that truthfulness is possibly the least of these concerns – the majority of people genuinely do want to contribute to knowledge. Also, in many research studies the therapist never gets to see the questionnaires (and the client will know this), so pleasing the therapist does not come into it. Interviews allow some of these issues to be addressed, by checking things out with the person and establishing a quality of rapport that encourages honesty. In my view, it is important for therapy researchers to get better at using other sources of information that can be triangulated against self-report. For example, in schools counselling, actual school attendance, exam performance, and the views of peer group, family members and teachers may be relevant outcomes of therapy (along with other types of outcome such as self-reports of well-being). At the same time, it would be strange if client self-report was *not* part of the counselling and psychotherapy evidence base. It is therefore a matter of achieving a balance between self-report questionnaire data and other sources of information. Recent systematic case study research provides many examples of how diverse sources of information can be incorporated in a single investigation. The ease of administering and analysing self-report questionnaires, and the illusion of objectivity that accompanies them, has led to an over-use of this form of data. It seems likely that further advances in counselling and psychotherapy research knowledge will be associated with further innovation around different sources of information.

Each client that I work with is a unique individual. This uniqueness gets lost in research, because the person is defined and categorised, and their experience is aggregated alongside the responses of other people. Isn't this a major problem, in terms of the application of research to an area of practice such as counselling and psychotherapy?

The issue of uniqueness is important, presenting significant challenges for researchers, but it also needs to be viewed in context. Yes, each person is unique. Human beings are biologically programmed to be responsive to uniqueness, for example in the area of face recognition. Yet, at the same time, our appreciation of the individual qualities of a person is constructed from categories or concepts (such as 'tall', 'intelligent' and 'kind') that allow us to compare this unique other person to all the other people we have come across in our lives, as well as comparing them to our own self. An experience of some kind of 'pure' sense of another person as a wholly unique 'other' is a powerful event, but probably quite rare, even in the therapy room. One of the functions of research is to generate categories and concepts which can then be used to achieve a more nuanced or differentiated perception of the qualities of other people. Theory-building or theory-oriented research plays this kind of role. There are other kinds of research, such as case studies and qualitative research, that seek to document and explore the complex ways in which different processes can come together in individual cases, and explore the texture of specific moments within therapy. These are research traditions that are particularly sensitive to uniqueness. There are also other research traditions that are more concerned with making general statements at a group or population level. It is useful to know, for example, that some interventions tend to be more helpful than others for certain problems – even if there may be some individual clients for whom this pattern does not apply. In the early years of research into the processes and outcomes of counselling and psychotherapy, it was probably true that the (largely quantitative) methodologies that were adopted by researchers were mainly 'nomothetic' in nature (i.e. seeking to identify generalities). More recently, the balance has begun to shift, with many researchers adopting a more 'idiographic' approach. Another factor that is relevant to this debate concerns the ethical sensitivity of publishing research that might make it possible to identify individuals. In fields such as political science or history, it is possible to study the unique circumstances that contributed to, for example, the outbreak of war in 1914. In medicine, it is possible to report detailed information on individual patients, because what is being described is concerned with symptoms and bio-data, rather than social identity. Therapy research is different, in that the closer the research gets to the unique aspects of an individual case, the more that identifiable aspects of the client or therapist's particular life-story are opened up. Nevertheless, some therapy researchers have still been able to produce richly described accounts of individual experiences of therapy.

As a therapist, I am very interested in unconscious aspects of human experience – emotions, thought-process and patterns of behaviour that are not readily accessible to conscious awareness, but that nevertheless exert a powerful influence on how people live their lives. The research that I read does not seem to take account of unconscious factors. Is it possible to do research that does justice to the concept of 'the unconscious', and advances our understanding of this domain?

In my experience, there are two sides to this question. Some people who raise this type of question seem to take the view that any information that is based on the person's perception or account of his or her own behaviour is virtually worthless, because the true reasons for their action are always outside of their conscious awareness. At a personal level, I have a strong negative reaction to this position, because it implies that the researcher, therapist or other external observer 'knows better'. For me, such a standpoint is morally and politically unacceptable. I believe that the starting point for developing an understanding of any aspect of therapy is to begin by asking people what they think, and asking them to describe their experience, and then seeing how far that takes us. However, it is also clear that the conscious awareness of most people, in most situations, is only part of the story. Usually, there is a lot of stuff happening that is outside of awareness, including stuff that may be impossible to retrieve even if the person is given a lot of assistance in directing their attention to specific aspects of their experience (e.g. by a skilled interviewer). A classic paper by Nisbett and Wilson (1977) brought together the findings of many experimental studies which showed that people were generally unaware of aspects of their environment that affected their decision-making and other types of behaviour. More recently, the best-selling book *Blink: The Power of Thinking Without Thinking* (Gladwell, 2006) offers an accessible and entertaining account of this area of research. What is reflected in these sources is a vast amount of research that has been carried out by psychologists into the nature of unconscious processing. This line of inquiry has also been pursued within the field of counselling and psychotherapy research. Walsh (1996) provides a thoughtful discussion of how the analysis of qualitative data (e.g. from interviews) can be used to identify implicit or unconscious aspects of the meaning of the events and experiences that are described by informants. Qualitative methods that enable fine-grained exploration of language use, such as discourse analysis, conversation analysis and narrative analysis, are able to pick up on patterns of interaction that are outside of conscious awareness. For example, a paper by Billig (1997) uses detailed analysis of language to develop new insights into the unconscious dynamics of one of Freud's cases. Other researchers, such as Ramseyer and Tschacher (2011) have studied out-of-awareness interactional synchronies in the bodily movements of clients and therapists during sessions. Many therapy researchers (see Chapter 9) have devised ways to study the operation of classical psychoanalytic processes such as transference. There also exists a growing body of research into the biochemical basis of such experiences as attachment, loss and anger. To return to the question, there is no doubt that there does exist a substantial interest in unconscious processes within the field of counselling and psychotherapy research. It is reasonable to suggest, however, that there has been a predominance of research into consciously available information (which is easier to collect), and that there has been limited progress in understanding the ways in which conscious and unconscious factors interact with each other, or take precedence at different points in therapy (the assimilation model – Stiles, 2002 – represents a notable exception). To some extent, the resolution of these questions probably depends on the achievement of a satisfactory explanation of the nature of human consciousness, which remains a major scientific mystery.

I am a lecturer/trainer in counselling and psychotherapy. The curriculum that I teach is overflowing with essential topics that must be covered, in areas such as theory, skills, personal development, ethics and reflection on practice. How can research skills and awareness be integrated into this curriculum without leading to students becoming completely overwhelmed?

This is an arena of real difficulty for many tutors and trainers, who have a great deal to offer students in the form of clinical experience and leadership, but who have had little or no previous involvement in research. A recent therapy research training manual compiled by McLeod et al. (2010) includes a wide range of ideas and examples around how to teach research in a way that contributes to the therapeutic competence of students, and energises them in respect of the value of research. There are many small ways in which these goals can be attained within a counselling or psychotherapy training programme. The key underlying principle involves teaching research through experiential activities, such as reflecting on the experience of completing a questionnaire or carrying out a group project. By contrast, research teaching that is based on lecture inputs from colleagues who are not therapists is rarely successful, even if these colleagues are expert and inspirational researchers within their own fields. To make the connection between research and practice, students on counselling and psychotherapy training programmes need to be exposed to trainers who are therapists but who also have a positive research identity that they are willing to share with trainees.

The image I have of research at the moment is that it is a mechanism for exerting government control over therapy, by ensuring that the only therapies that are offered are those that teach people to be obedient citizens and consumers. The types of therapy that have made a huge difference to me in my own life, and that I have been trained to deliver, are considered as worthless because they lack an evidence base. Surely we should be doing all we can to resist the encroachment of 'research' into our practice?

In recent years, not only in the UK but also in many other countries, there are many therapy practitioners who are angry about the way that research has been used to promote the interests of some approaches to therapy, and professional communities, at the expense of others. The problem here, I would suggest, is not 'research' but the way that 'research' is used. At its core, counselling and psychotherapy consists of a relationship between a client (or couple or family) and a therapist (or team of therapists). At that level, within most societies, the client has freedom to choose any practitioner that they regard as appropriate to their needs. Although the state, or professional licensing bodies, retain a right to intervene in situations of exploitation or harm to clients, the definition of what may be considered acceptable therapeutic practice remains very wide. What has happened over the past 20 years is that third-party funders of therapy, such as government departments and insurance companies, have increasingly demanded evidence of efficacy as a condition for investment in counselling and psychotherapy services (i.e. have implemented evidence-based practice policies). Various groups of therapists have responded to these developments by carrying out research that they believed would be convincing to these purchasers of care, and as a result have been successful in gaining recognition and getting work. It seems very unlikely that governments and insurance companies will abandon evidence-based practice policies any time soon, because to do so, they would need to devise some kind of alternative method of transparent and accountable resource allocation, and it is hard to see what this might look like. What seems more likely is that the pressure to demonstrate efficacy will gradually permeate the world of private practice, as self-paying consumers of therapy use the Internet as a source of information around which therapist they should choose. So even if the NHS started to hand out psychotherapy vouchers to patients, rather than directly employing psychotherapists, it is probable that they would seek out therapists or practices that can provide them with research-based evidence around outcomes, quality, previous satisfied users and so on. As far as I can see, there has been a fundamental shift in counselling and psychotherapy that has taken place since Carl Rogers and his colleagues started to do research in the 1940s. The shift is that research evidence is now part of the game. There is no escape from this. On the basis of my own experience, I know that in the UK there are several communities of gifted counsellors and psychotherapists, whose work is of a high standard, whose response to this scenario has been to deny the validity of all research, and who try to hang on to the way things were. This is not a sensible or constructive way to proceed. The field of contemporary counselling and psychotherapy embraces a wide range of methodologies. Engaging with research does not necessarily require using brief outcome questionnaires and conducting RCTs. There are many ways in which credible evidence can be collected. Yes, at the moment, proponents of CBT have a huge advantage in terms of the amount of research that supports their work. But in the 1960s, when the pioneers of CBT were beginning to disseminate their ideas, psychoanalysis and client-centre therapy were the dominant approaches and CBT was the new kid on the block. It is never too late to make a start.

It seems to me that counsellors and psychotherapists have been doing research for more than half a century. Is there evidence that what we are doing now is any more helpful for people than the therapy that was available in the 1950s and 1960s?

This is an important and difficult question. There are many areas of contemporary life where it has been possible to document progress in human well-being as a result of focused collective effort. Survival rates for many types of cancer have improved over the past few decades. Infant mortality has been reduced. Cars break down less often, and are more fuel-efficient. More people attend university. These kinds of statistics testify to the capacity of modern democratic states to deliver real benefits to citizens, and their dissemination reinforces public support for policies and services that demand considerable expenditures on the part of taxpayers. It would be reassuring if similar improvement figures could be compiled that demonstrated steady improvement in the quality and effectiveness of counselling and psychotherapy provision. To the best of my knowledge, no one has attempted this exercise, probably because it would be an extremely difficult undertaking. The first comprehensive meta-analysis of the effectiveness of psychotherapy was published by Smith et al. (1980). In principle, it would be possible to summarise the therapy effect sizes (i.e. magnitude of change) reported in current meta-analyses, then compare them to the results of the Smith et al. (1980) review. However, there have been significant shifts in the technology of outcome research over the past 30 years. Researchers are using measures that are more sensitive to change, are more likely to be studying manualised treatments, and are likely to be more selective about the inclusion and exclusion criteria for the clients admitted into a study. Each of these factors would have the effect of inflating the success rates of current therapies, compared to previous data, and would need to be taken into account in some way in a comparison analysis. Researchers who are perhaps more optimistic than I am about the rate of progress in being able to use research to enhance the effectiveness of therapy will want to point to innumerable examples of studies in which a new version of a therapy approach has been shown to be more effective than an older version. This evidence is relevant, but not necessarily wholly convincing. Research into organisational innovation tends to show that new ideas are promulgated by charismatic pioneers, taken up by enthusiastic 'early adopters', and hailed as landmark breakthroughs. But in the medium term, as new ideas and practice become routinised, and implemented by workers who are less committed to them, their effectiveness gradually diminishes. Another way of looking at this question is that it would clearly be in the interest of leaders and managers of counselling and psychotherapy services in the NHS and other large-scale healthcare systems to be able to report that the effectiveness of their services is getting a bit better, year on year. The fact that such good news is not being publicised must mean that the evidence does not exist. And the fact that it does not exist raises important questions about the role of research in driving quality improvement in counselling and psychotherapy provision: *Why* doesn't the evidence exist?

There is still a lack of research evidence in relation to many important practical issues in counselling and psychotherapy. What can be done to make sure that more good quality research gets carried out?

I receive a steady flow of mail from therapists and service managers asking me about what research can offer in relation to practical choices that they need to make. For example, a recent email enquired about the relative effectiveness of externally contracted employee assistance programmes, as against in-house counselling, as alternative ways of organising workplace counselling. I have reviewed this literature (McLeod, 2007, 2010b), and know that it has little to offer around this question. This is disappointing, because it is in fact a big question that has major implications for clients and counsellors. What can be done to improve matters, and allow more research to be carried out and published on issues of practical significance? I believe that a lot could be done, quite quickly, on the basis of some strategic realignment of the efforts and energies of academics, funding bodies, professional associations, and publishing houses. Here are my suggestions:

1 *Investment in creating and supporting practice research networks* (PRNs), in which academic researchers function as facilitators and sources of expertise to co-ordinate the activity of practitioners and students. Part of this policy would be an expectation that students undertaking master's and doctoral work would normally conduct their research within the context of a PRN. There would also be an expectation that the professional role of counsellor or psychotherapist would involve participation in a PRN, just as it currently involves participation in clinical supervision, CPD and personal therapy. Compared to research that is designed and carried out by individuals, PRN-based research has four major advantages: (i) to be implemented, a research idea needs to pass the 'common sense and practical relevance' test of being acceptable to members of the PRN; (ii) there is a much higher leverage, in terms of productivity, around the scarce expertise and research experience of those who have PhDs and hold academic positions; (iii) it is possible to access larger samples of participants, and hard-to-access participants, because a network of willing collaborators is already in existence; (iv) modest investment by funding bodies, to support regular meetings of a PRN, maintain a website and resources library, and allow short-term research sabbatical leave for practitioner members, would generate a greater volume of research output than any other funding arrangement.

2 *Take a fresh look at how the findings of research studies are published and disseminated.* Research journals are still organised and structured in much the same way as they were 40 years ago. However, the world of research has changed, and the way that people read research has changed. Getting an article published in a research journal takes a long time (as the paper proceeds through the review process) and calls for high-level academic writing skills (in the past, it was a reasonable assumption that almost everyone who submitted a paper to a journal would have a PhD). The largest research resource at the present time consists of unpublished work carried out by students and therapy agencies, who are deterred by the general stress and hassle associated with attempting to get their work published in a research journal. At the same time, the stuff in these journals is read by only a small minority of practitioners – in turn, this has the effect of damping down practitioner interest in research and motivation to do research. I wonder whether a different type of research journal, published on-line, might not represent a solution to some of these

barriers. This would be a journal that published work quickly, and had a different level of quality threshold ('readable, coherent, ethical' rather than 'perfect'). It would be a journal in which readers could respond to each article, using the kind of discussion/feedback forum programmes used in some newspapers or in TripdAdvisor and Amazon. Each paper would be subject to an initial editorial and peer review, as at present, but beyond an initial guidance to the author on any changes that he or she might need to make in order to be 'readable, ethical and coherent', the more substantive review and comment process would be open and transparent. My guess is that this would be much more interesting and engaging for readers. Rather than being faced with papers that were somewhat monolithic and impenetrable, they could follow the unfolding of a more detailed, critical account of the study by tracking the way in which authors responded to the views of readers. As a wholly on-line system, published material could be searched according to a wide range of key words, thus allowing connections to be made across different studies. This form of publication has the potential to be much more inclusive than traditional journals around what is published. However, a journal of this type would not only support the efforts of novice researchers, but also get the best out of expert researchers, who would be faced by a situation in which (perhaps for the first time) they could find out what colleagues really thought and felt about the research they had done.

3 *Get other people involved.* I would estimate that 99 per cent of research papers that are published on counselling and psychotherapy topics are written by people who are therapists. It is obviously a good thing that many therapists seek to be reflective practitioners, or practitioner-scientists, and want to do research. What is less good is that very little research on therapy topics is carried out by people who are not therapists. Despite the turf wars that are fought between therapists of different theoretical orientations, there is still a common professional identity and socialisation, and set of assumptions, that are distinct to therapists as a group. Research that is carried out by people from other backgrounds and disciplines has the value of taking a fresh and different look at issues and stimulating debate and further inquiry. In the field of psychiatry and mental health care, for example, there have been many crucial contributions in recent years from voices outside the profession. The research carried out by Goffman (1968a, 1968b), a sociologist, had a major impact on mental health policy and practice by drawing attention to the social role of the patient and the way that psychiatric institutions induced patients into fulfilling certain role expectations. Other social scientists have described the ways in which the prevalence of mental health issues is linked to levels of social inequality within a society, and also that the manifestation of psychological problems is shaped by cultural traditions and beliefs. Increasingly, the experiences and views of

service users are being documented by user organisations, leading to a reconceptualisation of mental health care in terms of a 'recovery' model. Each of these developments has encouraged dialogue and debate within professional arenas, and stimulated new approaches to treatment and care.

All right, I have got to the end of the book, and I am keen to carry on learning about research in therapy. What do you suggest that I should do next?

There are two main directions that I would suggest. One is to get involved in carrying out research, either in the context of a university qualification or the on-going work of a counselling or psychotherapy agency, or as a participant in a PRN. Just as books can never do justice to the lived reality of therapy, neither can they convey the reality of research. For example, it is easy to be critical and even dismissive of much research that is reported in journal articles, because any study is flawed or incomplete in one way or another. However, first-hand experience of the process of doing research tends to result in appreciation of the authentic work that has been put into any piece of research, no matter how flawed it might be. The choice of how to become directly involved in doing research depends on individual circumstances and local opportunities. My second direction can be pursued independently. I believe that one of the best ways to learn about research is to read research articles (i.e. papers that have a 'method' section). I usually advise my own students that if they read one research paper each week, then by the end of a few months they will be able to draw on a sub-stantial repertoire of knowledge about how research is done and what it can offer.

The research studies listed below have been selected on the basis of being interesting, relatively easy to read, and representative of different methodologies. This is my own list, rather than being derived from a systematic survey of 'most valued' therapy research studies – other researchers would come up with completely different lists. But at least it is a starting point. All of these items should be available through a university or public library, or some occupational libraries (e.g. NHS). Librarians are usually helpful in these matters, and are able to find any-thing, if provided with full reference details.

Borrill, J. and Foreman, E.I. (1996). Understanding cognitive change: A qualitative study of the impact of cognitive-behavioural therapy on fear of flying. *Clinical Psychology and Psychotherapy*, 3, 62–74. One of the first studies to ask clients about their experiences with CBT. An example of how qualitative research can open up new perspectives – these clients had a lot to say about the importance of their relationship with their therapist. Has led to many more qualitative studies of CBT.

Cushman, P. (1995). *Constructing the Self, Constructing America: A Cultural History of Psychotherapy*. New York: Addison-Wesley. Another study that should be essential reading on training courses. This is a historical account, based on detailed analysis of original sources, of the development and growth of psychotherapy in the USA. This is no congratulatory history of rolling back the frontiers of suffering. Instead, Cushman invites his readers to consider the social implications of therapy, and ultimately, the way that cultural values permeate their own work with clients.

Davis, K. (1986). The process of problem (re)formulation in psychotherapy. *Sociology of Illness and Health*, 8, 44–74. There have been several studies in recent years that have used a technique known as 'conversation analysis' to explore the ways in which therapists and clients use language within therapy sessions not only to convey meaning but also to exert control over each other. This is one of the first such studies to be published – it is clear, accessible and easy to read, and raises important questions about what really goes on in therapy.

Davis, S.D. (2005). Beyond technique: An autoethnographic exploration of how I learned to show love towards my father. *The Qualitative Report*, 10, 533–542. Autoethnography is a relatively new methodology (at least within the world of counselling and psychotherapy). It involves careful personal/autobiographical self-exploration as a source of insight into wider issues. So far, few autoethnographic studies have been published on therapy topics. This is a lovely example of what can be achieved.

Dreier, O. (1998). Client perspectives and uses of psychotherapy. *European Journal of Psychotherapy, Counselling and Health*, 1, 295–310. This study looks at what happens outside the therapy room, in the everyday life of the client, and generates a radical new way of thinking about therapy. If you enjoy this, you might also want to read Dreier (2000, 2008) and Mackrill (2008a).

Elliott, R., Partyka, R., Wagner, J., Alperin, R., Dobrenski, R., Messer, S.B., Watson, J.C. and Castonguay, L.G. (2009). An adjudicated Hermeneutic Single Case Efficacy Design study of experiential therapy for panic/phobia. *Psychotherapy Research*, 19, 453–457. This is the case of George, a man who had a phobia about driving across bridges. A superb example of the new genre of systematic, research-based case studies. The research team display a high level of openness to considering alternative interpretations of whether George's therapy was actually helpful for him. In doing so, they touch on profound questions around the nature of evidence in therapy research.

Kramer, U. (2009). Individualizing exposure therapy for PTSD: The case of Caroline. *Pragmatic Case Studies in Psychotherapy*, 5(2), 1–24. Available at http://hdl.rutgers.edu/1782.1/pcsp_journal. An example of a 'pragmatic' case study. This paper needs to be read alongside the accompanying commentary papers in the same issue of this (on-line) journal, which attack Kramer's flexible approach to this client on the grounds that he should have stuck to the guidelines in the treatment manual.

Kraus, D.R., Castonguay, L., Boswell, J.F., Nordberg, S.S. and Hayes, J.A. (2011). Therapist effectiveness: Implications for accountability and patient care. *Psychotherapy Research*, 21, 267–276. An example of a number-crunching study that has generated a lot of interest, and will probably continue to be debated for years to come. It offers the most detailed analysis so far of differences in effectiveness across individual therapists.

McKenna, P.A. and Todd, D.M. (1997). Longtitudinal utilization of mental health services: A time-line method, nine retrospective accounts, and a preliminary conceptualization. *Psychotherapy Research*, 7, 383–396. A neglected classic. Interviews with clients around their experiences of multiple therapy episodes over several years. A good example of how a research study can present individual case vignettes alongside general themes.

Morris, B. (2005). *Discovering Bits and Pieces of Me: Research Exploring Women's Experiences of Psychoanalytical Psychotherapy.* London: Women's Therapy Centre. Available at www.womenstherapycentre.co.uk/news/news.html. A carefully written and detailed exploration of the experience of therapy, and the way that therapy either did or did not help. An example of a qualitative study that provides a rich account of how a specific approach to therapy is received and used by clients.

Nilsson, T., Svensson, M., Sandell, R. and Clinton, D. (2007). Patients' experiences of change on cognitive behavioral therapy and psychodynamic therapy: A qualitative comparative study. *Psychotherapy Research*, 17, 553–566. Most qualitative studies look at the experiences of a single group of people (e.g. CBT clients in the Borrill and Foreman 1996 study mentioned above). The Nilsson study broke new ground by interviewing two groups of clients (psychodynamic and CBT) about how they had changed as a result of therapy, and comparing the stories that emerged. This is technically a very accomplished piece of work (state-of-the-art qualitative research) that opens the door to a whole new genre of inquiry.

Strupp, H.H. and Hadley, S.W. (1979). Specific vs nonspecific factors in psychotherapy: A controlled study of outcome. *Archives of General Psychiatry*, 36, 1125–1136. A fascinating piece of work, which should be required reading on all training courses. A randomised trial in which clients were allocated to either experienced therapists or untrained volunteer helpers. The value of the study is enhanced by the publication of a supplementary series of case studies (Strupp, 1980a, b, c and d).

References

Abram, D. (1996). *The Spell of the Sensuous: Perception and Language in a More-than-Human World.* New York: Vintage.

Addy, K.B.E. (2007). The treatment of depression and anxiety within the context of chronic obstructive pulmonary disease. *Clinical Case Studies,* 6, 383–393.

Agnew-Davies, R. (1999). Learning from research into the counselling relationship. In C. Feltham (ed.), *Understanding the Counselling Relationship.* London: Sage.

Agnew-Davies, R., Stiles, W.B., Hardy, G.E., Barkham, M. and Shapiro, D.A. (1998). Alliance structure assessed by the Agnew Relationship Measure (ARM). *British Journal of Clinical Psychology,* 37, 155–172.

Allen, M., Bromley, A., Kuyken, W. and Sonnenberg, S.J. (2009). Participants' experiences of mindfulness-based cognitive therapy: 'It changed me in just about every way possible'. *Behavioural and Cognitive Psychotherapy,* 37, 413–430.

Anderson, E. (2011). Feminist epistemology and philosophy of science. In Edward N. Zalta (ed.), *The Stanford Encyclopedia of Philosophy (Spring 2011 Edition).* Retrieved 30 January 2012 from http://plato.stanford.edu/archives/spr2011/entries/feminism-epistemology.

Anderson, R. (1998). Intuitive inquiry: A transpersonal approach. In W. Braud and R. Anderson (eds.), *Transpersonal Research Methods for the Social Sciences: Honoring Human Experience.* Thousand Oaks, CA: Sage.

Anderson, R. (2004). An epistemology of the heart for scientific inquiry. *The Humanistic Psychologist,* 32, 307–341.

Anderson, S. and Brownlie, J. (2011). Build it and they will come? Understanding public views of 'emotions talk' and the talking therapies. *British Journal of Guidance and Counselling,* 39, 53–66.

Anderson, T., Ogles, B.M., Patterson, C.L., Lambert, M.J. and Vermeersch, D.A. (2009). Therapist effects: Facilitative interpersonal skills as a predictor of therapist success. *Journal of Clinical Psychology,* 65, 755–768.

Andrews, W., Twigg, E., Minami, T. and Johnson, G. (2011). Piloting a practice research network: A 12-month evaluation of the Human Givens approach in primary care at a general medical practice. *Psychology and Psychotherapy: Theory, Research and Practice,* 84, 389–405.

Angus, L.E. and Rennie, D.L. (1988). Therapist participation in metaphor generation: collaborative and non-collaborative styles. *Psychotherapy*, 25, 552–560.

Angus, L.E. and Rennie, D.L. (1989). Envisioning the representational world: The client's experience of metaphoric expressiveness in psychotherapy. *Psychotherapy*, 26, 373–379.

Angus, L., Levitt, H. and Hardtke, K. (1999). The Narrative Process Coding System: Research applications and implications for psychotherapy practice. *Journal of Clinical Psychology*, 55, 1255–1270.

Argyrous, G. (2011). *Statistics for Research: With a Guide to SPSS*, 3rd edn. London: Sage.

Armstrong, J. (2010). How effective are minimally trained/experienced volunteer mental health counsellors? Evaluation of CORE outcome data. *Counselling and Psychotherapy Research*, 10, 22–31.

Arthern, J. and Madill, A. (1999). How do transition objects work? The therapist's view. *British Journal of Medical Psychology*, 72, 1–21.

Ashworth, M., Robinson, S., Evans, C., Shepherd, M., Conolly, A. and Rowlands, G. (2007). What does an idiographic measure (PSYCHLOPS) tell us about the spectrum of psychological issues and scores on a nomothetic measure (CORE-OM)? *Primary Care and Community Psychiatry*, 12, 7–16.

Ashworth, M., Evans, C. and Clement, S. (2009). Measuring psychological outcomes after cognitive behaviour therapy in primary care: A comparison between a new patient-generated measure, 'PSYCHLOPS' (Psychological Outcome Profiles), and 'HADS' (Hospital Anxiety Depression Scale). *Journal of Mental Health*, 18, 169–177.

Atkins, D.C., Bedics, J.D., McGlinchey, J.B. and Beauchaine, T.B. (2005). Assessing clinical significance: Does it matter which method we use? *Journal of Consulting and Clinical Psychology*, 73, 982–989.

Attkisson, C.C. and Greenfield, T.K. (1994). Client Satisfaction Questionnaire-8 and Service Satisfaction Scale-30. In M.E. Maruish (ed.), *The Use of Psychological Testing for Treatment Planning and Outcome Assessment*. Hillsdale, NJ: Lawrence Erlbaum.

Axline, V. (1950). Play therapy experiences as described by child participants. *Journal of Consulting Psychology*, 14, 53–63.

Bachelor, A. (1988). How clients perceive therapist empathy: A content analysis of 'received' empathy. *Psychotherapy*, 25: 227–240.

Bachelor, A. (1995). Clients perception of the therapeutic alliance: A qualitative analysis. *Journal of Counseling Psychology*, 42, 323–337.

Balmforth, J. (2006) Clients' experiences of how perceived differences in social class between a counsellor and client affect the therapeutic relationship. In G. Proctor, M. Cooper, P. Sanders and B. Malcolm (eds.), *Politicizing the Person-centred Approach: An Agenda for Social Change*. Ross-on-Wye: PCCS.

Barber, J.P., Luborsky, L., Crits-Christoph, P. and Diguer, L. (1995). A comparison of core conflictual relationship themes before psycho-therapy and during early sessions. *Journal of Consulting and Clinical Psychology*, 63, 145–148.

Barker, C. (1985). Interpersonal process recall in clinical training and research. In F.N. Watts (ed.), *New Developments in Clinical Psychology*. Chichester: Wiley/BPS.

Barker, C., Pistrang, N. and Elliott, R. (1994). *Research Methods in Clinical and Counselling Psychology*. Chichester: Wiley.

Barker, C., Pistrang, N. and Elliott, R. (2002). *Research Methods in Clinical Psychology: An Introduction for Students and Practitioners*, 2nd edn. Chichester: Wiley.

Barkham, M.J. and Shapiro, D.A. (1986). Counselor verbal response modes and experienced empathy. *Journal of Counseling Psychology*, 33, 3–10.

Barkham, M.J., Shapiro, D.A. and Firth-Cozens, J. (1989). Personal ques-tionnaire changes in prescriptive vs. exploratory psychotherapy. *British Journal of Clinical Psychology*, 28, 97–107.

Barkham, M.J., Stiles, W.B., Hardy, G.E. and Field, S.D. (1996). The Assimilation Model: Theory, research and practical guidelines. In W. Dryden (ed.), *Research in Counselling and Psychotherapy: Practical Applications*. London: Sage.

Barkham, M., Mellor-Clark, J., Connell, J. and Cahill, J. (2006). A core approach to practice-based evidence: A brief history of the origins and applications of the CORE-OM and CORE System. *Counselling and Psychotherapy Research*, 6, 3–15.

Barkham, M., Stiles, W.B., Connell, J., Twigg, E., Leach, C., Lucock, M., Mellor-Clark, J., Bower, P., King, M., Shapiro, D.A., Hardy, G.E., Greenberg, L.S. and Angus, L. (2008). Effects of psychological therapies in randomized trials and practice-based studies. *British Journal of Clinical Psychology*, 47, 397–415.

Barkham, M., Hardy, G.E. and Mellor-Clark, J. (eds.) (2010). *Developing and Delivering Practice-Based Evidence: A Guide for the Psychological Therapies*. Chichester: Wiley-Blackwell.

Barlow, D.H. and Hersen, M. (1986). *Single Case Experimental Designs: Strategies for Studying Behavior Change*, 2nd edn. New York: Pergamon.

Barrett-Lennard, G.T. (1979). The client-centered system unfolding. In F.J. Turner (ed.), *Social Work Treatment: Interlocking Theoretical Approaches*, 2nd edn. New York: Free Press.

Barrett-Lennard, G.T. (1981). The empathy cycle – refinement of a nuclear concept. *Journal of Counseling Psychology*, 28, 91–100.

Barrett-Lennard, G.T. (1986). The Relationship Inventory now: Issues and advances in theory, method and use. In L.S. Greenberg and W.M. Pinsof (eds.), *The Psychotherapeutic Process: A Research Handbook*. New York: Guilford Press.

Beck, A.T., Ward, C.H., Mendelson, M. et al. (1961). Inventory for measuring depression, *Archives of General Psychiatry*, 4, 561–571.

Beck, A.T., Steer, R.A. and Garbin, M.G. (1988). Psychometric properties
of the Beck Depression Inventory: Twenty-five years of evaluation.
Clinical Psychology Review, 8(1), 77–100.

Bedi, R.P., Davis, M.D. and Williams, M. (2005). Critical incidents in the
formation of the therapeutic alliance from the client's perspective.
Psychotherapy: Theory, Research, Practice, Training, 41, 311–323.

Bergin, A.E. (1963). The effects of psychotherapy: negative results revisited.
Journal of Counseling Psychology, 10, 244–250.

Berman, J.S. and Reich, C.M. (2010). Investigator allegiance and the
evaluation of psychotherapy outcome research. *European Journal of
Psychotherapy and Counselling*, 12, 11–21.

Berzon, B., Pious, C. and Farson, R.E. (1963). The therapeutic event in
group psychotherapy: a study of subjective reports by group members.
Journal of Individual Psychology, 19, 204–212.

Bevan, A., Oldfield, V.B. and Salkovskis, P.M. (2010). A qualitative study
of the acceptability of an intensive format for the delivery of cognitive-
behavioural therapy for obsessive-compulsive disorder. *British Journal
of Clinical Psychology*, 49, 173–191.

Billig, M. (1997). Freud and Dora: Repressing an oppressed identity.
Theory, Culture and Society, 14, 29–55.

Binder, J.L. and Henry, W.P. (2010). Developing skills in managing negative processes. In J.C. Muran and J.P. Barber (eds.), *The Therapeutic
Alliance: An Evidence-Based Approach to Practice*. New York: Guilford Press.

Bjelland, I., Dahl, A.A., Haug, T.T. et al. (2002). The validity of the
Hospital Anxiety and Depression Scale: an updated literature review.
Journal of Psychosomatic Research, 52, 69–77.

Blackburn, S. (1999). *Think: A Compelling Introduction to Philosophy*.
Oxford: Oxford University Press.

Bloch, S., Reibstein, J., Crouch, E., Holroyd, P. and Themen, J. (1979). A
method for the study of therapeutic factors in group psychotherapy.
British Journal of Psychiatry, 134, 257–263.

Bohart, A.C. and Greenberg, L.S. (eds.) (1997). *Empathy Reconsidered: New
Directions in Psychotherapy*. Washington, DC: American Psychological
Association.

Bohart, A.C. and Tallman, K. (2010). Clients as active self-healers:
Implications for the person-centered approach. In M. Cooper, J.C. Watson
and D. Holldampf (eds.), *Person-centered and Experiential Therapies Work: A
Review of the Research on Counseling, Psychotherapy and Related Practices*.
Ross-on-Wye: PCCS.

Bordin, E.S. (1979). The generalizability of the psychoanalytic concept
of working alliance. *Psychotherapy: Theory, Research and Practice*, 16,
252–260.

Borenstein, M., Hedges, L.V., Higgins, J.P.T. and Rothstein, H.R. (2009). *Introduction to Meta-analysis*. Oxford: Wiley-Blackwell.

Borrill, J. and Foreman, E.I. (1996). Understanding cognitive change: A qualitative study of the impact of cognitive-behavioural therapy on fear of flying. *Clinical Psychology and Psychotherapy*, 3, 62–74.

Brannen, J. and Collard, J. (1982). *Marriages in Trouble: The Process of Seeking Help*. London: Tavistock.

Branthwaite, A. and Lunn, T. (1983). Projective techniques in social and market research. In R. Walker (ed.), *Applied Qualitative Research*. Aldershot: Gower.

Braud, W. (1998). Integral inquiry: complementary ways of knowing, being and expression. In W. Braud and R. Anderson (eds.), *Transpersonal Research Methods for the Social Sciences: Honoring Human Experience*. Thousand Oaks, CA: Sage.

Braud, W. and Anderson, R. (eds.) (1998). *Transpersonal Research Methods for the Social Sciences: Honoring Human Experience*. Thousand Oaks, CA: Sage.

Brinegar, M.G., Salvi, L.M., Stiles, W.B. and Greenberg, L.S. (2006) Building a meaning bridge: Therapeutic progress from problem formulation to understanding. *Journal of Counseling Psychology*, 53, 165–180.

Brown, J.B. (ed.) (2012). *Philosophy of Science: The Key Thinkers*. New York: Continuum.

Brown, W. and Kandirikirira, N. (2007). *Recovering Mental Health in Scotland: Report on a Narrative Investigation of Mental Health Recovery*. Glasgow: Scottish Recovery Network.

Bruner, J. (1986). *Actual Minds, Possible Worlds*. Cambridge, MA: Harvard University Press.

Buckroyd, J. and Rother, S. (eds.) (2008). *Psychological Responses to Eating Disorders and Obesity: Recent and Innovative Work*. New York: Wiley-Blackwell.

Budge, S., Baardseth, T.P., Wampold, B.E. and Flückiger, C. (2010). Researcher allegiance and supportive therapy: Pernicious affects on results of randomized clinical trials. *European Journal of Psychotherapy and Health*, 12(1), 23–39.

Cahill, J., Barkham, M. and Stiles, W.B. (2010). Systematic review of practice-based research on psychological therapies in routine clinic settings. *British Journal of Clinical Psychology*, 49, 421–453.

Cahill, J., Stiles, W.B., Barkham, M., Hardy, G.E., Stone, G., Agnew-Davies, R. and Unsworth, G. (2012). Two short forms of the Agnew Relationship Measure: The ARM-5 and ARM-12. *Psychotherapy Research*, 22, 241–255.

Cain, D.J. and Seeman, J. (eds.) (2002). *Humanistic Psychotherapies: Handbook of Research and Practice*. Washington, DC: American Psychological Association.

Callahan, J.L. and Hynan, M.T. (2005). Models of psychotherapy outcome: Are they applicable in training clinics? *Psychological Services*, 2, 65–69.

Cartwright, D.S. (1957). Annotated bibliography of research and theory construction in client-centered therapy. *Journal of Counseling Psychology*, 4, 82–100.

Castonguay, L.G., Muran, J.C., Angus, L., Hayes, J.A., Ladany, N. and Anderson, T. (eds.) (2010a). *Bringing Psychotherapy Research to Life: Understanding Change Through the Work of Leading Clinical Researchers*. Washington, DC: American Psychological Association.

Castonguay, L.G., Nelson, D.L., Boutselis, M.A., Chiswick, N.R., Damer, D.D., Hemmelstein, N.A., Jackson, J.S., Morford, M., Ragusea, S.A., Roper, J.G., Spayd, C., Weiszer, T. and Borkovec, T.D. (2010b). Psychotherapists, researchers, or both? A qualitative analysis of psychotherapists' experiences in a practice research network. *Psychotherapy: Theory, Research, Practice, Training*, 47, 345–354.

Challacombe, F.L. and Salkovskis, P.M. (2011). Intensive cognitive-behavioural treatment for women with postnatal obsessive-compulsive disorder: A consecutive case series. *Behaviour Research and Therapy*, 49, 422–426.

Christodoulides, T., Dudley, R., Brown, S., Turkington, D. and Beck, A.T. (2008). Cognitive behaviour therapy in patients with schizophrenia who are not prescribed antipsychotic medication: A case series. *Psychology and Psychotherapy: Theory, Research and Practice*, 81, 199–207.

Clark, D.M., Fairburn, C.G. and Wessely, S. (2008) Psychological treatment outcomes in routine NHS services: A commentary on Stiles et al. (2007). *Psychological Medicine*, 38, 629–634.

Clark-Carter, D. (2009). *Quantitative Psychological Research*, 3rd edn. New York: Psychology Press.

Cohen, J. (1988). *Statistical Power Analysis for the Behavioural Sciences*, 2nd edn. Hillsdale, NJ: Lawrence Erlbaum.

Cohen, S., Kamarck, T., and Mermelstein, R. (1983). A global measure of perceived stress. *Journal of Health and Social Behavior*, 24, 386–396.

Combs, A.W. (1986). What makes a good helper? A person-centered approach. *Person-Centered Review*, 1, 51–61.

Comtois, K.A. and Linehan, M.M. (2006). Psychosocial treatments of suicidal behaviors: A practice-friendly review. *Journal of Clinical Psychology*, 62, 161–170.

Concato, J., Shah, N. and Horwitz, R.I. (2000). Randomized, controlled trials, observational studies, and the hierarchy of research designs. *New England Journal of Medicine*, 342, 1887–1892.

Cook, J.M., Biyanova, T., Elhai, J. and Schnurr, P.P. (2010). What do psychotherapists really do in practice? An internet study of over 2,000 practitioners. *Psychotherapy Theory, Research, Practice, Training*, 47, 260–267.

Coolidge, F.L. (2012). *Statistics: A Gentle Introduction*, 3rd edn. Thousand Oaks, CA: Sage.

Cooper, M. (2005). Therapists' experiences of relational depth: A qualitative interview study. *Counselling and Psychotherapy Research*, 5, 87–95.

Cooper, M. (2008). *Essential Research Findings in Counselling and Psychotherapy: The Facts Are Friendly.* London: Sage.

Cooper, M. and McLeod, J. (2011). *Pluralistic Counselling and Psychotherapy.* London: Sage.

Cooper, M., Watson, J.C. and Holldampf, D. (eds.) (2010). *Person-centered and Experiential Therapies Work: A Review of the Research on Counseling, Psychotherapy and Related Practices.* Ross-on-Wye: PCCS.

Cornelius, E.T., III (1983). The use of projective techniques in personnel selection. In K. Rowland and G. Ferris (eds.), *Research in Personnel and Human Resources Management*, Vol. 1. London: JAI Press.

Cornforth, S. (2011). Ethics for research and publication. In K. Crocket, M. Agee and S. Cornforth (eds.), *Ethics in Practice: A Guide for Counsellors.* Wellington, NZ: Dunmore.

Craig, P., Dieppe, P., Macintyre, S., Michie, S., Nazareth, I. and Petticrew, M. (2008). *Developing and Evaluating Complex Interventions: New Guidance.* London: Medical Research Council. Available at www.mrc.ac.uk/complex interventionsguidance.

Cramer, D. (1992). *Personality and Psychotherapy: Theory, Practice and Research.* Maidenhead: Open University Press.

Crits-Christoph, P., Cooper, A. and Luborsky, L. (1988). The accuracy of therapists' interpretations and the outcome of dynamic psychotherapy. *Journal of Consulting and Clinical Psychology*, 56, 490–495.

Crits-Christoph, P., Crits-Christoph, K. and Connolly Gibbons, M.B. (2010). Training in alliance-fostering techniques. In J.C. Muran and J.P. Barber (eds.), *The Therapeutic Alliance: An Evidence-Based Approach to Practice.* New York: Guilford Press.

Cuijpers, P., Andersson, G., Donker, T. and van Straten, A. (2011). Psychological treatment of depression: Results of a series of meta-analyses. *Nordic Journal of Psychiatry*, 65, 354–364.

Curtis, J.T., Weiss, J., Silberschatz, G., Sampson, H. and Rosenberg, S.E. (1988). Developing reliable psychodynamic case formulations: An illustration of the plan diagnosis method. *Psychotherapy*, 25, 256–265.

Cushman, P. (1995). *Constructing the Self, Constructing America: A Cultural History of Psychotherapy*. New York: Addison-Wesley.

Dale, P., Allen, J. and Measor, L. (1998). Counselling adults who were abused as children: Clients' perceptions of efficacy, client–counsellor communication, and dissatisfaction. *British Journal of Guidance and Counselling*, 26, 141–158.

Dalenberg, C.J. (2004). Maintaining the safe and effective therapeutic relationship in the context of distrust and anger: Countertransference and complex trauma. *Psychotherapy: Theory, Research, Practice, Training*, 41, 438–447.

Daniel, T. and McLeod, J. (2006). Weighing up the evidence: A qualitative analysis of how person-centred counsellors evaluate the effectiveness of their practice. *Counselling and Psychotherapy Research*, 6, 244–249.

Davidson, L., Harding, C. and Spaniol, L. (eds.) (2005). *Recovery from Severe Mental Illnesses: Research Evidence and Implications for Practice*, Volume 1. Boston, MA: Boston University Center for Psychiatric Rehabilitation.

Davidson, L., Harding, C. and Spaniol, L. (eds.) (2006). *Recovery from Severe Mental Illnesses: Research Evidence and Implications for Practice*, Volume 2. Boston, MA: Boston University Center for Psychiatric Rehabilitation.

Davis, K. (1986). The process of problem (re)formulation in psychotherapy. *Sociology of Illness and Health*, 8, 44–74.

Davis, S.D. (2005). Beyond technique: An autoethnographic exploration of how I learned to show love towards my father. *The Qualitative Report*, 10, 533–542.

Deane, F.P., Spicer, J. and Todd, D.M. (1997). Validity of a simplified target complaints measure. *Assessment*, 4, 119–130.

Denker, P.G. (1937). Prognosis and life expectancy in the psychoneuroses. *Proceedings of the Association of Life Insurance Medical Directors of America*, 24, 179.

Denzin, N.K. and Lincoln, Y.S. (eds.) (2011). *The Sage Handbook of Qualitative Research*, 4th edn. Thousand Oaks, CA: Sage.

Dersch, C.A., Shumway, S.T., Harris, S.M. and Arredondo, R. (2002). A new comprehensive measure of EAP satisfaction: A factor analysis. *Employee Assistance Quarterly*, 17, 55–60.

Dreier, O. (1998). Client perspectives and uses of psychotherapy. *European Journal of Psychotherapy, Counselling and Health*, 1, 295–310.

Dreier, O. (2000). Psychotherapy in clients' trajectories across contexts. In C. Mattingly and L. Garro (eds.) *Narratives and the Cultural Construction of Illness and Healing*. Berkeley, CA: University of California Press.

Dreier, O. (2008). *Psychotherapy in Everyday Life*. Cambridge: Cambridge University Press.

Duncan, B.L., Miller, S.D., Sparks, J.A., Claud, D.A., Reynolds, L.R., Brown, J. and Johnson, L.D. (2003). The Session Rating Scale: Preliminary psychometric properties of a 'working' alliance measure. *Journal of Brief Therapy*, 3, 3–12.

Eames, V. and Roth, A. (2000). Patient attachment orientation and the early working alliance: A study of patient and therapist reports of alliance quality and ruptures. *Psychotherapy Research*, 10, 421–434.

Egan, S.J. and Hine, P. (2008). Cognitive behavioural treatment of perfectionism: A single case experimental design series. *Behaviour Change*, 25, 245–258.

Eisenstein, C. (2007). *The Ascent of Humanity.* Harrisburg, PA: Panenthea Press.

Elkin, I. (1994). The NIMH Treatment of Depression Collaborative Research Program: Where we began and where we are. In A.E. Bergin and S.L. Garfield (eds.), *Handbook of Psychotherapy and Behavior Change,* 4th edn. Chichester: Wiley.

Elkin, I., Parloff, M.B., Hadley, S.W. and Autry, J.H. (1985). NIMH Treatment of Depression Collaborative Research Program: Background and research plan. *Archives of General Psychiatry,* 42(3), 305–316.

Elkin, I., Shea, M.T., Watkins, J.T., Imber, S.D., Sotsky, S.D., Collins, J.F., Glass, D.R., Pilkonis, P.A., Leber, W.R., Docherty, J.P., Fiester, S.J. and Parloff, M.B. (1989). National Institute of Mental Health Treatment of Depression Collaborative Research Program: General effectiveness of treatments. *Archives of General Psychiatry,* 46, 971–982.

Elliott, R. (1983). 'That in your hands . . .': A comprehensive process analysis of a significant event in psychotherapy. *Psychiatry,* 46, 113–29.

Elliott, R. (1984). A discovery-oriented approach to significant change events in psychotherapy: Interpersonal Process Recall and Comprehensive Process Analysis. In L.N. Rice and L.S. Greenberg (eds.), *Patterns of Change: Intensive Analysis of Psychotherapy Process.* New York: Guilford Press.

Elliott, R. (1986). Interpersonal Process Recall (IPR) as a psychotherapy process research method. In L.S. Greenberg and W.M. Pinsof (eds.), *The Psychotherapeutic Process: A Research Handbook.* New York: Guilford Press.

Elliott, R. (1991). Five dimensions of therapy process. *Psychotherapy Research,* 1, 92–103.

Elliott, R. (1999). Editor's introduction to special issue on qualitative psychotherapy research: Definitions, themes and discoveries. *Psychotherapy Research,* 9, 251–257.

Elliott, R. (2001). Hermeneutic single-case efficacy design: An overview. In K.J. Schneider, J. Bugental and J.F. Pierson (eds.), *The Handbook of Humanistic Psychology: Leading Edges in Theory, Research and Practice.* Thousand Oaks, CA: Sage.

Elliott, R. (2002a). Hermeneutic single case efficacy design. *Psychotherapy Research,* 12, 1–20.

Elliott, R. (2002b). The effectiveness of humanistic therapies: A meta-analysis. In D.J. Cain and J. Seeman (eds.), *Humanistic Psychotherapies: Handbook of Research and Practice.* Washington, DC: American Psychological Association.

Elliott, R. and Farber, B.A. (2010). Carl Rogers: Idealist, pragmatist and psychotherapy research pioneer. In L.G. Castonguay, J.C. Muran, L. Angus, J.A. Hayes, N. Ladany and T. Anderson (eds.), *Bringing Psychotherapy Research to Life: Understanding Change Through the*

Work of Leading Clinical Researchers. Washington, DC: American Psychological Association.

Elliott, R. and Shapiro, D.A. (1988). Brief Structured Recall: A more efficient method for studying significant therapy events. *British Journal of Medical Psychology*, 61, 141–153.

Elliott, R. and Shapiro, D.A. (1992). Client and therapist as analysts of significant events. In S.G. Toukmanian and D.L. Rennie (eds.), *Psychotherapy Process Research: Paradigmatic and Narrative Approaches*. London: Sage.

Elliott, R. and Zucconi, A. (2010). Organizational and conceptual framework for practice-based research on the effectiveness of psychotherapy and psychotherapy training. In M. Barkham, G.E. Hardy and J. Mellor-Clark (eds.), *Developing and Delivering Practice-based Evidence: A Guide for the Psychological Therapies*. Chichester: Wiley-Blackwell.

Elliott, R., Barker, C.B., Caskey, N. and Pistrang, N. (1982). Differential helpfulness of counselor verbal response modes. *Journal of Counseling Psychology*, 29, 354–361.

Elliott, R., Hill, C.E., Stiles, W.B., Friedlander, M.L., Mahrer, A.R. and Margison, F.R. (1987). Primary therapist response modes: Comparison of six rating systems. *Journal of Consulting and Clinical Psychology*, 55, 223–228.

Elliott, R., Fischer, C.T. and Rennie, D.L. (1999). Evolving guidelines for the publication of qualitative research studies in psychology and related fields. *British Journal of Clinical Psychology*, 38, 215–229.

Elliott, R., Slatick, E. and Urman, M. (2001). Qualitative change process research on psychotherapy: Alternative strategies. *Psychologische Beiträge*, 43, 69–111.

Elliott, R., Partyka, R., Wagner, J., Alperin, R., Dobrenski, R., Messer, S.B., Watson, J.C. and Castonguay, L.G. (2009). An adjudicated Hermeneutic Single Case Efficacy Design study of experiential therapy for panic/phobia. *Psychotherapy Research*, 19, 453–457.

Elliott, R., Greenberg, L.S., Watson, J., Timulak, L. and Freire, E. (2012). Research on experiential psychotherapies. In M.J. Lambert (ed.), *Bergin and Garfield's Handbook of Psychotherapy and Behavior Change*, 6th edn. New York: Wiley.

Ellis, C. and Bochner, A.P. (2000). Auto-ethnography, personal narrative, reflexivity: Researcher as subject. In N.K. Denzin and Y.S. Lincoln (eds.), *Handbook of Qualitative Research*, 2nd edn. Thousand Oaks, CA: Sage.

Ellis, C. and Flaherty, M. (eds.) (1992). *Investigating Subjectivity: Research on Lived Experience*. Thousand Oaks, CA: Sage.

Ellis, C., Kiesinger, C.E. and Tillmann-Healy, L.M. (1997). Interactive interviewing: Talking about emotional experience. In R. Hertz (ed.), *Reflexivity and Voice*. Thousand Oaks, CA: Sage.

Ellis, P.D. (2010). *The Essential Guide to Effect Sizes: Statistical Power, Meta-Analysis, and the Interpretation of Research Results*. Cambridge: Cambridge University Press.

Etherington, K. (1996). The counsellor as researcher: Boundary issues and critical dilemmas. *British Journal of Guidance and Counselling*, 24, 339–346.

Etherington, K. (ed.) (2003). *Trauma, the Body and Transformation: A Narrative Inquiry*. London: Jessica Kingsley.

Etherington, K. and Bridges, N. (2011). Narrative case study research: On endings and six session reviews. *Counselling and Psychotherapy Research*, 11(1), 11–22.

Eubanks-Carter, C., Muran, J.C. and Safran, J.D. (2010). Alliance ruptures and resolution. In J.C. Muran and J.P. Barber (eds.), *The Therapeutic Alliance: An Evidence-based Approach to Practice*. New York: Guilford Press.

Evans, I.M. and Robinson, C.H. (1978). Behavior therapy observed: The diary of a client. *Cognitive Therapy and Research*, 2, 335–355.

Eysenck, H.J. (1952). The effects of psychotherapy: An evaluation. *Journal of Consulting Psychology*, 16, 319–324.

Eysenck, H.J. (1960). The effects of psychotherapy. In H.J. Eysenck (ed.), *Handbook of Abnormal Psychology*. New York: Basic Books.

Eysenck, H.J. (1965). The effects of psychotherapy. *International Journal of Psychiatry*, 1, 97–178.

Eysenck, H.J. (1992). The outcome problem in psychotherapy. In W. Dryden and C. Feltham (eds.), *Psychotherapy and its Discontents*. Maidenhead: Open University Press.

Farber, B.A. (2006). *Self-disclosure in Psychotherapy*. New York: Guilford Press.

Farsimadan, F., Draghi-Lorenz, R. and Ellis, J. (2007). Process and outcome of therapy in ethnically similar and dissimilar therapeutic dyads. *Psychotherapy Research*, 17, 567–575.

Farsimadan, F., Khan, A. and Draghi-Lorenz, R. (2011). On ethnic matching: A review of the research and considerations for practice, training and policy. In C. Lago (ed.), *The Handbook of Transcultural Counselling and Psychotherapy*. Maidenhead: Open University Press.

Feyerabend, P. (2010). *Against Method*, 4th edn. New York: Verso.

Fidler, F., Cumming, G., Thomason, N., Pannuzzo, D., Smith, J., Fyffe, P., Edmonds, H., Harrington, C. and Schmitt, R. (2005). Toward improved statistical reporting in the *Journal of Consulting and Clinical Psychology*. *Journal of Consulting and Clinical Psychology*, 73, 136–143.

Field, A. (2009). *Discovering Statistics Using SPSS*, 3rd edn. London: Sage.

Finlay, L. (2006). The body's disclosure in phenomenological research. *Qualitative Research in Psychology*, 3, 19–30.

Finlay, L. (2008). A dance between the reduction and reflexivity: Explicating the 'phenomenological psychological attitude'. *Journal of Phenomenological Psychology*, 39, 1–32.

Finlay, L. and Evans, K. (eds.) (2009). *Relational-centred Research for Psychotherapists: Exploring Meanings and Experiences.* Chichester: Wiley-Blackwell.

Finlay, L. and Gough, B. (eds.) (2003). *Reflexivity: A Practical Guide for Researchers in Health and Social Sciences.* Oxford: Blackwell.

Fischer, C.T. (2006). *Qualitative Research Methods for Psychologists: Introduction Through Empirical Case Studies.* San Diego, CA: Academic Press.

Fishman, D.B. (1999). *The Case for a Pragmatic Psychology.* New York: New York Universities Press.

Fishman, D.B. (2011). Another strategy for critically evaluating case studies: Introduction to an issue on the adjudicated case study method. *Pragmatic Case Studies in Psychotherapy*, 7(1), 1–5.

Fitts, W. (1965). *The Experience of Psychotherapy: What it's Like for Client and Therapist.* Princeton, NJ: Van Nostrand.

Fletcher, J., Fahey, T. and McWilliam, J. (1995). Relationship between the provision of counselling and the prescribing of antidepressants, hypnotics and anxiolytics in general practice. *British Journal of General Practice*, 45, 467–469.

Fluckiger, C. and Holtforth, M.G. (2008). Focusing the therapist's attention on the patient's strengths: A preliminary study to foster a mechanism of change in outpatient psychotherapy. *Journal of Clinical Psychology*, 64, 876–890.

Flyvbjerg, B. (2001). *Making Social Science Matter: Why Social Inquiry Fails and How It Can Succeed Again.* New York: Cambridge University Press.

Fonagy, P. (1999). Achieving evidence-based psychotherapy practice: A psychodynamic perspective on the general acceptance of treatment manuals. *Clinical Psychology: Science and Practice*, 6, 442–444.

Frommer, J. and Rennie, D.L. (eds.) (2000). *Qualitative Psychotherapy Research: Methods and Methodology.* Lengerich, Germany: Pabst.

Gabbay, J. and le May, A. (2010). *Practice-based Evidence for Healthcare: Clinical Mindlines.* London: Routledge.

Gabriel, L. (2005). *Speaking the Unspeakable: The Ethics of Dual Relationships in Counselling and Psychotherapy.* London: Routledge.

Gallagher, M., Tracey, A. and Millar, R. (2005). Ex-clients' evaluation of bereavement counselling in a voluntary sector agency. *Psychology and Psychotherapy: Theory, Research and Practice*, 78, 59–76.

Geertz, C. (1973). *The Interpretation of Culture: Selected Essays.* New York: Basic Books.

Geller, S.M. and Greenberg, L.S. (2002). Therapeutic presence: Therapists' experience of presence in the psychotherapeutic encounter. *Person-Centered & Experiential Psychotherapies*, 1, 71–86.

Geller, S.M., Greenberg, L.S. and Watson, J.C. (2010). Therapist and client perceptions of therapeutic presence: The development of a measure. *Psychotherapy Research*, 20, 599–610.

Gibbard, I. and Hanley, T. (2008). A five-year evaluation of the effectiveness of person-centred counselling in routine clinical practice in primary care. *Counselling and Psychotherapy Research*, 8, 215–222.

Gladwell, M. (2006). *Blink: The Power of Thinking Without Thinking*. New York: Penguin.

Glasman, D., Finlay, W.M.L. and Brock, D. (2004). Becoming a self-therapist: Using cognitive-behavioural therapy for recurrent depression and/or dysthymia after completing therapy. *Psychology and Psychotherapy: Theory, Research and Practice*, 77, 335–351.

Goffman, E. (1968a). *Asylums: Essays on the Social Situation of Mental Patients and Other Inmates*. Harmondsworth: Penguin.

Goffman, E. (1968b). *Stigma*. Harmondsworth: Penguin.

Grafanaki, S. (1996). How research can change the researcher: The need for sensitivity, flexibility and ethical boundaries in conducting qualitative research in counselling/psychotherapy. *British Journal of Guidance and Counselling*, 24, 329–338.

Grafanaki, S. (2001). What counselling research has taught us about the concept of congruence: Main discoveries and unresolved issues. In G. Wyatt (ed.), *Rogers' Therapeutic Conditions: Evolution, Theory and Practice. Volume 1: Congruence*. Ross-on-Wye: PCCS Books.

Greenberg, G. (2011). *Manufacturing Depression: The Secret History of a Modern Disease*. London: Bloomsbury.

Greenberg, L.S. (1984). Task analysis: The general approach. In L.N. Rice and L.S. Greenberg (eds.), *Patterns of Change: Intensive Analysis of Psychotherapy Process*. New York: Guilford Press.

Greenberg, L.S. (1992). Task analysis: Identifying components of interpersonal conflict resolution. In S.G. Toukmanian and D.L. Rennie (eds.), *Psychotherapy Process Research: Paradigmatic and Narrative Approaches*. London: Sage.

Greenberg, L.S. and Pascual-Leone, A. (2006). Emotion in psychotherapy: A practice-friendly research review. *Journal of Clinical Psychology*, 62, 611–630.

Greenberg, L.S. and Pinsof, W.M. (eds.) (1986). *The Psychotherapeutic Process: A Research Handbook*. New York: Guilford Press.

Greenberg, L.S., Rice, L.N. and Elliott, R. (1993). *Facilitating Emotional Change: The Moment-by-Moment Process*. New York: Guilford Press.

Greenberg, L.S., Watson, J.C. and Lietaer, G. (eds.) (1998). *Handbook of Experiential Psychotherapy: Foundations and Differential Treatment*. New York: Guilford Press.

Greenhalgh, T. (2006). *How to Read a Paper: The Basis of Evidence-based Medicine,* 3rd edn. Oxford: Wiley-Blackwell.

Guthrie, E., Moorey, J., Margison, F., Barker, H., Palmer, S., McGrath, G., Tomenson, B. and Creed, F. (1999). Cost-effectiveness of brief psychodynamic-interpersonal therapy in high utilizers of psychiatric services. *Archives of General Psychiatry*, 56, 519–526.

Gyani, A., Shafran, R., Layard, R. and Clark, D.M. (2011). *Enhancing Recovery Rates in IAPT Services: Lessons from Analysis of the Year One Data*. London: NHS. Available at www.iapt.nhs.uk/silo/files/enhancing-recovery-rates–iapt-year-one-report.pdf.

Hannan, C., Lambert, M.J., Harmon, C., Nielsen, S.L, Smart, D.W., Shimokawa, K. and Sutton, S.W. (2005). A lab test and algorithms for identifying clients at risk for treatment failure. *Journal of Clinical Psychology*, 61, 155–163.

Hansen, S. and Rapley, M. (2008) Editorial: Special Issue of *Qualitative Research in Psychology* on 'Teaching Qualitative Methods'. *Qualitative Research in Psychology*, 5, 171–172.

Hardy, G. (1995). Organisational issues: Making research happen. In M. Aveline and D.A. Shapiro (eds.), *Research Foundations for Psychotherapy Practice*. Chichester: Wiley.

Hardy, G., Rees, A., Barkham, M., Field, S.D., Elliott, R. and Shapiro, D.A. (1998). Whingeing versus working: Comprehensive process analysis of a 'vague awareness' event in psychodynamic-interpersonal therapy. *Psychotherapy Research*, 8, 334–353.

Hatcher, R.L. (2010). Alliance theory and measurement. In J.C. Muran and J.P. Barber (eds.), *The Therapeutic Alliance: An Evidence-based Approach to Practice*. New York: Guilford Press.

Hatcher, R.L. and Gillaspy, J.A. (2006). Development and validation of a revised short form of the Working Alliance Inventory. *Psychotherapy Research*, 16, 12–25.

Hatfield, D., McCullough, L., Frantz, S.H.B. and Krieger, K. (2010). Do we know when our clients get worse? An investigation of therapists' ability to detect negative client change. *Clinical Psychology and Psychotherapy*, 17, 25–32.

Healy, D. (1999). *The Antidepressant Era*. Cambridge, MA: Harvard University Press.

Healy, D. (2006). *Let Them Eat Prozac: The Unhealthy Relationship Between the Pharmaceutical Industry and Depression*. New York: New York University Press.

Hersoug, A.G., Høglend, P., Havik, J., von der Lippe, A. and Monsen, J. (2009). Therapist characteristics influencing the quality of alliance in long-term psychotherapy. *Clinical Psychology and Psychotherapy*, 16, 100–110.

Hesse, E. (1999). The Adult Attachment Interview: Historical and current perspectives. In J. Cassidy and P.R. Shaver (eds.), *Handbook of Attachment: Theory, Research and Clinical Applications*. New York: Guilford Press.

Higgins, J.P.T. and Green, S. (eds.) (2008). *Cochrane Handbook for Systematic Reviews of Interventions*. Oxford: Wiley-Blackwell.

Hill, C.E. (1986). An overview of the Hill Counselor and Client Verbal Response Modes Category Systems. In L.S. Greenberg and W.M. Pinsof (eds.), *The Psychotherapeutic Process: A Research Handbook*. New York: Guilford Press.

Hill, C.E. (1989). *Therapist Techniques and Client Outcomes: Eight Cases of Brief Psychotherapy*. London: Sage.

Hill, C.E. (1991). Almost everything you ever wanted to know about how to do process research on counseling and psychotherapy but didn't know who to ask. In C.E. Watkins and L.J. Schneider (eds.), *Research in Counseling*. Hillsdale, NJ: Lawrence Erlbaum.

Hill, C.E. (ed.) (2012). *Consensual Qualitative Research: A Practical Resource for Investigating Social Science Phenomena*. Washington, DC: American Psychological Association.

Hill, C.E. and Corbett, M.M. (1993). A perspective on the history of process and outcome research in counseling psychology. *Journal of Counseling Psychology*, 40, 3–24.

Hill, C.E. and Knox, S. (2001). Self-disclosure. *Psychotherapy: Theory, Research, Practice, Training*, 38, 413–425.

Hill, C.E. and O'Grady, K.E. (1985) List of therapist intentions illustrated by a case study and with therapists of varying theoretical orientations. *Journal of Counseling Psychology*, 32, 3–22.

Hill, C.E., Helms, J.E., Tichenor, V., Spiegel, S.B., O'Grady, K.E. and Perry, E.S. (1988). Effects of therapist response modes in brief psychotherapy. *Journal of Counseling Psychology*, 35, 222–233.

Hill, C.E., Sim, W.E., Spangler, P., Stahl, J., Sullivan, T. and Teyber, E. (2008). Therapist immediacy in brief psychotherapy: Case Study 2. *Psychotherapy: Theory, Research, Practice, Training*, 45(3), 298–315.

Hill, C.E., Knox, S. and Hess, S.A. (2012). Qualitative meta-analysis of consensual qualitative research studies. In C.E. Hill (ed.), *Consensual Qualitative Research: A Practical Resource for Investigating Social Science Phenomena*. Washington, DC: American Psychological Association.

Honos-Webb, L., Stiles, W.B., Greenberg, L.S. and Goldman, R. (1998). Assimilation analysis of process-experiential psychotherapy: A comparison of two cases. *Psychotherapy Research*, 8, 264–286.

Honos-Webb, L., Surko, M., Stiles, W.B. and Greenberg, L.S. (1999). Assimilation of voices in psychotherapy: The case of Jan. *Journal of Counseling Psychology*, 46, 448–460.

Honos-Webb, L., Stiles, W.B., Greenberg, L.S. and Goldman, R. (2006). An assimilation analysis of psychotherapy: Responsibility for 'being there'. In C.T. Fischer (ed.), *Qualitative Research Methods for Psychologists: Introduction Through Empirical Studies*. New York: Academic Press.

Horvath, A.O. and Greenberg, L.S. (1986). Development of the Working Alliance Inventory. In L.S. Greenberg and W.M. Pinsof (eds.), *The Psychotherapeutic Process: A Research Handbook*. New York: Guilford Press.

Horvath, A.O. and Greenberg, L.S. (1989). Development and validation of the Working Alliance Inventory. *Journal of Counseling Psychology*, 36, 223–233.

Hoshmand, L.T. and Martin, J. (eds.) (1995). *Research as Praxis: Lessons from Programmatic Research in Therapeutic Psychology*. New York: Teachers College Press.

Howard, G.S. (1983). Toward methodological pluralism. *Journal of Counseling Psychology*, 30, 19–21.

Howe, D. (1989). *The Consumer's View of Family Therapy*. Aldershot: Gower.

Howe, D. (1996). Client experiences of counselling and treatment interventions: A qualitative study of family views of family therapy. *British Journal of Guidance and Counselling*, 24, 367–376.

Jacobson, N.S. and Revenstorf, D. (1988). Statistics for assessing the clinical significance of psychotherapy techniques: Issues, problems and new developments. *Behavioral Assessment*, 10, 133–145.

Jacobson, N.S., Follette, W.C. and Revenstorf, D. (1984). Psychotherapy outcome research: Methods for reporting variability and evaluating clinical significance. *Behavior Therapy*, 15, 336–352.

Jennings, L. and Skovholt, T.M. (1999). The cognitive, emotional and relational characteristics of master therapists. *Journal of Counseling Psychology*, 48, 3–11.

Jones, E.E. and Pulos, S.M. (1993). Comparing the process in psychodynamic and cognitive-behavioral therapies. *Journal of Consulting and Clinical Psychology*, 61, 306–316.

Jones, P. (1975). *Philosophy and the Novel*. Oxford: Clarendon Press.

Josselson, R. (ed.) (1996). *Ethics and Process in the Narrative Study of Lives*. Thousand Oaks, CA: Sage.

Josselson, R., Lieblich, A. and McAdams, D.P. (eds.) (2003). *Up Close and Personal: The Teaching and Learning of Narrative Research*. Washington, DC: American Psychological Association.

Kagan, N. (1980). Influencing human interaction: 18 years with IPR. In A.K. Hess (ed.), *Psychotherapy Supervision: Theory, Research and Practice*. Chichester: Wiley.

Kagan, N. (1984). Interpersonal Process Recall: Basic methods and recent research. In D. Larsen (ed.), *Teaching Psychological Skills*. Monterey, CA: Brooks/Cole.

Kagan, N., Krathwohl, D.R. and Miller, R. (1963). Stimulated recall in therapy using videotape – a case study. *Journal of Counseling Psychology*, 10, 237–243.

Kasper, L.B., Hill, C.E. and Kivlighan, D.E. (2008). Therapist immediacy in brief psychotherapy: Case Study 1. *Psychotherapy: Theory, Research, Practice, Training*, 45(3), 281–297.

Kincheloe, J.L. and McLaren, P. (2008). Rethinking critical theory and qualitative research. In N.K. Denzin and Y.S. Lincoln (eds.), *The Landscape of Qualitative Research*, 3rd edn. Thousand Oaks, CA: Sage.

King, A. (2011). When the body speaks: Tummy rumblings in the therapeutic encounter. *British Journal of Psychotherapy*, 27, 156–174.

Kitchener, K.S. (1984). Intuition, critical evaluation and ethical principles: The foundation for ethical decisions in counseling psychology. *Counseling Psychologist*, 12, 43–55.

Kivlighan, D.M., Patton, M.J. and Foote, D. (1998). Moderating effects of client attachment on the counselor experience-working alliance relationship. *Journal of Counseling Psychology*, 45, 274–278.

Klein, M.J. and Elliott, R. (2006). Client accounts of personal change in process-experiential psychotherapy: A methodologically pluralistic approach. *Psychotherapy Research*, 16, 91–105.

Klein, M.H., Greist, J.H., Gurman, A.S., Neimeyer, R.A., Lesser, D.P., Bushnell, N.J. and Smith, R.E. (1985). A comparative outcome study of group psychotherapy vs. exercise treatments for depression. *International Journal of Mental Health*, 13, 148–176.

Klein, M.H., Mathieu-Coughlan, P. and Kiesler, D.J. (1986). The experiencing scales. In L.S. Greenberg and W.M. Pinsof (eds.), *The Psychotherapeutic Process: A Research Handbook*. New York: Guilford Press.

Knight, R.P. (1941). Evaluation of the results of psychoanalytic therapy. *American Journal of Psychiatry*, 98, 434–446.

Knox, R. (2008). Clients' experiences of relational depth in person-centred counselling. *Counselling and Psychotherapy Research*, 8, 118–124.

Knox, R. and Cooper, M. (2010). Relationship qualities that are associated with moments of relational depth: The client's perspective. *Person-Centered and Experiential Psychotherapies*, 9, 236–256.

Knox, R. and Cooper, M. (2011). A state of readiness: An exploration of the client's role in meeting at relational depth. *Journal of Humanistic Psychology*, 51, 61–81.

Knox, S. and Hill, C.E. (2003). Therapist self-disclosure: Research-based suggestions for practitioners. *Journal of Clinical Psychology*, 59, 529–539.

Knox, S., Goldberg, J.L., Woodhouse, S.S. and Hill, C.E. (1999). Clients' internal representations of their therapists. *Journal of Counseling Psychology*, 46, 244–256.

Knox, S., Adrians, N., Everson, E., Hess, S., Hill, C. and Crook-Lyon, R. (2011). Clients' perspectives on therapy termination. *Psychotherapy Research*, 21, 154–167.

Kraus, D.R., Castonguay, L., Boswell, J.F., Nordberg, S.S. and Hayes, J.A. (2011). Therapist effectiveness: Implications for accountability and patient care. *Psychotherapy Research*, 21, 267–276.

Kroenke, K., Spitzer, R.L. and Williams, J.B. (2001). The PHQ-9: Validity of a brief depression severity measure. *Journal of General Internal Medicine*, 16, 606–613.

Kuhn, T.S. (1962). *The Structure of Scientific Revolutions*. Chicago, IL: University of Chicago Press.

Kuhnlein, I. (1999). Psychotherapy as a process of transformation: The analysis of posttherapeutic autobiographical narrations. *Psychotherapy Research*, 9, 274–288.

Kunz, R. and Oxman, A.D. (1998). The unpredictability paradox: Review of empirical comparisons of randomised and non-randomised clinical trials. *British Medical Journal*, 317, 1185–1190.

Kuyken, W., Byford, S., Taylor, R.S., Watkins, E., Holden, E., White, K., Barrett, B., Byng, R., Evans, A., Mullan, E. and Teasdale, J.D. (2008). Mindfulness-based cognitive therapy to prevent relapse in recurrent depression. *Journal of Consulting and Clinical Psychology*, 76, 966–978.

Kvale, S. (2001). The psychoanalytic interview as qualitative research. In J. Frommer and D. Rennie (eds.), *Qualitative Psychotherapy Research: Methods and Methodology*. Lengerich, Germany: Pabst.

Kvale, S. and Brinkmann, S. (2009). *InterViews: Learning the Craft of Qualitative Research Interviewing*, 2nd edn. Thousand Oaks, CA: Sage.

Laing, R.D. (1960). *The Divided Self: An Existential Study in Sanity and Madness*. Harmondsworth: Penguin.

Laing, R.D. (1961). *Self and Others*. Harmondsworth: Penguin.

Laing, R.D. and Esterson, A. (1964). *Sanity, Madness and the Family: Families of Schizophrenics*. Harmondsworth: Penguin.

Lambert, M.J. (1989). The individual therapist's contribution to psychotherapy process and outcome. *Clinical Psychology Review*, 9, 469–485.

Lambert, M.J. (ed.) (2004). *Bergin and Garfield's Handbook of Psychotherapy and Behavior Change*, 5th edn. New York: Wiley.

Lambert, M.J. (2007). What we have learned from a decade of research aimed at improving psychotherapy outcome in routine care. *Psychotherapy Research*, 17, 1–14.

Lambert, M.J. (ed.) (2013) *Bergin and Garfield's Handbook of Psychotherapy and Behavior Change*, 6th edn. New York: Wiley.

Lambert, M.J. and Finch, A.E. (1999). The outcome questionnaire. In M.E. Maruish (ed.), *The Use of Psychological Testing for Treatment Planning and Outcome Assessment*, 2nd edn. Mahwah, NJ: Lawrence Erlbaum.

Lambert, M.J. and Ogles, B.M. (2004). The efficacy and effectiveness of psychotherapy. In M.J. Lambert (ed.), *Bergin and Garfield's Handbook of Psychotherapy and Behavior Change*, 5th edn. New York: Wiley.

Lambert, M.J., Burlingame, G.M., Umphress, V., Hansen, N.B., Yancher, S.C., Vermeersch, D. and Clouse, G.C. (1996). The reliability and validity of a new psychotherapy outcome questionnaire. *Clinical Psychology and Psychotherapy*, 3, 249–258.

Landis, C. (1938). Statistical evaluation of psychotherapeutic methods. In S.E. Hinsie (ed.), *Concepts and Problems of Psychotherapy*. London: Heinemann.

Lane, D.A. and Corrie, S. (2006). *The Modern Scientist-Practitioner: A Guide to Practice in Psychology*. Hove: Routledge.

Larsen, D., Flesaker, K. and Stege, R. (2008). Qualitative interviewing using interpersonal process recall: Investigating internal experiences during professional–client conversation. *International Journal of Qualitative Methods*, 7, 18–37.

Lazarus, A.A. and Zur, O. (eds.) (2002). *Dual Relationships in Psychotherapy*. New York: Springer.

Lees, J. and Freshwater, D. (eds.) (2008). *Practitioner-based Research: Power, Discourse and Transformation*. London: Karnac.

Lepper, G. and Riding, N. (2006). *Researching the Psychotherapy Process: A Practical Guide to Transcript-based Methods*. Basingstoke: Palgrave Macmillan.

Levine, B.E. (2007). *Surviving America's Depression Epidemic: How to Find Morale, Energy, and Community in a World Gone Crazy*. White River Junction, VT: Chelsea Green.

Levitt, H.M. and Williams, D.C. (2010). Facilitating client change: Principles based upon the experience of eminent psychotherapists. *Psychotherapy Research*, 20, 337–352.

Levitt, H.M., Butler, M. and Hill, T. (2006). What clients find helpful in psychotherapy: Developing principles for facilitating moment-to-moment change. *Journal of Counseling Psychology*, 53, 314–324.

Levy, R. and Ablon, S. (eds.) (2009). *Handbook of Evidence-Based Psychodynamic Psychotherapy: Bridging the Gap between Science and Practice*. New York: Humana.

Lewis, A.J., Dennerstein, M. and Gibbs, P.M. (2008). Short-term psychodynamic psychotherapy: Review of recent process and outcome studies. *Australian and New Zealand Journal of Psychiatry*, 42, 445–455.

Lewis, J., Clark, D. and Morgan, D. (1992). *Whom God Hath Joined Together: The Work of Marriage Guidance*. London: Routledge.

Leykin, Y. and DeRubeis, R.J. (2009). Allegiance in psychotherapy outcome research: Separating association from bias. *Clinical Psychology: Science and Practice*, 16: 54–65.

Liddle, B.J. (1997). Gay and lesbian clients' selection of therapists and utilization of therapy. *Psychotherapy*, 34, 11–18.

Lietaer, G. (1990). The client-centered approach after the Wisconsin project: A personal view on its evolution. In G. Lietaer, J. Rombauts and R. Van Balen (eds.), *Client-Centered and Experiential Therapy in the Nineties*. Leuven, Belgium: University of Leuven Press.

Lietaer, G. (1992). Helping and hindering processes in client-centered/experiential psychotherapy: A content analysis of client and therapist post-session perceptions. In S.G. Toukmanian and D.L. Rennie (eds.), *Psychotherapy Process Research: Paradigmatic and Narrative Approaches*. London: Sage.

Lilliengren, P. and Werbart, A. (2005). A model of therapeutic action grounded in the patients' view of curative and hindering factors in psychoanalytic psychotherapy. *Psychotherapy: Theory, Research, Practice, Training*, 42, 324–339.

Lilliengren, P. and Werbart, A. (2010). Therapists' view of therapeutic action in psychoanalytic psychotherapy with young adults. *Psychotherapy: Theory, Research, Practice, Training*, 47, 570–585.

Lincoln, Y.S. and Guba, E.G. (1989). Judging the quality of case study reports. *Qualitative Studies in Education*, 3, 53–59.

Lindgren, A., Werbart, A. and Philips, B. (2010). Long-term outcome and post-treatment effects of psychoanalytic psychotherapy with young adults. *Psychology and Psychotherapy: Theory, Research and Practice*, 83, 27–43.

Lipkin, S. (1948). The client evaluates nondirective psychotherapy. *Journal of Consulting Psychology*, 12, 137–146.

Lipkin, S. (1954). Clients' feelings and attitudes in relation to the outcome of client-centered therapy. *Psychological Monographs*, 68, 1–30.

Llewelyn, S.P., Elliott, R., Shapiro, D.A., Hardy, G. and Firth-Cozens, J. (1988). Client perceptions of significant events in prescriptive and exploratory periods of individual therapy. *British Journal of Clinical Psychology*, 27, 105–114.

Lock, A. and Strong, T. (2010). *Social Constructionism: Sources and Stirrings in Theory and Practice*. Cambridge: Cambridge University Press.

Logan, D.E. and Marlatt, G.A. (2010). Harm reduction therapy: A practice-friendly review of research. *Journal of Clinical Psychology*, 66, 201–214.

Luborsky, L., Singer, B. and Luborsky, L. (1975). Comparative outcome studies of psychotherapy. *Archives of General Psychiatry*, 32, 995–1008.

Luborsky, L., Crits-Christoph, P. and Mellon, J. (1986). Advent of objective measures of the transference concept. *Journal of Consulting and Clinical Psychology*, 54, 39–47.

Luborsky, L., Barber, J.P. and Diguer, L. (1992). The meanings of narratives told during psychotherapy: The fruits of a new observational unit. *Psychotherapy Research*, 2, 277–290.

Luborsky, L., Popp, C., Luborsky, E. and Mark, D. (1994). The core conflictual relationship theme. *Psychotherapy Research*, 4, 172–183.

Luborsky, L., McLellan, A.T., Diguer, L., Woody, G. and Seligman, D.A. (1997). The psychotherapist matters: Comparison of outcomes across twenty-two therapists and seven patient samples. *Clinical Psychology: Science and Practice*, 4, 53–65.

Luborsky, L., Diguer, L., Seligman, D.A., Rosenthal, R., Krause, E.D., Johnson, S., Halperin, G., Bishop, M., Berman, J.S. and Schweizer, E. (1999). The researcher's own therapy allegiances: A 'wild card' in comparisons of treatment efficacy. *Clinical Psychology: Science and Practice*, 6, 95–106.

Lundahl, B. and Burke, B.L. (2009). The effectiveness and applicability of motivational interviewing: A practice-friendly review of four meta-analyses. *Journal of Clinical Psychology*, 65, 1232–1245.

Macaskie, J. and Lees, J. (2011). Dreaming the research process: A psychotherapeutic contribution to the culture of healthcare research. *British Journal of Guidance & Counselling*, 39, 411–424.

Mackrill, T. (2007). Using a cross-contextual qualitative diary design to explore client experiences of psychotherapy. *Counselling and Psychotherapy Research*, 7, 233–239.

Mackrill, T. (2008a). Exploring psychotherapy clients' independent strategies for change while in therapy. *British Journal of Guidance and Counselling*, 36, 441–453.

Mackrill, T. (2008b). Solicited diary studies of psychotherapeutic practice – pros and cons. *European Journal of Psychotherapy and Counselling*, 10, 5–18.

Mahrer, A. and Nadler, W. (1986). Good moments in psychotherapy: A preliminary review, a list and some promising research avenues. *Journal of Consulting and Clinical Psychology*, 54, 10–15.

Mahrer, A., Nadler, W., Gervaize, P. and Markow, R. (1986). Discovering how one therapist obtains some very good moments in psychotherapy. *Voices*, 22, 72–83.

Mahrer, A., Dessaulles, A., Nadler, W.P., Gervaize, P.A. and Sterner, I. (1987). Good and very good moments in psychotherapy: Content, distribution and facilitation. *Psychotherapy*, 24, 7–14.

Main, M. (1991). Metacognitive knowledge, metacognitive monitoring, and singular (coherent) versus multiple (incoherent) model of attachment: Findings and directions for future research. In C.M. Parkes, J. Stevenson-Hinde and P. Marris (eds.), *Attachment across the Life-cycle*. London: Routledge.

Mains, J.A. and Scogin, F.R. (2003). The effectiveness of self-administered treatments: A practice-friendly review of the research. *Journal of Clinical Psychology*, 59, 237–246.

Maluccio, A. (1979). *Learning from Clients: Interpersonal Helping as Viewed by Clients and Social Workers*. New York: Free Press.

Manthei, R.J. (2006). Clients talk about their experience of seeking counselling. *British Journal of Guidance and Counselling*, 34, 519–528.

Martin, J. and Stelmazonek, K. (1988). Participants' identification and recall of important events in counselling. *Journal of Counseling Psychology*, 35, 385–390.

Martin, J., Martin, W. and Slemon, A.G. (1989). Cognitive-mediational models of action-act sequences in counselling. *Journal of Counseling Psychology*, 36, 8–16.

Mayer, J. and Timms, N. (1970). *The Client Speaks: Working-Class Impressions of Casework*. London: Routledge and Kegan Paul.

McCarthy, K.S. and Barber, J.P. (2009). The Multitheoretical List of Therapeutic Interventions (MULTI): Initial report. *Psychotherapy Research*, 19, 96–113.

McClelland, D.C. (1980). Motive dispositions: The merits of operant and respondent measures. In L. Wheeler (ed.), *Review of Personality and Social Psychology*. Beverly Hills, CA: Sage.

McClelland, D.C. (1981). Is personality consistent? In A.I. Rabin, J. Aronoff, A.M. Barclay and R.A. Zucher (eds.), *Further Explorations in Personality*. New York: Wiley.

McKenna, P.A. and Todd, D.M. (1997). Longitudinal utilization of mental health services: A time-line method, nine retrospective accounts, and a preliminary conceptualization. *Psychotherapy Research*, 7, 383–396.

McLennan, J. (1990). Clients' perceptions of counsellors: A brief measure for use in counselling research, evaluation and training. *Australian Psychologist*, 25, 133–46.

McLeod, B.D. (2009) Understanding why therapy allegiance is linked to clinical outcomes. *Clinical Psychology: Science and Practice*, 16, 69–72.

McLeod, J. (1996). Qualitative approaches to research in counselling and psychotherapy: Issues and challenges. *British Journal of Guidance and Counselling*, 24, 309–316.

McLeod, J. (1997). Reading, writing and research. In I. Horton and V. Varma (eds.), *The Needs of Counsellors and Psychotherapists*. London: Sage.

McLeod, J. (2001a). *Counselling in the Workplace: the Facts. A systematic study of the research evidence*. Rugby: British Association for Counselling and Psychotherapy.

McLeod, J. (2001b). An administratively created reality: Some problems with the use of self-report questionnaire measures of adjustment in counselling/psychotherapy outcome research. *Counselling and Psychotherapy Research*, 1, 215–226.

McLeod, J. (2002). Research policy and practice in person-centered and experiential therapy: Restoring coherence. *Person-Centered and Experiential Psychotherapies*, 1, 87–101.

McLeod, J. (2007). *Counselling in the Workplace: A Comprehensive Review of the Research Evidence*, 2nd edn. Lutterworth: BACP.

McLeod, J. (2009). *An Introduction to Counselling*, 4th edn. Maidenhead: Open University Press.

McLeod, J. (2010a). *Case Study Research in Counselling and Psychotherapy*. London: Sage.

McLeod, J. (2010b). The effectiveness of workplace counselling: A systematic review. *Counselling and Psychotherapy Research*, 10, 238–248.

McLeod, J. (2011). *Qualitative Research in Counselling and Psychotherapy*, 2nd edn. London: Sage.

McLeod, J. (2012). What do clients want from therapy? A practice-friendly review of research into client preferences. *European Journal of Psychotherapy, Counselling and Health*, 14, 19–32.

McLeod, J. (forthcoming). *Doing Research in Counselling and Psychotherapy*. London: Sage.

McLeod, J. and Cooper, M. (2011). A protocol for systematic case study research in pluralistic counselling and psychotherapy. *Counselling Psychology Review*, 26, 47–58.

McLeod, J. and Elliott, R. (2011). Systematic case study research: A practice-oriented introduction to building an evidence base for counselling and psychotherapy. *Counselling and Psychotherapy Research*, 11, 1–10.

McLeod, J., Elliott, R. and Wheeler, S. (2010). *A Training Manual in Research Skills and Awareness for Counsellors and Psychotherapists*. Lutterworth: BACP.

McMillan, M. and McLeod, J. (2006). Letting go: The client's experience of relational depth. *Person-Centered and Experiential Psychotherapies*, 5, 277–292.

McNeilly, C.L. and Howard, K.I. (1991). The Therapeutic Procedures Inventory: Psychometric properties and relationship to phase of treatment. *Journal of Psychotherapy Integration*, 1, 223–234.

Meekums, B. (2008). Embodied narratives in becoming a counselling trainer: An autoethnographic study. *British Journal of Guidance and Counselling*, 36, 287–301.

Meier, S.T. (2008). *Measuring Change in Counseling and Psychotherapy*. New York: Guilford Press.

Mellor-Clark, J. and Barkham, M. (2006). The CORE system: Quality evaluation to develop practice-based evidence base, enhanced service delivery and best practice management. In C. Feltham and I. Horton (eds.), *Handbook of Counselling and Psychotherapy*. London: Sage.

Mellor-Clark, J., Jenkins, A.C., Evans, R., Mothersole, G. and Mcinnes, B. (2006). Resourcing a CORE Network to develop a National Research Database to help enhance psychological therapy and counselling service provision. *Counselling and Psychotherapy Research*, 6, 16–22.

Messer, S.B., Sass, L.A. and Woolfolk, R.L. (eds.) (1988). *Hermeneutics and Psychological Theory: Interpretive Perspectives on Personality, Psychotherapy and Psychopathology*. New Brunswick, NJ: Rutgers University Press.

Michel, L., Kramer, U. and De Roten, Y. (2011). Alliance evolutions over the course of short-term dynamic psychotherapy: A case study. *Counselling and Psychotherapy Research*, 11, 43–54.

Michell, J. (1999). *Measurement in Psychology: Critical History of a Methodological Concept*. New York: Cambridge University Press.

Michell, J. (2000). Normal science, pathological science and psychometrics. *Theory and Psychology*, 10, 639–667.

Michell, J. (2013). Constructs, inferences, and mental measurement. *New Ideas in Psychology*, 13, 13–21.

Miles, M. and Huberman, A. (1994). *Qualitative Data Analysis: A Sourcebook of New Methods*, 2nd edn. London: Sage.

Miller, B. (2007). What creates and sustains commitment to the practice of psychotherapy? *Psychiatric Services*, 58, 174–176.

Miller, N.E. and Magruder, K.M. (eds.) (1999). *Cost-effectiveness of Psychotherapy: A Guide for Practitioners, Researchers and Policymakers*. New York: Oxford University Press.

Miller, S.D., Duncan, B.L. and Hubble, M.A. (2005). Outcome-informed clinical work. In J.C. Norcross and M.R. Goldfried (eds.), *Handbook of Psychotherapy Integration*. New York: Oxford University Press.

Minami, T., Wampold, B.E., Serlin, R.C., Kircher, J.C. and Brown, G.S. (2007). Benchmarks for psychotherapy efficacy in adult major depression. *Journal of Consulting and Clinical Psychology*, 75, 232–243.

Moerman, M. and McLeod, J. (2006). Person-centered counseling for alcohol-related problems: The client's experience of self in the therapeutic relationship. *Person-centered and Experiential Psychotherapies*, 5, 21–35.

Morgan, D.L. and Morgan, R.K. (2009). *Single-case Research Methods for the Behavioural and Health Sciences*. Thousand Oaks, CA: Sage.

Morley, S. (2007). Single case methodology in psychological therapy. In S.J.E. Lindsay and G.E. Powell (eds.), *A Handbook of Clinical Adult Psychology*, 3rd edn. London: Brunner-Routledge.

Morris, B. (2005). *Discovering Bits and Pieces of Me: Research Exploring Women's Experiences of Psychoanalytical Psychotherapy*. London: Women's Therapy Centre. Available at www.womenstherapycentre.co.uk/news/news.html.

Morrison, K.H., Bradley, R. and Westen, D. (2003). The external validity of controlled clinical trials of psychotherapy for depression and anxiety. *Psychology and Psychotherapy*, 76, 109–132.

Morrow, S.L. (2005). Quality and trustworthiness in qualitative research in counselling psychology. *Journal of Counseling Psychology*, 52, 250–260.

Morrow-Bradley, C. and Elliott, R. (1986). Utilization of psychotherapy research by practicing psychotherapists. *American Psychologist*, 41, 188–197.

Moustakas, C. (1990). *Heuristic Research: Design, Methodology and Applications*. Thousand Oaks, CA: Sage.

Mullin, T., Barkham, M., Mothersole, G., Bewick, B.M. and Kinder, A. (2006). Recovery and improvement benchmarks for counselling and the psychological therapies in routine primary care. *Counselling and Psychotherapy Research*, 6, 68–80.

Muran, J.C. and Barber, J.P. (eds.) (2010). *The Therapeutic Alliance: An Evidence-based Approach to Practice*, 2nd edn. New York: Guilford Press.

Muran, J.C., Safran, J.D. and Eubanks-Carter, C. (2010). Developing therapist abilities to negotiate alliance ruptures. In J.C. Muran and J.P. Barber (eds.), *The Therapeutic Alliance: An Evidence-based Approach to Practice*. New York: Guilford Press.

Murray, H.A. (1938). *Explorations in Personality: A Clinical and Experimental Study of Fifty Men of College Age*. New York: Oxford University Press.

Najavits, L.M. (1993). How do psychotherapists describe their work? A study of metaphors for the therapy process. *Psychotherapy Research*, 3, 294–299.

Najavits, L.M., Weis, R.D., Shaw, S.R. and Dierbeger, A.E. (2000). Psychotherapists' views of treatment manuals. *Professional Psychology: Research and Practice*, 31, 404–408.

Nezu, A.M. and Nezu, C.M. (2007a). Ensuring treatment integrity. In A.M. Nezu and C.M. Nezu (eds.), *Evidence-based Outcome Research: A Practical Guide to Conducting Randomized Controlled Trials for Psychosocial Interventions*. Cary, NC: Oxford University Press.

Nezu, A.M. and Nezu, C.M. (eds.) (2007b). *Evidence-based Outcome Research: A Practical Guide to Conducting Randomized Controlled Trials for Psychosocial Interventions*. Cary, NC: Oxford University Press.

Nilsson, T., Svensson, M., Sandell, R. and Clinton, D. (2007). Patients' experiences of change on cognitive-behavioral therapy and psychodynamic therapy: A qualitative comparative study. *Psychotherapy Research*, 17, 553–566.

Nisbett, R.E. and Wilson, T.D. (1977). Telling more than we can know: Verbal reports on mental processes. *Psychological Review*, 84, 231–259.

Norcross, J.C. (ed.) (2011). *Psychotherapy Relationships that Work: Evidence-based Responsiveness*, 2nd edn. New York: Oxford University Press.

Oei, T.P.S. and Shuttlewood, G.J. (1999). Development of a satisfaction with therapy and therapist scale. *Australian and New Zealand Journal of Psychiatry*, 33, 748–753.

Okasha, S. (2002). *Philosophy of Science: A Very Short Introduction*. Oxford: Oxford University Press.

Okiishi, J., Lambert, M.J., Nielsen, S.L. and Ogles, B.M. (2003). Waiting for supershrink: An empirical analysis of therapist effects. *Clinical Psychology and Psychotherapy*, 10, 361–373.

Orlinsky, D.E. and Howard, K.I. (1975). *Varieties of Psychotherapeutic Experience: Multivariate Analyses of Patients and Therapists Reports*. New York: Teachers College Press.

Orlinsky, D.E. and Howard, K.I. (1986). The psychological interior of psychotherapy: Explorations with the Therapy Session reports. In L.S. Greenberg and W.M. Pinsof (eds.), *The Psychotherapeutic Process: A Research Handbook*. New York: Guilford Press.

Orlinsky, D.E., Ronnestad, M.G. and Willutzki, U. (2004). Fifty years of psychotherapy process-outcome research: Continuity and change. In M.J. Lambert (ed.), *Bergin and Garfield's Handbook of Psychotherapy and Behavior Change*, 5th edn. New York: Wiley.

Pallant, J. (2010). *SPSS Survival Manual: A Step-by-Step Guide to Data Analysis Using SPSS*, 4th edn. Maidenhead: Open University Press.

Panhofer, H. (2011). Languaged and non-languaged ways of knowing in counselling and psychotherapy. *British Journal of Guidance and Counselling*, 39, 455–470.

Parry, G., Castonguay, L.G., Borkovec, T.D. and Wolf, A.W. (2010). Practice research networks and psychological services research in the

UK and USA. In M. Barkham, G.E. Hardy and J. Mellor-Clark (eds.), *Developing and Delivering Practice-based Evidence: A Guide for the Psychological Therapies*. Chichester: Wiley-Blackwell.

Paterson, C. (1996). Measuring outcome in primary care: A patient-generated measure, MYMOP, compared to the SF-36 health survey. *British Medical Journal*, 312, 1016–1020.

Paterson, C. and Britten, N. (2000). In pursuit of patient-centred outcomes: A qualitative evaluation of MYMOP, Measure Yourself Medical Outcome Profile. *Journal of Health Service Research and Policy*, 5, 27–36.

Patterson, C.H. (1984). Empathy, warmth and genuineness in psychotherapy: A review of reviews. *Psychotherapy*, 21, 431–438.

Paulson, B., Everall, R.D. and Stuart, J. (2001). Client perceptions of hindering experiences in counselling. *Counselling and Psychotherapy Research*, 1, 53–61.

Pearson, M. and Coomber, R. (2010). The challenge of external validity in policy-relevant systematic reviews: A case study from the field of substance misuse. *Addiction*, 105, 136–145.

Peräkylä, A., Antaki, C., Vehviläinen, S. and Leudar, I. (eds.) (2011). *Conversation Analysis and Psychotherapy*. New York: Cambridge University Press.

Perren, S., Godfrey, M. and Rowland, N. (2009). The long-term effects of counselling: The process and mechanisms that contribute to ongoing change from a user perspective. *Counselling and Psychotherapy Research*, 9, 241–249.

Persons, J.B. (1998). Are results of randomized controlled trials useful to psychotherapists? *Journal of Consulting and Clinical Psychology*, 66, 126–135.

Philips, B., Werbart, A. and Schubert, J. (2005). Private theories and psychotherapeutic technique. *Psychoanalytic Psychotherapy*, 19, 48–70.

Philips, B., Wennberg, P. and Werbart, A. (2007a). Ideas of cure as a predictor of premature termination, early alliance, and outcome in psychoanalytic psychotherapy. *Psychology and Psychotherapy: Theory Research and Practice*, 80, 229–245.

Philips, B., Werbart, A., Wennberg, P. and Schubert, J. (2007b). Young adults' ideas of cure prior to psychoanalytic psychotherapy. *Journal of Clinical Psychology*, 63, 213–232.

Polkinghorne, D.E. (1994). Reaction to special section on qualitative research in counseling process and outcome. *Journal of Counseling Psychology*, 41, 510–512.

Polkinghorne, D.E. (1999). Traditional research and psychotherapy practice. *Journal of Clinical Psychology*, 55, 1429–1440.

Ponterotto, J.G. (2002). Qualitative research methods: The fifth force in psychology. *The Counseling Psychologist*, 30, 394–496.

Ponterotto, J.G. (2005). Qualitative research in counseling psychology: A primer on research paradigms and philosophy of science. *Journal of Counseling Psychology*, 52, 126–136.

Ponterotto, J.G. and Grieger, I. (2007). Effectively communicating qualitative research. *The Counseling Psychologist*, 35, 404–430.

Pope, K.S. (1991). Dual relationships in psychotherapy. *Ethics and Behavior*, 1, 21–34.

Popper, K.R. (1959). *The Logic of Scientific Discovery*. New York: Basic Books.

Popper, K.R. (1962). *Conjectures and Refutations*. New York: Basic Books.

Popper, K.R. (1972). *Objective Knowledge*. Oxford: Oxford University Press.

Post, B.C. and Wade, N.G. (2009). Religion and spirituality in psychotherapy: A practice-friendly review of research. *Journal of Clinical Psychology*, 65, 131–146.

Prochaska, J.O. (2010). With science and service we can survive and thrive. In S. Sold. and L. McCullough (eds.), *Reconciling Empirical Knowledge and Clinical Experience: The Art and Science of Psychotherapy*. Washington, DC: American Psychological Association.

Råbu, M., Halvorsen, M.S. and Haavind, H. (2011). Early relationship struggles: A case study of alliance formation and reparation. *Counselling and Psychotherapy Research*, 11, 23–33.

Ramseyer, F. and Tschacher, W. (2011). Nonverbal synchrony in psychotherapy: Coordinated body movement reflects relationship quality and outcome. *Journal of Consulting and Clinical Psychology*, 79, 284–295.

Ravitz, P., Maunder, R., Hunter, J., Sthankiya, B. and Lancee, W. (2010). Adult attachment measures: A 25-year review. *Journal of Psychosomatic Research*, 69, 419–432.

Reason, P. (1988). Whole person medical practice. In P. Reason (ed.), *Human Inquiry in Action: Developments in New Paradigm Research*. London: Sage.

Reason, P., Chase, H.D., Desser, A. et al. (1992). Towards a clinical framework for collaboration between general and complementary practitioners: Discussion paper. *Journal of the Royal Society of Medicine*, 85, 161–164.

Rennie, D.L. (1990). Toward a representation of the client's experience of the psychotherapy hour. In G. Lietaer, J. Rombauts and R. Van Balen (eds.), *Client-Centered and Experiential Therapy in the Nineties*. Leuven, Belgium: University of Leuven Press.

Rennie, D.L. (1992). Qualitative analysis of the client's experience of psychotherapy: The unfolding of reflexivity. In S.G. Toukmanian and D.L. Rennie (eds.), *Psychotherapy Process Research: Paradigmatic and Narrative Approaches*. London: Sage.

Rennie, D.L. (1994a). Clients' deference in psychotherapy. *Journal of Counseling Psychology*, 41, 427–437.

Rennie, D.L. (1994b). Storytelling in psychotherapy: The client's subjective experience. *Psychotherapy*, 31, 234–243.

Rennie, D.L. (1994c). Clients' accounts of resistance in counselling: A qualitative analysis. *Canadian Journal of Counselling*, 28, 43–57.

Rennie, D.L. (2000). Aspects of the client's conscious control of the psychotherapeutic process. *Journal of Psychotherapy Integration*, 10, 151–167.

Rennie, D.L. (2001). The client as self-aware agent in counselling and psychotherapy. *Counselling and Psychotherapy Research*, 1, 82–89.

Rennie, D.L., Phillips, J.R. and Quartaro, J.K. (1988). Grounded theory: A promising approach for conceptualization in psychology? *Canadian Psychology*, 29, 139–150.

Reynolds, S. (1997). Psychological wellbeing at work: Is prevention better than cure? *Journal for Psychosomatic Research*, 43, 93–102.

Rice, L.N. (1992). From naturalistic observation of psychotherapy process to micro theories of change. In D.L. Rennie and S.G. Toukmanian (eds.), *Psychotherapy Process Research: Narrative and Paradigmatic Approaches*. London: Sage.

Rice, L.N. and Greenberg, L.S. (eds.) (1984). *Patterns of Change: Intensive Analysis of Psychotherapy Process*. New York: Guilford Press.

Rice, L.N. and Kerr, G.P. (1986). Measures of client and therapist voice quality. In L.S. Greenberg and W.M. Pinsof (eds.), *The Psychotherapeutic Process: A Research Handbook*. New York: Guilford Press.

Rice, L.N. and Saperia, E.P. (1984). Task analysis of the resolution of problematic reactions. In L.N. Rice and L.S. Greenberg (eds.), *Patterns of Change: Intensive Analysis of Psychotherapy Process*. New York: Guilford Press.

Rodgers, B. (2006). Life space mapping: Preliminary results from the development of a new method for investigating counselling outcomes. *Counselling and Psychotherapy Research*, 6, 227–232.

Rogers, C.R. (1942). The use of electrically recorded interviews in improving psychotherapy techniques. *American Journal of Orthopsychiatry*, 12, 429–434. Reprinted in H. Kirschenbaum and V. Henderson (eds.) (1990) *The Carl Rogers Reader*. London: Constable.

Rogers, C.R. (1951). *Client-centered Therapy*. Boston, MA: Houghton Mifflin.

Rogers, C.R. (1957). The necessary and sufficient conditions of therapeutic personality change. *Journal of Consulting Psychology*, 21, 95–103.

Rogers, C.R. and Dymond, R.F. (eds.) (1954). *Psychotherapy and Personality Change*. Chicago, IL: University of Chicago Press.

Rogers, C.R. and Stevens, B. (eds.) (1968). *Person to Person: The Problem of Being Human*. Lafayette, CA: Real People Press.

Rogers, C.R., Gendlin, E.T., Kiesler, D.J. and Truax, C.B. (eds.) (1967). *The Therapeutic Relationship and its Impact: A Study of Psychotherapy with Schizophrenics*. Madison, WI: University of Wisconsin Press.

Ronnestad, M.H. and Skovholt, T.M. (2001). Learning arena for professional development: Retrospective accounts of senior psychotherapists. *Professional Psychology: Research and Practice*, 32, 181–187.

Ronnestad, M.H. and Skovholt, T.M. (2013). *The Developing Practitioner. Growth and Stagnation of Therapists and Counselors*. New York: Routledge.

Rosenthal, R. and Rosnow, R.L. (2009). *Artifacts in Behavioral Research: Robert Rosenthal and Ralph L. Rosnow's Classic Books*. New York: Oxford University Press.

Rosenthal, R. and Rubin, D.B. (1978). Interpersonal expectancy effects: The first 345 studies. *Behavioral and Brain Sciences*, 3, 377–415.

Roth, A.D. and Fonagy, P. (2005). *What Works for Whom?* 2nd edn. New York: Guilford Press.

Royal College of Psychiatrists (2011). *National Audit of Psychological Therapies for Anxiety and Depression: National Report 2011*. London: RCP.

Rubino, G., Barker, C, Roth, T. and Fearon, P. (2000). Therapist empathy and depth of interpretation in response to potential alliance ruptures: The role of patient and therapist attachment styles. *Psychotherapy Research*, 10, 408–420.

Russell, R.L. (1989). Language and psychotherapy. *Clinical Psychology Review*, 9, 505–520.

Rust, J. and Golombok, S. (2008). *Modern Psychometrics: The Science of Psychological Assessment*, 3rd edn. London: Routledge.

Sachs, J.S. (1983). Negative factors in brief psychotherapy: An empirical assessment. *Journal of Consulting and Clinical Psychology*, 51, 557–564.

Sachse, R. and Elliott, R. (2002). Process-outcome research on humanistic therapy variables. In D.J. Cain and J. Seeman (eds.), *Humanistic Psychotherapies: Handbook of Research and Practice*. Washington, DC: American Psychological Association.

Safran, J.D. (1993). Breaches in the therapeutic alliance: An arena for negotiating authentic relatedness. *Psychotherapy*, 30, 11–24.

Safran, J.D. and Muran, J.C. (2006). Has the concept of the therapeutic alliance outlived its usefulness? *Psychotherapy: Theory, Research, Practice, Training*, 43, 286–291.

Salkind, N.J. (2010). *Statistics for People Who (Think They) Hate Statistics*, 4th edn. Thousand Oaks, CA: Sage.

Sampson, H. and Weiss, J. (1986). Testing hypotheses: The approach of the Mount Zion Psychotherapy Research Group. In L.S. Greenberg and W.M. Pinsof (eds.), *The Psychotherapeutic Process: A Research Handbook*. New York: Guilford Press.

Schielke, H.J., Fishman, J.L., Osatuke, K. and Stiles, W.B. (2009). Creative consensus on interpretations of qualitative data: The Ward method. *Psychotherapy Research*, 19, 558–565.

Schneider, K.J., Bugental, J.F.T. and Pierson, J.F. (eds.) (2001). *The Handbook of Humanistic Psychology: Leading Edges in Theory, Research and Practice*. Thousand Oaks, CA: Sage.

Schnellbacher, J. and Leijssen, M. (2008). The significance of therapist genuineness from the client's perspective. *Journal of Humanistic Psychology*, 49, 207–228.

Schulz, K.F., Chalmers, I., Hayes, R.J. and Altman, D.G. (1995). Empirical evidence of bias: Dimensions of methodological quality associated with estimates of treatment effects in controlled trials. *Journal of the American Medical Association*, 273, 408–441.

Seligman, M.E.P. (1995). The effectiveness of psychotherapy: The *Consumer Reports* study. *American Psychologist*, 50, 965–974.

Semeonoff, B. (1976). *Projective Techniques*. Chichester: Wiley.

Shapiro, D.A., Barkham, M., Hardy, G. and Morrison, L. (1990). The Second Sheffield Psychotherapy Project: Rationale, design and preliminary outcome data. *British Journal of Medical Psychology*, 63, 97–108.

Shea, M.T., Elkin, I., Imber, S.D., Sotsky, S.M., Watkins, J.T., Collins, J.F., Pilkonis, P.A., Beckman, E., Glass, D.R., Dolan, R.T. and Parloff, M.B. (1992). Course of depressive symptoms over follow-up: Findings from the National Institute for Mental Health Treatment of Depression Research Program. *Archives of General Psychiatry*, 49, 782–787.

Shin, C.-M., Chow, C., Camacho-Gonsalves, T., Levy, R.J., Allen, I.E. and Leff, H.S. (2005). A meta-analytic review of racial-ethnic matching for African American and Caucasian American clients and clinicians. *Journal of Counseling Psychology*, 52, 45–56.

Shumway, S.T., Dersch, C., Harris, S.M. and Arredondo, R. (2004). Two outcome measures of EAP satisfaction: A factor analysis. *Employee Assistance Quarterly*, 16, 71–79.

Sibbald, B., Addington-Hall, J., Brenneman, D. and Freeling, P. (1996). Investigation of whether on-site general practice counsellors have an impact on psychotropic drug prescribing rates and costs. *British Journal of General Practice*, 46, 63–67.

Silberschatz, G., Fretter, P.B. and Curtis, J.T. (1986). How do interpretations influence the progress of psychotherapy? *Journal of Consulting and Clinical Psychology*, 54, 646–652.

Silberschatz, G., Curtis, J.T. and Nathans, S. (1989). Using the patient's plan to assess progress in psychotherapy. *Psychotherapy*, 26, 40–46.

Silverman, D. (2009). *Doing Qualitative Research*, 3rd edn. London: Sage.

Sin, N.L. and Lyubomirsky, S. (2009). Enhancing well-being and alleviating depressive symptoms with positive psychology interventions: A practice-friendly meta-analysis. *Journal of Clinical Psychology*, 65, 467–487.

Skovholt, T.M., Ronnestad, M.H. and Jennings, L. (1997). Searching for expertise in counseling, psychotherapy and professional psychology. *Educational Psychology Review*, 9, 361–369.

Skovholt, T.M. and Jennings, L. (2004). *Master Therapists: Exploring Expertise in Therapy and Counseling*. New York: Allyn and Bacon.

Slade, M. and Priebe, S. (2001). Are randomised controlled trials the only gold that glitters? *British Journal of Psychiatry*, 178, 286–287.

Sloane, R.B., Staples, F.R., Cristol, A.H., Yorkston, N.J. and Whipple, K. (1975). *Psychotherapy vs Behavior Therapy*. Cambridge, MA: Harvard University Press.

Sloboda, J.A., Hopkins, J.S., Turner, A., Rogers, D. and McLeod, J. (1993). An evaluated staff counselling programme in a public sector organization. *Employee Counselling Today*, 5, 4–12.

Smith, J.A. (ed.) (2007). *Qualitative Psychology: A Practical Guide to Research Methods*, 2nd edn. London: Sage.

Smith, L.T. (1999) *Decolonizing Methodologies: Research and Indigenous Peoples*. London: Zed Books.

Smith, M., Glass, G. and Miller, T. (1980). *The Benefits of Psychotherapy*. Baltimore, MD: Johns Hopkins Press.

Soldz, S. and McCullough, L. (eds.) (2000). *Reconciling Empirical Knowledge and Clinical Experience: The Art and Science of Psychotherapy*. Washington, DC: American Psychological Association.

Solomon, S.D. and Johnson, D.M. (2002). Psychosocial treatment of posttraumatic stress disorder: A practice-friendly review of outcome research. *Journal of Clinical Psychology*, 58, 947–959.

Sørensen, P., Birket-Smith, M., Wattar, U., Buemann, I. and Salkovskis, P.M. (2011). A randomized clinical trial of cognitive behavioural therapy versus short-term psychodynamic psychotherapy versus no intervention for patients with hypochondriasis. *Psychological Medicine*, 41, 431–441.

Speedy, J. (2008). *Narrative Inquiry and Psychotherapy*. Basingstoke: Palgrave Macmillan.

Spence, D.P. (1982). *Narrative Truth and Historical Truth: Meaning and Interpretation in Psychoanalysis*. New York: Norton.

Spence, D.P. (1986). Narrative smoothing and clinical wisdom. In T.R. Sarbin (ed.), *Narrative Psychology: The Storied Nature of Human Conduct*. New York: Praeger.

Spence, D.P. (1989). Rhetoric vs. evidence as a source of persuasion: A critique of the case study genre. In M.J. Packer and R.B. Addison (eds.), *Entering the Circle: Hermeneutic Investigation in Psychology*. New York: Addison-Wesley.

Spence, D.P. (2001). Dangers of anecdotal reports. *Journal of Clinical Psychology*, 57, 37–41.

Spitzer, R.L., Kroenke, K., Williams, J.B., et al. (2006). A brief measure for assessing generalized anxiety disorder: The GAD-7. *Archives of Internal Medicine*, 166, 1092–1097.

Stevenson, I. (1961). Processes of 'spontaneous' recovery from the psychoneuroses. *American Journal of Psychiatry*, 117, 1057–1064.

Stewart, R.E. and Chambless, D.L. (2010). Interesting practitioners in training in empirically supported treatments: Research reviews versus case studies. *Journal of Clinical Psychology*, 66, 73–95.

Stiglera, M., de Roten, Y., Drapeau, M. and Despland, J. (2007). Process research in psychodynamic psychotherapy: A combined measure for accuracy and conflictuality of interpretations. *Schweizer Archive fur Neurolgie und Psychiatrie*, 168, 225–232.

Stiles, W.B. (1980). Measurement of the impact of psychotherapy sessions. *Journal of Consulting and Clinical Psychology*, 48, 176–185.

Stiles, W.B. (1986). Development of a taxonomy of verbal response modes. In L.S. Greenberg and W.M. Pinsof (eds.), *The Psychotherapeutic Process: A Research Handbook*. New York: Guilford Press.

Stiles, W.B. (1993). Quality control in qualitative research. *Clinical Psychology Review*, 13, 593–618.

Stiles, W.B. (2001). Assimilation of problematic experiences. *Psychotherapy: Theory, Research, Practice, Training*, 38, 462–465.

Stiles, W.B. (2002). Assimilation of problematic experiences. In J.C. Norcross (ed.), *Psychotherapy Relationships that Work*. New York: Oxford University Press.

Stiles, W.B. (2003). When is a case study scientific research? *Psychotherapy Bulletin*, 38(1), 6–11.

Stiles, W.B. (2005). Case studies. In J.C. Norcross, L.E. Beutler and R.F. Levant (eds.), *Evidence-based Practices in Mental Health: Debate and Dialogue on the Fundamental Questions*. Washington, DC: American Psychological Association.

Stiles, W.B. (2007). Theory-building case studies of counselling and psychotherapy. *Counselling and Psychotherapy Research*, 7, 122–127.

Stiles, W.B. (2009). Responsiveness as an obstacle for psychotherapy outcome research: It's worse than you think. *Clinical Psychology: Science and Practice*, 16, 86–91.

Stiles, W.B. and Snow, J. (1984). Dimensions of psychotherapy session impact across sessions and across clients. *British Journal of Clinical Psychology*, 23, 59–63.

Stiles, W.B., Elliott, R., Llewelyn, S., Firth-Cozens, J., Margison, F., Shapiro, D.A. and Hardy, G. (1990). Assimilation of problematic experiences by clients in psychotherapy. *Psychotherapy*, 27, 411–420.

Stiles, W.B., Morrison, L.A., Haw, S.F., Harper, H., Shapiro, D.A. and Firth-Cozens, J. (1991). Longitudinal study of assimilation in exploratory psychotherapy. *Psychotherapy*, 28, 195–206.

Stiles, W.B., Meshot, C.N., Anderson, T.M. and Sloan, W.W. (1992). Assimilation of problematic experiences: The case of John Jones. *Psychotherapy Research*, 2, 81–101.

Stiles, W.B., Gordon, L.E. and Lani, J.A. (2002). Session evaluation and the Session Evaluation Questionnaire. In G.S. Tryon (ed.), *Counseling*

Based on Process Research: Applying What We Know. Boston, MA: Allyn and Bacon.

Stiles, W.B., Barkham, M., Twigg, E., Mellor-Clark, J. and Cooper, M. (2006). Effectiveness of cognitive-behavioural, person-centred and psychodynamic therapies as practised in UK National Health Service settings. *Psychological Medicine*, 36, 555–566.

Stiles, W.B., Barkham, M., Mellor-Clark, J. and Connell, J. (2007). Effectiveness of cognitive-behavioural, person-centred, and psychodynamic therapies as practised in UK primary care routine practice: Replication in a larger sample. *Psychological Medicine*, 38, 677–688.

Stiles, W.B., Barkham, M., Mellor-Clark, J. and Connell, J. (2008). Routine psychological treatment and the Dodo verdict: A rejoinder to Clark et al. (2007). *Psychological Medicine*, 38, 905–910.

Stratton, P., Bland, J., Janes, E. and Lask, J. (2010). Developing a practicable outcome measure for systemic family therapy: The SCORE. *Journal of Family Therapy*, 32, 232–258.

Strauss, A. and Corbin, J. (1998). *Basics of Qualitative Research: Techniques and Procedures for Developing Grounded Theory,* 2nd edn. Thousand Oaks, CA: Sage.

Strupp, H.H. (1980a). Success and failure in time-limited psychotherapy. A systematic comparison of two cases: Comparison 1. *Archives of General Psychiatry*, 37, 595–603.

Strupp, H.H. (1980b). Success and failure in time-limited psychotherapy. A systematic comparison of two cases: Comparison 2. *Archives of General Psychiatry*, 37, 708–716.

Strupp, H.H. (1980c). Success and failure in time-limited therapy: With special reference to the performance of the lay counselor. *Archives of General Psychiatry*, 37, 831–841.

Strupp, H.H. (1980d). Success and failure in time-limited psychotherapy. Further evidence: Comparison 4. *Archives of General Psychiatry*, 37, 947–954.

Strupp, H.H. and Hadley, S.W. (1979). Specific vs nonspecific factors in psychotherapy: A controlled study of outcome. *Archives of General Psychiatry*, 36, 1125–1136.

Suh, C.S., Strupp, H.H. and O'Malley, S.S. (1986). The Vanderbilt process measures: The Psychotherapy Process Scale (VPPS) and the Negative Indicators Scale (VNIS). In L.S. Greenberg and W.M. Pinsof (eds.), *The Psychotherapeutic Process: A Research Handbook*. New York: Guilford Press.

Sundet, R. (2009). Therapeutic collaboration and formalized feedback: Using perspectives from Vygotsky and Bakhtin to shed light on practices in a family therapy unit. *Clinical Child Psychology and Psychiatry*, 15, 81–95.

Sundet, R. (2012). Therapist perspectives on the use of feedback on process and outcome: Patient-focused research in practice. *Canadian Psychology*, 53, 122–130.

Sussman, S. (2001). The significance of psycho-peristalsis and tears within the therapeutic relationship. *Counselling and Psychotherapy Research*, 1, 90–100.

Swift, J.K. and Callahan, J.L. (2009). The impact of client treatment preferences on outcome: A meta-analysis. *Journal of Clinical Psychology*, 65, 368–381.

Taylor, C. (1979). Interpretation and the science of man. In P. Rabinow and W. Sullivan (eds.), *Interpretive Social Science: A Reader*. Berkeley, CA: University of California Press.

Thoma, N.C. and Cecero, J.J. (2009). Is integrative use of techniques in psychotherapy the exception or the rule? Results of a national survey of doctoral-level practitioners. *Psychotherapy*, 46, 405–417.

Thompson, C. and Jenal, S. (1994). Interracial and intraracial quasi-counselling interactions: When counselors avoid discussing race. *Journal of Counseling Psychology*, 41, 484–491.

Thompson, V.L.S., Bazile, A. and Akbar, M. (2004). African Americans' perceptions of psychotherapy and psychotherapists. *Professional Psychology: Research and Practice*, 35, 19–26.

Timulak, L. (2007). Identifying core categories of client-identified impact of helpful events in psychotherapy – A qualitative meta-analysis. *Psychotherapy Research*, 17, 305–314.

Timulak, L. (2008). *Research in Counselling and Psychotherapy*. London: Sage.

Timulak, L. (2009). Meta-analysis of qualitative studies: A tool for reviewing research findings in psychotherapy. *Psychotherapy Research*, 19, 591–600.

Tolley, K. and Rowland, N. (1995). *Evaluating the Cost-Effectiveness of Counselling in Health Care*. London: Routledge.

Toukmanian, S.G. (1986). A measure of client perceptual processing. In L.S. Greenberg and W.M. Pinsof (eds.), *The Psychotherapeutic Process: A Research Handbook*. New York: Guilford Press.

Toukmanian, S.G. (1992). Studying clients' perceptual processes and their outcomes in psychotherapy. In S.G. Toukmanian and D.L. Rennie (eds.), *Psychotherapy Process Research: Paradigmatic and Narrative Approaches*. London: Sage.

Toukmanian, S.G. and Rennie, D.L. (eds.) (1992). *Psychotherapy Process Research: Paradigmatic and Narrative Approaches*. London: Sage.

Trijsburg, R.W., Frederiks, G.C.F.J., Gorlee, M., Klouwer, E., den Hollander, A.M. and Duivenvoorden, H.J. (2002). Development of the Comprehensive Psychotherapeutic Interventions Rating Scale (CPIRS). *Psychotherapy Research*, 12, 287–317.

Truax, C.B. and Carkhuff, R.R. (1967). *Toward Effective Counseling and Psychotherapy: Training and Practice*. Chicago: Aldine.

Trudeau, K., Mostofsky, E., Stuhr, J.K. and Davidson, K.W. (2007). Explanation of the CONSORT statement with application to psychosocial interventions. In A.M. Nezu and C.M. Nezu (eds.), *Evidence-based Outcome Research: A Practical Guide to Conducting Randomized Controlled Trials for Psychosocial Interventions*. Cary, NC: Oxford University Press.

Trusty, J., Thompson, B. and Petrocelli, J.V. (2004). Practical guide for reporting effect size in quantitative research in the *Journal of Counseling and Development*. *Journal of Counseling and Development*, 82, 107–110.

Tryon, G.S. (ed.) (2002). *Counselling Based on Process Research: Applying What We Know*. Boston, MA: Allyn and Bacon.

Tuckwell, G. (2001). 'The threat of the Other': Using mixed quantitative and qualitative methods to elucidate racial and cultural dynamics in the counselling process. *Counselling and Psychotherapy Research*, 1, 154–162.

Valkonen, J., Hanninen, V. and Lindfors, O. (2011). Outcomes of psychotherapy from the perspective of the users. *Psychotherapy Research*, 21, 227–240.

von Below, C., Werbart, A. and Rehnberg, S. (2010). Experiences of overcoming depression in young adults in psychoanalytic psychotherapy. *European Journal of Psychotherapy and Counselling*, 12, 129–147.

von Consbruch, K., Clark, D.M. and Stangier, U. (2012). Assessing therapeutic competence in cognitive therapy for social phobia: Psychometric properties of the Cognitive Therapy Competence Scale for Social Phobia (CTCS-SP). *Behavioural and Cognitive Psychotherapy*, 40, 149–161.

von Wright, G.H. (1971). *Explanation and Understanding*. London: Routledge.

Wachholz, S. and Stuhr, U. (1999). The concept of ideal types in psychoanalytic follow-up research. *Psychotherapy Research*, 9, 327–341.

Wagner, J. and Elliott, R. (2001). The Simplified Personal Questionnaire. Unpublished manuscript, Department of Psychology, University of Toledo.

Waldram, J.B. (2007a). Narrative and the construction of 'truth' in a prison-based treatment program for sexual offenders. *Ethnography*, 8, 145–169.

Waldram, J.B. (2007b). 'Everybody's Got a Story': Listening to imprisoned sexual offenders. *Qualitative Health Research*, 17, 963–970.

Waldram, J.B. (2012). *Hound Pound Narrative: Sexual Offender Habilitation and the Anthropology of Therapeutic Intervention*. Berkeley: University of California Press.

Walker, J. and Almond, P. (2010). *Interpreting Statistical Findings: A Guide for Health Professionals and Students*. Maidenhead: Open University Press.

Walsh, R.A. (1996). The problem of unconsciousness in qualitative research. *British Journal of Guidance and Counselling*, 24, 377–384.

Wampold, B.E. (2001). *The Great Psychotherapy Debate: Models, Methods and Findings*. Mahwah, NJ: Erlbaum.

Wampold, B.E. and Brown, G.S. (2005). Estimating variability in outcomes attributable to therapists: A naturalistic study of outcomes in managed care. *Journal of Consulting and Clinical Psychology, 73*, 914–923.

Ward, E.C. (2005). Keeping it real: A grounded theory study of African American clients engaged in counseling at a community mental health agency. *Journal of Counseling Psychology, 52*, 471–481.

Ward, G. (2010). *Teach Yourself Postmodernism*. London: Teach Yourself Books.

Watson, N. (1984). The empirical status of Rogers' hypotheses of the necessary and sufficient conditions for effective psychotherapy. In R. Levant and J. Shlien (eds.), *Client-Centered Therapy and the Person-Centered Approach: New Directions in Theory, Research and Practice*. New York: Praeger.

Weersing, V.R. (2005). Benchmarking the effectiveness of psychotherapy: Program evaluation as a component of evidence-based practice. *Journal of the American Academy of Child and Adolescent Psychiatry, 44*, 1058–1062.

Weersing, V.R. and Weisz, J.R. (2002). Community clinic treatment of depressed youth: Benchmarking usual care against CBT clinical trials. *Journal of Consulting and Clinical Psychology, 70*, 299–310.

Werbart, A. and Levander, S. (2006). Two sets of private theories in analysands and their analysts: Utopian versus attainable cures. *Psychoanalytic Psychology, 23*, 108–127.

Wessely, S. (2006). Randomised, controlled trials. In M. Slade and S. Priebe (eds.), *Choosing Methods in Mental Health Research*. London: Routledge.

West, M.A. and Reynolds, S. (1995). Employee attitudes to work-based counselling services. *Work and Stress, 9*, 31–44.

Westen, D., Novotny, C.M. and Thompson-Brenner, H. (2004). The empirical status of empirically-supported psychotherapies: Assumptions, findings, and reporting in controlled clinical trials. *Psychological Bulletin, 130*, 641–663.

Wheeler, S., Aveline, M. and Barkham, M. (2011). Practice-based supervision research: A network of researchers using a common toolkit. *Counselling and Psychotherapy Research, 11*, 88–96.

Widdowson, M. (2012). TA treatment of depression – A Hermeneutic Single-Case Efficacy Design study – 'Peter'. *International Journal of Transactional Analysis Research, 3*, 3–13.

Williams, E.N. and Hill, C.E. (2012). Establishing trustworthiness in Consensual Qualitative Research studies. In C.E. Hill (ed.), *Consensual Qualitative Research: A practical Resource for Investigating Social Science Phenomena*. Washington, DC: American Psychological Association.

Williams, E.N. and Morrow, S.L. (2009). Achieving trustworthiness in qualitative research: A panparadigmatic perspective. *Psychotherapy Research*, 19, 576–582.

Willig, C. (2008). *Introducing Qualitative Research in Psychology*, 2nd edn. Maidenhead: Open University Press.

Wise, E.A. (2004). Methods for analysing psychotherapy outcomes: A review of clinical significance, reliable change and recommendations for future directions. *Journal of Personality Assesssment*, 82, 50–59.

Yalom, I.D. and Elkin, G. (1974). *Every Day Gets a Little Closer: A Twice-Told Therapy*. New York: Basic Books.

Zigmond, A.S. and Snaith, R.P. (1983). The Hospital Anxiety and Depression scale. *Acta Psychiatrica Scandinavica*, 67, 361–370.

Index